my story

BRUNO TONIOLI

with Matt Allen

headline

First published in 2012
by HEADLINE PUBLISHING GROUP

1

Cataloguing in Publication Data is available from the British Library

Hardback ISBN 978 0 7553 6407 7
Trade paperback ISBN 978 0 7553 6408 4

Typeset in Bliss Light by Avon DataSet Ltd,
Bidford-on-Avon, Warwickshire

Printed and bound in Great Britain by
Clays Ltd, St Ives plc

Headline's policy is to use papers that are natural, renewable
and recyclable products and made from wood grown in sustainable forests.
The logging and manufacturing processes are expected to conform
to the environmental regulations of the country of origin.

HEADLINE PUBLISHING GROUP
An Hachette UK Company
338 Euston Road
London NW1 3BH
www.headline.co.uk

I dedicate this book to the memory of my parents
and Michael Summerton.
Wish you were here.

I would like to take this opportunity to thank the long list of people who have kept me working in this wonderful industry for nearly forty years. There are so many of you around the world that I would run out of paper if I namechecked you all. A special thank you goes to the team behind the creation of *Strictly Come Dancing* and *Dancing With The Stars* at the BBC, BBC Worldwide and ABC for taking a chance on me and changing my life.

Thank you to Paul Stevens and Laura Hill at Independent Talent and to Jonathan Taylor and his team at Headline for all their support and encouragement in the making of this book.

FANTASIA

Hollywood, 2012. It was in the Paramount Studios, Los Angeles, where I first made my mark on the silver screen. I, Bruno Tonioli, was announcing my arrival as an actor in Hollywood – the pinnacle for any performer of ambition and a playground stage for the crème de la crème of 'thespianism'. (It's my made-up word and I like it.) In the grand Studio 16 building, a shooting location for the golden-age movie *Sunset Boulevard*, I was surrounded by actors, make-up girls, camera crews, a fearsome-looking director and tonnes and tonnes of stardust. Oh my god: *heaven*.

Of course, this wasn't my first Rumba with razzmatazz. As you know, I've been a judge on the Saturday night variety show sensation *Strictly Come Dancing* for nearly a decade now. From the sanctuary of a judging panel it's been my job, alongside fellow experts Craig Revel Horwood, Arlene Phillips, Alesha Dixon and Len Goodman, not to mention the doyen of show business himself Sir

Bruce Forsyth, to watch as countless celebrities have shimmied and strutted their wobbly bottoms and bingo wings across the nation's TV screens. Meanwhile, in America, I've done a similar job on *Dancing With the Stars*, where the levels of dazzlement, excitement and ineptitude among our contestants have been equally unsettling and bewildering.

Anyway, I was well versed in working on televisual extravaganzas by the time my Hollywood acting debut arrived. I was ready – that was the good news. The bad news involved my role, because somewhat embarrassingly for me I hadn't been earmarked for a villainous cameo in the new Bond saga. Nor was I set for a singing and dancing part in *Mission Impossible 5: The Musical*. No, for my entrance on the grand stage of Tinsel Town, I would be making an advert for a well-known fruit drink. And what would I have to do in order to wow my audience, I wondered out loud?

'Bruno, we're dressing you up like a mariachi singer and trussing you up like a sausage on that crane there,' said my director for the day, the legendarily antagonistic advertising Midas, Paul Weiland, as he pointed first to the assistant holding a sparkly jacket and some maracas, then to the large winch device which loomed over me in the studio like a mechanical T-Rex.

My heart sank, but deep down I knew it had been my own fault. When Paul first asked me to do the advert, I had agreed, with the proviso that I was allowed to sing. Once he had relented, I became so excited at my musical role that I completely forgot to look at the storyboard, so I had no idea that I would have to shake my stuff, suspended, in a harness that belonged in *Fifty Shades of Grey*. I was also unaware that, with the help of some video trickery, I was to be shrunk to the size of a jar of mustard because my miniaturised figure was going to be performing from the inside of a fridge.

However, as you'll soon discover, I've never been one to turn down a challenge, so I dressed up in my frilly uniform, climbed into the extremely uncomfortable harness, grabbed my props and proceeded to do one of the first of many uncomfortable dance routines.

'Now, Bruno, I want you to spin around like a whirling dervish,' shouted Paul, getting his camera crew into position.

'That's fine,' I said. 'But you'd better catch me if I topple over.'

The response was reassuring. 'Don't worry, Bruno. I'll be here to break your fall,' he said, readying himself like a removal man awaiting a sofa of considerable heft. *The cheek.*

On his cue, I began twirling and spinning, pirouetting and twist-ing, until I collapsed to the floor with a crash. I yelled in pain. Paul had neglected to break my fall. My knees were throbbing, the palms of my hands stung like fury and my dignity was in ruins. When I looked up, everybody was laughing their heads off.

'You were supposed to bloody catch me!' I screamed at Paul, picking myself up.

'I thought about it for a second,' he wheezed. 'But then I realised you would be too heavy.'

Well, that's when my brain started to burn, my ears began to steam. I was overheating with rage, which is a very bad thing. I let fly with a volley of expletives and four-letter words so foul it would have embarrassed a trucker.

'*******!' I screamed.

Paul was falling around in hysterics, which made me even more furious and I let fly with another barrage of abuse.

'You ******* ****!'

'You *******

'You pillock!'

It was at that moment that Paul grabbed me by the arm and gesticulated to the stunned faces alongside him – a five-year-old boy and a man waring a sharp suit and a look of bemusement. He was clearly a high-flying executive.

'Bruno,' said Paul, the smirk still spread across his chops. 'Meet the client . . . and the client's son.'

My heart sank. I was mortified, I had made an utter fool of myself. But in an instant I transformed into vision of charm – like Dame Judi Dench – and fluttered my eyelashes at the pair of them.

'Good day, sir,' I purred, extending my manicured fingers for a handshake. 'So lovely to meet you. And what a delightful child.'

My ego was in tatters, my body ached, and as I stood there, huiliated, I asked myself the same question I've raised on many occasions during my life.

'Bruno, how the flippin' heck did you get here?'

☆

The answer to that, as you'll find out shortly, is hard work, a lot of determination and the occasional duet with luck, not that you would have guessed from my acting debut in Hollywood. My journey began in northern Italy where the creative talents I possessed were mainly ignored by my parents, so I ran away to the theatre at eighteen; I broke my back perfecting different styles of dance in schools around the globe before becoming an instructor to the actress Goldie Hawn, albeit for the briefest of moments.

What followed was a whirlwind of jobs on TV shows, films and pop videos, as I worked with the likes of The Rolling Stones, Freddie Mercury and Duran Duran. It was then that I landed my role as a judge on *Strictly Come Dancing*, where I've since drawn attention to myself with a series of madcap performances. Since 2004 I've been filmed straddling the studio desk, falling out of my seat with excitement and gesticulating wildly like a horny octopus with every performance, thankfully for the entertainment of millions. What fun!

Along the way there have been highs and lows, as one would expect. In my bleaker moments, I struggled to express my sexuality in a very backward-thinking, provincial community in Italy. Before I made my name on telly, I had dalliances with drugs, including LSD and cocaine (on one occasion, a session with a friend became so 'intense' that I ended up speaking in tongues; he developed lockjaw). There have also been times where I've been forced to question my own sanity, particularly during my time on the *Strictly Come Dancing* panel where calamity and chaos have made for randy bedfellows.

The presence of Craig Revel Horwood, for example, is usually enough to send me into a spin because he can be a terrible tart. He spends his days shopping in the sales, his evenings laying waste to the vineyards of France, and when he's not spending or sipping, he's spray-painting his skin with ill-advised fake tans.

One such occasion took place when we were working on *Strictly Come Dancing Live!*, a touring version of the show. The crew were in Glasgow and Craig, after a night on the vino, decided to have a late night 'treatment'. On the face of it, that wasn't enough to cause a kerfuffle but because he had passed out in his hotel room afterwards without showering (which, as anyone know, is very important after a spray tan), the results were disastrous.

The following day, he resembled a barrage balloon-sized bottle of Tango. His face was a blotchy mess, apart from his teeth which shone like illuminated tombstones; the colour of his eyes, had they been painted by Dulux, would have been described as 'Hungover Pink'.

'What the flippin' heck have you done?' I said as he settled down for the show with his pad and pen.

'Darling, it's just a bit of a spray tan,' he quipped back.

'But it's ridiculous!'

Craig didn't like that one bit.

'It'll settle down, don't fret, darling,' he hissed.

Well, I can tell you, it didn't. As the hour progressed, Craig kept getting more and more orange. His skin tones became darker and darker. The orange turned to muddy brown and he looked like a creosoted fence, but even worse, he smelt like a digestive biscuit – the sure sign of a fake tan. By the end of the evening, the brown had turned to black and Len couldn't talk to him without collapsing in hysterics. When Craig took his clothes off at the end of the evening, he was dripping in gunk and mess. It was beyond disgusting. You wouldn't put up with it for a second.

The highs of my life, though: *Oh, the highs*! There are many to tell you about and some of them have been mind-blowing. I've worked with cinematic acting greats such as Sir Michael Caine and the American actress Anne Hathaway. I've put together shows with comedy masterminds including Rowan Atkinson and Steve Coogan.

Meanwhile, *Strictly Come Dancing* and *Dancing With the Stars* have earned plaudits around the globe.

It was only when I visited America that I realised just how big an impact the show had made. Around the same time as my eventful visit to Paramount Studios, I was invited to dinner in a very chi chi Beverly Hills restaurant. When I arrived, I was confronted by a vision of glamour and elegance dressed in high heels, a snappy leather jacket and sunglasses the size of SAS night-vision goggles.

'Hey, I know you!' she cried, as we collided in the lobby. I stepped back, startled, and eyed the prowling tigress in front of me. It was only Jane bloody Fonda, *Barbarella*, one of the greatest actresses in cinematic history. For once I was speechless.

'You're the one from *Dancing With Stars*,' she said. 'You can be pretty catty when you want to be, can't you?'

I winced. I knew I'd gathered a reputation. I had once described the singer Billy Ray Cyrus as a 'crazy bear lost in a swamp' during his particularly off-kilter attempt at the Cha Cha Cha. Cattiness was very much in character for my racy, frothy, occasionally over-exuberant TV persona, where some of my descriptions for our more hapless contestants had been particularly savage, but I didn't want Jane Fonda to think of me as evil. For a split second, I floundered. I knew I had to act fast – I was being gently scolded by the star of *On Golden Pond*.

'No, Jane, dear,' I said, desperately reaching for a white lie. 'I think you'll find that was one of the others. Probably my fellow judge, the senior sex symbol and bridge club heart-throb, Len Goodman.'

'Ah yes,' said Jane Fonda – *Jane bloody Fonda* – stroking my arm. 'You would never do that, would you? You're the nice one . . .'

The exciting news is that these adventures have been fun, a wild ride, and all my ups and downs and *pas de basques* into the frying pan and out of the fire are in this book for you to enjoy. Hopefully you'll laugh, maybe you'll weep – not at the jokes but at some of the sadder moments in my life (and there have been a few), but for the most part, darling, I'd like to think you might come to the same conclusion that I have in life: all that glitters is not gold. And if it is gold, it's usually the cheap rubbish that Craig would pick up in the sales.

Los Angeles, 2012

CHAPTER 1

BRINGING
UP BABY

When I first clapped my eyes on Lucy he was parading across the picture-postcard Piazza Trento Trieste in Ferrara, the small town in northern Italy where I grew up as a stubborn, impulsive, occasionally crazy little boy. He was sucking on a cigarette like a frumpy fishwife. Lipstick had been smeared around his mouth and stubble. He wore a short skirt, weightlifter's thighs and high heels that sometimes caught the cobbles in the street, causing him to wobble about like a Kung Fu Panda dancing the Samba.

From a distance — well, the bar of the local taverna where the red-blooded blokes used to break away from their football chinwags to whistle and jeer at his graceless strutting — Lucy could have passed for Joan Collins, or maybe Joanna Lumley's Patsy, the chain-smoking lush from BBC One's hit comedy series *Absolutely Fabulous*. Up close and personal, however, he looked more like Craig Revel Horwood. My darling, let me tell you, this cross-dresser was not a looker.

Anyway, as the local trannie, Lucy became something of a celeb and he divided opinion throughout the town. Some people in Ferrara, the women mostly, thought of him as an amusing nutter. They laughed good-naturedly whenever he appeared on the street and waved out to say hello as he spritzed through the shops. But the men? Well, they often spat out their feathers whenever he dared to bring his padded bra and fur coat into broad daylight.

'If my son is a Lucy, I'm going to shoot him,' they would hiss with macho bravado in their bar conversations, angrily clinking glasses together. Then they would return to whatever they had been vigorously fighting about moments earlier – the sports news, or which Italian car maker from the region they considered to be the greatest: Ferrari, Maserati or Lamborghini.

The funny thing was, I was thirteen when I first saw Lucy, and he played an important part in my formative years because whenever I heard the cruel insults from the men in town it made me feel terrible and uncomfortable. Not because I knew their victim or spoke to him as he tottered around the streets, but because I knew that I was different, too. I could feel it almost from the beginning of my life. I wasn't the stereotypical, lady-killing Marcello Mastroianni-type; I knew girls weren't for me. I was gay, and even as a very young boy without a sexual experience to my name, well, apart from a quick grope with a local boy in a local park, I sensed I would be isolated forever if I remained in a town like Ferrara during my adult life, just as Lucy had chosen to do. It was a quiet, pretty place, but not the town for a restless spirit like myself, as you'll soon discover. (For those of you who might not know,

Marcello Mastroianni was the heart-throb Italian actor and the ultimate Latin lover who bedded beautiful women. I think every teenage boy was envious of him at the time, including me because he looked so fabulous.)

I was convinced at the back of my head that there was something else for me in the world, something very different from the dull-as-ditchwater future my parents had planned for me. They dreamed that someday I would work towards becoming a successful accountant or a banker in a backwater Italian office, something with security and stability. In reality, all I wanted to do was dance the Cha Cha Cha in a Sunday afternoon dance club, watch Elizabeth Taylor movies and listen to The Beatles, even though I didn't understand a word of what John Lennon was bloody well singing.

I suppose that sense of impatience and not belonging began from the minute I popped out of my mother Fulvia on 25 November 1955. I was so desperate to get on with life that even the timing of my arrival was catastrophically bad. I was a whole month out of step, premature, and my grand entrance on her birthday was my first attempt at the big, show-stopping performance. *Because I just had to escape!* I think, in retrospect, the poor woman had no idea what she was letting herself in for when she brought me into the world.

Thankfully I was a happy baby, which probably had a lot to do with my idyllic surroundings. Ferrara was off the beaten track, quiet and sleepy. The streets were cobbled, picturesque and lined with beautiful buildings, the type usually seen in black-and-white movies or Bond films. Old ladies hung their bloomers over balconies, and grizzled, chain-smoking men sipped espressos outside roadside cafés; the grand Castle Estense was moat-lined and towering with its impressive battlements.

Ferrara looked like something out of a romantic, fairytale book. The town hall had beautiful arches and a lot of the houses were architecturally unique; one building was even nicknamed the Palace of the Diamonds because it was built with strange, pointed bricks. Bicycles were the preferred way of getting around town and you would always hear the tinkle of bells and the screech of brakes if you ever stepped onto the road without looking. I don't want to turn this into a history book, but Ferrara used to be a city of the d'Este dynasty, one of the most splendid and powerful duchys in Italy. At its peak it was as powerful as Florence.

Not that *we* strutted around like royalty, *amore mio*. The whole Tonioli family lived together in a rented house, and though the building had a turret, it was hardly the Castle Estense because it was so overcrowded. It had been built at the bottom of an embankment and outside was a canal that stunk to high heaven in the summer months. Inside, the building had a large kitchen which served as our communal room. Everybody had their own bedrooms – the one in the turret had been the scene of my birth. In that respect I was like Rapunzel – a fairytale about to begin. Or maybe a horrific nightmare, depending on your point of view.

Anyway, my mother, my father Werther, his brother Silvano and Silvano's wife Nella all lived under the same roof. To add a few degrees of extra warmth to the cold and damp building, my grandfather Giovanni and grandmother Ines were stuffed into another room, which meant that most days were spent tripping over one another en route to the toilet.

We didn't have anything back then, we were working class. My grandfather was a *mediator*, which meant he acted as an agent between the fruit farmers in the region and the buyers in the market. Every Monday he would go to the piazza (long before Lucy had arrived on the scene, thank god) to strike deals between the two parties. Whenever an agreement or sale was made, he would take a very modest percentage. Meanwhile, Dad was a car painter and Silvano a carpenter; Silvano's wife, like my mother, was a seamstress though she worked with lingerie, but we'll get to that later.

Behind the scenes, my grandmother ran the whole show and – oh my goodness – the woman was a saint, what with the palaver and general chaos of family life in a house so packed with people it could have been a sardine tin. During the day she would babysit me when my mother went to work. During the evening she suffered the language of my uncle who had a potty mouth like a trucker. He would swear with the most colourful and blasphemous turns of phrase I have ever heard and my poor grandmother would turn blue with embarrassment and anger.

'Oh Jesus and Mary!' she would wail tearfully as Silvano let fly with another round of four-letter words, though it never dissuaded him from cursing at any little incident that annoyed him. Because of the shouting and swearing, the Tonioli household was a very colourful and noisy place. By contrast, my father was almost the exact opposite in terms of personality, and whereas Silvano was always powerful and loud, Dad remained quiet and reserved. He was a very handsome man, with dark hair. He had the look of young Frank Sinatra about him. He loved to dress up at weekends and wore smart suits, despite our modest wealth. One of our cousins from my mother's side was a tailor in a nearby village and whenever he could afford it, my dad would buy a tailor-made outfit at a reasonable rate.

In the house, my father liked to live quietly in the background. I think the clash of styles between the brothers must have annoyed them both, though it proved a fertile environment for a boy like myself – I later grew up with dad's love of dance and style. Meanwhile, my uncle's vile gob would inspire some colourful tirades as I became older (not that I would ever talk that way in front of you).

My father could express himself in other ways though, and when it came to the stylish and graceful art of ballroom dancing, the man was a king of the clubs, a prowling tiger, and a wonderfully natural mover. He was besotted with Fred Astaire and Gene Kelly. On a Saturday night he would take my mother dancing and when I was older I would accompany them, watching as they glided around the floor. Later, as I learned to dance myself, I would stand on my mother's feet as she taught me the steps that made up the Jive and the Cha Cha Cha. Little did I know that these lessons would later afford me a role on Saturday night's favourite ballroom dancing show, starring Sir Bruce Forsyth himself and the modern day, thinking-grandmother's crumpet, the Cockney cavalier, Len Goodman. (Len has promised me a handsome reward for this gushing praise.)

My parents' flamboyance had a profound effect on me, almost from the minute I was pushed out, because I loved an audience. I was a showman, and as a baby there were very few occasions where I wasn't performing, or trying to gather rave reviews for one little stunt or another. In those days there wasn't a TV in the entire neighbourhood, let alone our family home, so instead we used to gather around a wireless that was operated in the kitchen. Whenever my grandmother switched it on I would move and wriggle in my cot to the rhythm of the music. It wasn't long before I was making my Royal Variety Performance debut in the Tonioli Palladium when, months before I'd uttered my first words, I clambered onto the dining table to shake my booty to the hits of the day. It was my way of entertaining the crowds.

I loved to perform for other families too, whether they liked it or not. Whenever the Toniolis could afford it, they would send their children on holiday with my grandmother. We would often head for the seaside town of Cervia for air because the dampness in our house was so bad that everybody was always coughing and spluttering and wheezing the place down. One year, my grandmother rented a holiday room which was more a bedsit than a seaside paradise. It had four beds and a stove, and I, my cousin Massimo and friend Licia (the daughter of my grandmother's niece) went there for a month. We were so cash-strapped that my grandmother, bless her, only had one outfit for the beach. I would watch, amazed, when she would wear her flowery dress all day and then wash it in the evening as the children got ready for bed. The following morning, having been baked in the morning sun on a window ledge, it would be fresh and dry enough for another outing.

Anyway, whenever I could sneak away from my grandmother's clutches at the seafront I would spend my time dancing for the German tourists in a nearby bar, even though I was only four years old. My disappearance would always cause a noisy, cat-among-the-pigeons panic on the beach as everyone would go mental looking for me among the umbrellas and towels. Shouts of 'Where's Bruno?

Bruno!' could be heard everywhere by everyone, but not by me because I would be in the middle of a wildly enthusiastic and knowledgeable audience, laughing and clapping as I danced to the music from a jukebox. Whenever my grandmother tore me away from the scene, a member of my fan club would always reward me with an ice-cream. Even then, I knew the value of working for a fee.

My behaviour must have driven my grandmother crackers. As if possessed I would spend the rest of our days on the beach moving from umbrella to umbrella, sun lounger to sun lounger, stealing women's shoes for fun. Wooden clogs were all the rage at the time and I became obsessed with them, often running around the rock pools and shallow water in a pair I had 'borrowed' from a snoozing sunbather. There was always an embarrassing scene as my grand-mother shamefacedly returned them to their rightful owner afterwards with the excuse that 'Bruno is a *fa contrario*'. Which, loosely translated, meant that I did whatever I bloody well wanted.

It wasn't long before I became a creative whirlwind at home and I'd spend dinner time making Tom Cruise-style cocktails for everyone at the table. Rather than plying them with booze and freshly squeezed fruit juices, however, I would grab anything and everything around me – bread crust, pasta, water, apples, tomatoes – and push the crazy recipes into a china cup. My creations always tasted vile and very few attempts were ever made to drink them, but my behaviour quickly became the chatter of the family: 'Bruno is clearly an artiste and craves attention!' they would declare in their daily gossiping sessions.

With hindsight, I must have been a nice distraction for everyone in the home because the place was overflowing with people who were always performing one laborious chore or another. I suppose you could say I grew up in a very traditional, post-war Italian household. When the women of the house weren't working, they would help my grandmother with the cooking, the cleaning and any other jobs that needed to be done around the home. When the men of the house weren't working they would go to the bar and drink espressos, play cards, and talk football and politics; to round the evening off they would drink a bitter digestif called an *amaro*. Their lack of elbow grease indoors was never questioned though, and I later learned that my father was unable to cook an egg, that's how limited the domestic skills of your typically Italian male were in those days.

The ladies certainly had their work cut out. On a Sunday, my mother, my aunt Nella and grandmother would boil the washing in a huge cauldron in the yard because we didn't have Zanussi washers and Persil non-bio tablets to work with back then. Instead they would light a fire and throw all the sheets and clothing into the water, stirring the material for hours. When it was suitably boiled, they would take the load out and wash it all over again. It really was an incredible effort.

Even though we weren't wealthy enough to wash our pants inside, we ate like the d'Este dukes at home. As a small child I used to live in the kitchen and I'd watch as my grandmother prepared the family dinners. She never worked from a cookbook; fine dining was part of our DNA because we were Italian and my grandfather came from a farming background. Every day she would make her dinners with recipes picked up from friends and family, all the while putting her imagination to good use. I'll never forget her wild rabbit and polenta suppers, the animal caught by my grandfather in the fields nearby. As she prepared the meat, our kitchen tops quickly became a mess of herbs and vegetables as pots and pans simmered and steamed away. When the family sat down as one for dinner, it looked like a colourful feast complete with fresh breads and beautiful wine from the region.

If there was one downside to the rustic lifestyle, then it was the traditional pig slaughter that would take place in the back yard every autumn. Flippin' heck, it was like something out of *The Texas Chainsaw Massacre*! As I got older, maybe five years of age, I remember the sounds being horrific – the high-pitched squealing of the pig as it wobbled around the yard, fearful for its life. I remember the violence was gory – the pig was stabbed, bled, scalded in a bathtub of hot water and cut up into little bits to make prosciutto, chops, bacon. You name it, we made it.

After the slaughter we would eat as a family, barbecuing chunks of meat on a smoking pile of embers. The smell of the sizzling, cooking pork was fantastic. Wine was passed around and the mood was always excitable as plate after plate of different cuts were prepared. Once the slaughter had been forgotten, I loved eating it all. Well, everything apart from the salami. At my first pig banquet, I watched in disgust as bits of meat were stuffed into a length of saggy intestine, the casing for a traditional salami sausage. I knew then that it would never be the *antipasto* for me, but everything else I scoffed like an emperor at a sexless Roman orgy. And I loved every mouthful.

☆

Given my pain-in-the-backside antics at home, I suppose my mother and father couldn't wait to pack me off to education, where I could inflict my madness and excitability on people other than themselves. At the age of four I was sent to pre-school, which was run by the local nuns, and a very serious place it was too; certainly not the type of place that would suffer shoe theft and cocktail-making lightly. Day-to-day life there was so strict that we were only allowed one glass of water when we ate lunch and even then we could only drink after we had finished the whole meal. If any of us were caught cheating we were beaten. And those nuns weren't messing about: 'Smack! Take that in the back of the head!' they would cry. It was terrifying.

Even as children we were taught religious studies and had to learn about Catholicism, but I just couldn't get my head around it. I never got the whole idea of burning in eternal flame if ever I did something wrong. That was a load of rubbish as far as I was concerned and I think it was a view shared by most of my family because we weren't very churchy people. We lived off the land, we were probably closer to being communists than anything else, and when my family went to church — which was only really at Christmas or Easter — it was because my grandparents were worried that if we didn't show our face at least once or twice a year then we would go to hell.

Me, I had to go to church every week because it was an intrinsic part of pre-school life. I was forever in confession for various misdemeanours, which usually involved impure thoughts, and I lost count of the Hail Marys I had to perform. I never understood why I had to admit my sins to a man who appeared to be locked in a closet. Make of that little metaphor what you will.

When the Toniolis did go to church, they went in style. On the Saturday night before those rare excursions to Mass, the family would always pay a visit to the local hairdressers to get their look just right. Mother and father would order a sharp hairdo and they would always wear new outfits, regardless of how much work it took to afford the bloody ensemble. It was a valuable lesson: carrying a sharp sense of style was always an important part of being a member of the Tonioli family.

Everybody viewed the church visit as an annoying inconvenience, but there was a plus side: it gave my family an excuse to moan and bitch and cry.

'You know he's seeing a hooker?' they would say of somebody they had spotted in the pews.

'Why did so and so have to call her mother a battle-axe?'

'What was it that the baker's daughter did with the fruit stall owner's sons?'

Forget the internet, if anyone wanted to know who was getting it on with who, or which man was having it away with the local boot, then they only had to ask at church. All the talk was about what somebody else was doing or not doing: who is marrying her? Why is she not marrying him? What is that she's wearing? Why does he look like this? Chat, chat, chat; gossip, gossip, gossip.

I started picking up valuable information at school too, but I quickly realised that this boy was not for turning when it came to traditional education. Although I was good at all subjects, I was really becoming a creative person. The problem was, I couldn't find a way to release my ideas, especially not in something such as maths. I wanted to perform, to *express myself*, and there was no way I could do that by working out bloody multiplication tables with a pencil and a piece of paper.

Thankfully, there was help at hand. One time an uncle who was a very talented painter brought over some oils and brushes for me to play with. I soon began making my own masterpieces at home, but to be honest I'd make use of anything around the house just to occupy my mind. Aunt Nella used to do her seamstress work in her bedroom and would often work on items of lingerie. There were always lots of pieces of lace and cotton lying around the place and I would gather them together to make my own dresses and haute couture constructions – thinking about it, I could have been another Giorgio Armani, given the opportunity. I stole anything that was close to me. I even used to make mosaics with broken glass and glue. There were all these ideas going on inside me and I desperately wanted a way of expressing them, but I just couldn't do it at school.

It was around this time that I saw my first vision of beauty: a white Giulietta Sprint, a sleek, sexy car that was crafted by the Italian car maker, Alfa Romeo. It was driven by my cousin Mary who arrived at the house looking for all the world like the movie star Claudia Cardinale with her beautiful dress, big sunglasses and long, jet black hair that flowed behind her in the breeze as she sat at the wheel of her gleaming coupé.

My love affair with cars had begun already when my father took me to work one day and showed me a Ferrari he had been painting, a two-seater Barchetta. My jaw just dropped when I saw it, I was taken aback by its beauty. I knew nothing about engines or exhausts but I was startled by the look of the body, the design of the chassis and its artistry. It blew my mind. My dad was in love with it too and even though he couldn't have afforded the Barchetta, he treated it as if it were part of his heritage and something to be proud of.

At the time, my mother had started working for her uncle, Signor Alberti, an importer of cars from Turin. She would work on the upholstery of his latest purchases and I remember he had a fantastical menagerie of second-hand masterpieces – I saw my first Mercedes there, and a Maserati, too – and I soon developed a passion for motor vehicles that were synonymous with the area. Ferrari, Lamborghini and Maserati all had their factories within thirty miles of Ferrara and the people in the town were divided between the cars as if they were football teams. The arguments! Fans of Maserati thought that Ferraris were *vulgar*; the Ferrari people thought that Maseratis were big barges. Lamborghini was an upstart, a tractor maker. And the fans of the different cars would argue in the bars and cafés as if they were supporters of the Italian football clubs, Juventus or AC Milan. I remember hearing men – who could probably only afford to ride a bike – talking about these cars with expert knowledge, as if the whole range had been parked inside their tiny courtyards.

Nobody looked upon the different cars with envy though, they looked upon them with pride and admiration because the *Ferraresi* were working class and aspirational. People believed that if they worked enough, then maybe one day they would be rewarded with enough money to buy a Lamborghini, and to hell with it if one-third of the town thought it was a flippin' tractor. That spirit ran through my entire family, too: we had a 'get on with it' attitude. We didn't have central heating, a TV, or a car, but we had a sense of pride in working hard and I was taught by my family that if I put the effort in at school and worked well, I would be rewarded later on in life. And how right they were.

☆

I lived in a fantasy world as a child. Our street was a dirt track surrounded by countryside, which was great for me because I could run in the fields and play with all the girls that lived nearby. I never joined in with the boys because they were always kicking a football around and there was no way they were going to let me join in with them because I was a disaster. They moaned because I had no real concept of the game – I never passed the ball or ran in the right direction.

The only thing I wanted to do was sing and dress up, it was a great laugh and I felt very free, even for a six- or seven-year-old. I never had any concept of it being weird or bizarre because I was too innocent. Living in the countryside also meant that I experienced a great sense of nature and the seasons. I loved the outdoors world and I would often hide myself away in one corner of a field and create a little universe for myself where I was King Bruno. There was The Land of the Butterflies and The Land of the Toad; I would concoct stories in my mind and I became completely lost in a fantasy kingdom.

One time I got so carried away that I forgot to go home and by the time I came to my senses it was dark. I ran to my front door and when I arrived, my family went flippin' mental. They dragged me into the house, shouting and screaming. My uncle was swearing the house down; my grandmother must have said a hundred Jesus and Marys, and my dad gave me such a beating with the belt that I couldn't sit down for hours afterwards. They weren't afraid of dishing out a little discipline in the Tonioli household.

What they didn't realise was that running away to the Land of the Toad had become an important escape route for me because there were so many arguments at home that staying indoors was almost unbearable, even in winter when it was so cold that my fingers would feel like they were falling off. The cause of all the shouting and yelling and crying was because my mother and father decided that they wanted their own home. That meant that they had to pull their money out of the property co-owned with Uncle Silvano. Oh, the arguments! My father felt like he wasn't allowed to take out the right amount of money and he became very resentful because of the squabbling that was going on. The pair of them really fell out and by the time we moved home, to an apartment in a newly built block down the road in Ferrara called Villa Barlaam, I was spending a lot of time on my own, just for some peace and quiet.

Hollywood films, with all their glitz and glamour, were providing some comfort, too. Before that turbulent and disruptive period began, my mother and father had started taking me to the cinema. I probably went for the first time when I was around five years old and in those days the local theatre would screen *Third Visione* films, which were classic movies that hadn't been shown before because nobody could afford to see them during the belt-tightening that took place following World War II; *Third Visione* basically meant 'Third Time Around', a bit like watching 2004 repeats of *Top Gear* on the TV channel Dave.

It didn't matter to me how old they were though because I was transfixed. Mother would always take me to the melodramas. With Father I would watch Gene Kelly movies. He also loved Tom and Jerry cartoons, so between them I had the full range of Hollywood.

Gene Kelly and Fred Astaire graced the screen with their wonderful dance moves! Elizabeth Taylor and Lana Turner blew my trousers off with their glamour! For the first time, I saw a world outside the cobbled streets, boiling bloomers and pig massacres of Ferrara, and I absolutely loved it. I wanted to be there, on the silver screen, singing and dancing, though at the time I had no idea of how I was going to make it.

During these early cinematic adventures, my mother took me to see *Madame X*, which starred Lana Turner. I was around nine years old but because of my wild over-imagination and dramatic nature as a child, I was incredibly sensitive and receptive to any form of tragedy, particularly something as powerful and well choreographed as a movie. As I sat in my seat and the plot began to unfold in front of me, I sobbed uncontrollably, my sniffs and snorts becoming louder and louder. I blew my nose and blubbered so hard that a woman in the seats behind us leaned forward to enquire about my well-being.

'What are you doing to that child?' she said, tapping my mother on the shoulder.

Mum turned around angrily. 'There's nothing I can do!' But it was no good. We had to leave the theatre shortly afterwards, mainly for fear that my mother might get reported to the police for abusing me.

The cinema was a godsend, though, and with it I entered a world of fabulous excitement. Mother used to style her hair like Liz Taylor (La Liz they used to call her; oh, wonderful Liz!). Father loved Rita Hayworth (it won't come as a surprise to learn that she was called La Rita, or when a little more imagination was required, *L'atomica*). The pair of them adored the actor Monty Clift, though they probably wouldn't have been so enamoured had they known how Monty would turn out eventually.

At the time, everybody loved all the Hollywood stars. They delivered a world of beauty and glamour that took audiences away from the grind and hardship of living in post-war Europe. I was just as passionate and would do anything to catch a film, especially if it came from one of the classical Italian directors such as Federico Fellini, Luchino Visconti or Pier Paolo Pasolini, who I fell in love with when I got a bit older. The trouble was, most of their movies were restricted viewing; people under the age of fourteen couldn't go in because there was lots of good stuff on show, like sex and swearing, so a few years after my emotional viewing of *Madame X*, when I was thirteen years old, I began falsifying my identity card to get in, even though it was an imprisonable offence. To increase my chances of success, I would steal my mother's make-up and draw stubble on my face. I must have looked like a daughter of Lucy, the town trannie (but much better looking).

It was crazy, but it was worth it. With each movie, I was drawn into a fantasy, a glimpse of an existence outside Ferrara. In my parents' eyes, the life of La Liz or *L'atomica* was unobtainable, a pipe dream, but I had other ideas. I wanted to enter a world starring Sophia Loren and Monty Clift, La Rita and Gene Kelly. And let me tell you, nothing was going to get in the way of my ambition.

CHAPTER 2

YOUNG MAN WITH A HORN

The boys . . . oh, the boys!

I was probably only around ten when I felt my first *tingle*. A sexual thought, a funny moment, something I couldn't truly understand in my head. I was an innocent child studying at an elementary school in Ferrara. It was a warm summer's day in 1965 and I was playing in a field opposite our new house with some of the girls who lived nearby – Patricia, Valentina, Daniella, Natalina and Loretta. The six of us had become best friends because we walked to school together, but a bunch of rough boys had also moved into our road. Rowdy, noisy boys who loved football and fighting and swimming in a nearby pond.

My grandmother would always wail, 'Oh they're from a family that are a lot rougher than us. Be careful!' But to be honest, nobody really paid any attention to her scaremongering and my mother and father always tried to welcome anyone new into the community.

If ever we had any spare clothing or hand-me-downs, we would always give it to the new gang in town. They looked like they needed all the help they could get.

Anyway, on this particular day, I decided to ditch the girls and I cycled down to the pond on my bike where the boys were swimming. Without thinking about it I jumped in, completely stark naked. There was no real drama in what I was doing; it was something all the kids did, if only to save our clothes from getting wet, but as we started playing around, something happened, something I couldn't quite explain. A feeling, a buzz; a sensation that definitely didn't happen when I played doctors and nurses with Patricia, Valentina, Daniella, Natalina or Loretta.

I admit it: I'd already tried it on with one girl that year, but it won't come as a surprise to you to learn that it didn't go very well. I won't name her now for fear of giving the *bella donna* a heart attack, but the moment came when the pair of us snuck into my family's basement. We did the drop-the-pants thing. We played the 'You show me yours and I'll show you mine' game. But as I stared at her bits and she stared at me, nothing really happened. It felt like a medical examination rather than a sexual awakening and after a few minutes of looking and giggling, we gave up.

'Hmm, maybe we should go and get an ice-cream instead?' I said.

As I splashed about in the pond that afternoon, I couldn't explain the feelings I was experiencing. I definitely didn't know it was my first sexual stirring – that I was gay – but it was my earliest inkling that I might be different from everybody else around me and that I might not belong. I just didn't know quite why or how.

Thinking about it now, that whole period in my life was an awakening. I was learning about myself and who I was. I knew I was becoming increasingly different from the other kids at school – I was definitely more and more expressive and flamboyant. I loved being artistic and as my flair with painting improved, I began to sell the work I'd created with the oils and brushes my uncle had given to me. Sometimes a family member would give me the equivalent of ten quid for a painting of a flower, which was a particular speciality of mine, or a still life of a bowl of fruit. Without ever having seen one before in my life, I started to create splatter paintings in the style of Jackson Pollock. The flowers always sold better.

It was also around this time that my obsession with dancing and music took hold of me. Singing was huge in Italy in the 50s and 60s, as it is now, and every year there was a big event called The Festival of Song in Sanremo. All the biggest Italian stars of the time would perform there, the TV cameras would descend upon the place and any new acts who performed would become national sensations overnight because the radio stations would always play their songs. It's probably where Simon Cowell got his idea for *The X Factor* all those years later.

I became obsessed with The Festival of Song in Sanremo. Whenever I listened to the radio and heard a tune that had exploded out from the show, I used to learn it off by heart. I would then sing it in music lessons at school the following week, but oh-my-god I must have sounded awful because I always used to pick a composition that was way too high for my range. When my moment came to perform, I would howl and screech like the dogs that slept out in the Ferrara streets at night.

The reason I was lucky enough to watch The Festival of Song in Sanremo was because television had arrived and it was like a miracle. The first set I remember seeing was at a flat in a courtyard in our neighbourhood. Even though the apartment was two storeys up, its owner would always leave his balcony doors open and as the fabulous invention blared out into the street, people from all around the nearby houses would gather below and look up, as if to snatch a glimpse of the magical box. Of course, I couldn't see what was happening, but very occasionally I caught a corner of flickering light or a flash, as some world-changing event took place.

It wasn't long afterwards that we were able to afford our own set and what a proud moment that was for the Tonioli family. Everyone sat around the living room and when it was tuned in for the first time I was transfixed, especially when I saw a Saturday night variety show called *Studio Uno*, which starred two German performers known as the Kessler Twins (even then I had a penchant for prime-time telly featuring song and dance, my darling). The two girls resembled something out of Moulin Rouge. They wore burlesque outfits and had beautiful feathers fixed in their hair. As they sang and danced, I became hypnotised by them. In my mind I felt that I belonged on a show like *Studio Uno*, even with my squealing, caterwauling singing performances at school.

And then there was dance. *Dance!* I loved it! Falling in love with its rhythms and movement felt like a eureka moment for me. I was only eleven or so, but I had style and a natural sense of timing. Moving to the music of *Studio Uno* – or whatever music was playing on the radio – became another form of self-expression and I discovered that when I danced, it replaced the idyllic innocence I'd experienced in the fields near my house, though instead of behaving like Sir David Attenborough in The Land of the Toad I was developing the moves and techniques that would serve me well for the rest of my life.

Everything was either self-taught or picked up from the steps my mother had taught me. I was graceful. Watching my father as he swooped across the dance floor had given me a sense of delivery, something most children of my age would have been without. Everything felt so natural. The tragedy of it all was that my parents could see my dancing ability and creative desires, but they didn't know how to channel the artistic streak within me. They were from a world where art school and dance colleges didn't exist. To them, a successful existence meant gaining several qualifications and getting a job for life, a career with security. Nobody close to them had ever worked in a vocation that was artistic or creative, so it was a fantasy world to them, like the movies of La Liz or La Rita, who were creatures of dreams and not for the likes of us.

'Bruno,' they said. 'Dancing is a hobby, not a career.'

And that was when the rows started.

As a child I was finding a voice for myself. I could argue and debate and scream and shout. I had a fiery side. And because my creative urges were unfulfilled, I felt frustrated; I was isolated and perplexed. I knew there was another life for me and I wanted to find it. As my impatience increased my poor father found it more difficult to communicate with me, firstly because he was either working or playing cards in the bar with his friends, but mainly because he didn't have the skills to negotiate with my demands.

His education was at fault. Just after World War II, Dad, like most boys of his age, had been taken out of school to help build the railways that would crisscross Italy. Of course, he had his own fantasies and hopes as a child, but because he had been removed from classes he hadn't been able to fulfill them. After his work on the railways had finished, he carried on working, working, working like a cart horse.

I couldn't understand his frustrations at the time, but now that I'm older and wiser I can see where his problems stemmed from: knowledge gives people power and Dad had that power taken away from him. There was no opportunity for him to get it back either. He didn't receive the schooling that later generations would enjoy and I think a lot of the issues my father had in life came about because he felt uneducated.

Meanwhile I was becoming more and more feisty. As I went into *scuola media* – or secondary school – I began devouring culture and literature. I read *Love in the Time of Cholera* by Gabriel Garcia Marquez and fell in love with its beautiful prose. I used to obsess over science fiction and horror novels by Edgar Allan Poe and Isaac Asimov because I adored the fantasy worlds they created and the twisted fiction they conjured up.

I bought a book on Hollywood and became more and more obsessed with the movie world. Because I was looking for an escape, I used to have a map on my bedroom wall. I would stare at it for ages, fantasising about the places I hoped to explore: America, London, Paris and Australia. I felt so trapped that I even tried to change my speaking voice. In Ferrara, the accent was coarse and vulgar. We spoke in a working-class dialect. The *Ferraresi* pronounced the letter 's' as if it were a 'ch'. We dropped the letter 'l' altogether, as if it weighed a tonne. Ordering a Coca Cola made me shudder whenever I went into the town café. My voice was grotesque, ugly

– far worse than the accent inflicted upon Cheryl Cole. She would have sounded like Dame Helen Mirren in comparison to me, had she hung around Ferrara's Piazza Trento Trieste back then. To improve my public image, I decided to adopt the more accessible and well-spoken Italian way of speaking.

My father couldn't understand any of this. He must have thought, 'What the flippin' heck have I got on my hands with this boy here?' and we butted heads constantly at home. There were terrible rows; the house was a war zone. Because of my education, Dad found he could never win an argument with me because he didn't have the tools to compete. He was like an angry bear without claws. It drove him crazy. Thankfully my mother seemed to understand me better. She was more worldly and could sense my frustration. Still, I don't think for one minute that they ever suspected that I was completely different, that I was *gay*. God knows what would have happened if they had.

☆

It probably didn't help matters when, at twelve, thirteen years of age, the hormones started to fly all over the place. My body started to change, there were all sorts of things going on inside me. New hair started sprouting in strange places and growth spurts took place. I turned into an ugly duckling; I puffed up because my diet was terrible, though a lot of that had to do with the calorific snacks I made at home when my mother wasn't looking. A favourite trick of mine was to take all the leftover pasta dough that had been put to one side and I would roll it into a ball, stuffing the mixture with cheese and tomato. Then I would fry it. It was incredibly unhealthy, but it tasted wonderful. Sadly I ate too many and it wasn't long before I'd ballooned to the size of Castle Estense.

But it got much worse. I also had a problem with one of my eyes. It was lazy, it had a mind of its own. So to cure the problem (and add to the mounting traumas that were already dogging me every day, what with the fatness and the arguments at home) I was given a patch to wear. I suppose it might have helped me medically, but for the first time in my life I felt inadequate. Suddenly I looked like a chubby pirate with a voice worse than Cheryl Cole. It was a nightmare.

If there was one hope for me it was that *scuola media* in Italy only lasted for three years and after that I could move into *liceo* – the equivalent of sixth form; the superior level of teaching which allowed me to choose between a *liceo classico* (grammar school), *instituto tecnico commerciale* (technical school) or *liceo artistico*, the nearest art college which was based in Bologna, a major town in the region. Well, my mind was made up: I was only fourteen years old but I wanted to leave Ferrara and pursue my dreams of making it as an artist, a singer, a painter, or a poet, any life in which my talents would be adored and my glass and glue mosaics would be appreciated.

Typically my mother and father had other ideas. They wanted me to go to the technical college where I would learn German, French and accountancy skills so I could begin my search for a proper job. A proper job! My darling, can you imagine? I was incensed, the rows increased and I was in such a state that I wanted to kill myself because I couldn't see any way of escaping the life of drudgery my parents had plotted out for me. They just couldn't comprehend how anyone would be able to earn a living as an artist; they couldn't recognise my talents.

I was so upset that I sat down and wrote a note, a diary entry, which my mother must have found and kept because I discovered it in her possessions some years after she had passed away.

'I don't know what to do,' I had written. 'I feel so different, I feel so outcast. I'm going to kill myself . . .'

Talk about drama! Thankfully the eye patch went some time afterwards, which probably helped my mood, but despite the pleas and screaming rows, my mother and father weren't going to change their minds about my dream of going to art school. I was put firmly in my place.

'You can't do anything until you're eighteen,' they said. 'Until then you're legally under our control. You'll have to do what we say.'

I was devastated, hurt. At that moment, I made a pact with myself, and a promise to them.

'OK, fine,' I screamed, crying and wailing. 'But at eighteen, I will leave. And you won't be able to stop me.'

It's so crazy how the survivor's mentality can kick in, especially once a person has made a drastic decision to change their life forever. At that moment, it was almost as if a new set of wheels had been put in motion. When my parents settled down for dinner and the house became quiet later that night, I went out on the town alone and met my first boyfriend. Well, he wasn't really a boyfriend, more somebody I'd bumped into on the streets in Ferrara: a young man, who was very, very handsome (well, what did you bloody expect?) and friendly. He gave me a look as we passed one another, and after some chatting and then some flirting, I had my first snog in a nearby park, away from prying eyes.

'Well, well, well,' I thought, as I walked home with a big grin on my face afterwards. 'That was a little bit different!'

For a brief moment, I was happy. Despite all the rows and the frustrations, I suddenly felt less confused. I understood the person I was becoming. The sexual side of my experience hadn't meant anything to me, I was more excited at the realisation that I could be appreciated for who I really was. It was a selfish feeling I know, but I felt valued. The penny had dropped, big time.

After my secret snog in the park, I became more aware of myself. I secretly met other boys in town. None of them ever became boyfriends, because I was just experimenting like a kid in the randy candy shop. My fleeting fancies were just people I would meet in the cinema; there wasn't a gay community in Ferrara at the time because nobody would have known what a gay community was, least of all in rural Italy, but there were, shall we say, encounters. Everything was incredibly innocent and experimental, though.

These introductions always began with a look, a sideways glance. One boy in the pictures would stare at me in a funny way and off we would go, in secret. It was probably a boy who would have never have admitted to his friends that he was gay, but it didn't stop him from sneaking out and having a kiss and a cuddle with me in a nearby park (it was always in the park). In those days, there wasn't a gay bar where people could meet, especially not for a teenager; there wasn't even any concept of being gay. Homosexuality, especially in a country as macho as Italy, was so under the carpet it was ridiculous. Instead it needed a random encounter

– like two boats passing in the night – for people who felt the same way to get together. Isn't it funny how things have changed?

☆

The domestic dramas and squabbling continued for months and months and by the time I'd made it into my mid teens I was causing even more of a kerfuffle around the place, especially as I'd discovered fashion. I slimmed down, my hair grew long; I became a pretty boy. I would leave the family home in trousers that were tight and bright, colourful and hip. I wore my hair long and my shirts sheer with big lapels and more frills than Versailles. I'd even ask Mother, with her seamstress expertise, to fashion trousers from the bundles of cheap cloth that I often brought home from the local market. One time I handed her a sheet of turquoise polyester and she constructed a pair of leggings so clingy that whenever I pulled them on it looked as if somebody had stuffed a zeppelin into my undercarriage. If Mother didn't know I was gay back then, well, she must have been mental.

Other people knew, or at least suspected, like some of the children at my school. They made cruel jokes, they couldn't help themselves. Anything that might have been slightly different to them or their way of living was perceived as a threat – it became a target. I was one of the biggest threats in the playground because I didn't want to play football or go to the gym. That meant I was picked on, pointed at and teased mercilessly as I sat in a corner and read my science-fiction book.

People would corner me and poke fun. Fortunately I was bright and sharp, and I could always come back at them with a line or a joke that would deflect any unpleasant attention. If that failed I would take my cues from Uncle Silvano and unleash a torrent of abuse and filth on the bully jabbing his fingers into my face.

'You ******g son of a b*****, your mother is a ***t and she s**** ****s. *******!' I would scream at the top of my voice.

Oh my god, you have no idea. When I let loose with one of my hysterical episodes, it was like a scene from *The Exorcist*. All it took was for me to start with one swear word and it built into a projectile vomit of curses and insults. When I was pushed, I went crazy and people could never really tell just how far I was going to go. They always backed off. I think they must have thought I was a mad person.

Thank god for the girls. I could talk to them at school. I liked their company and they liked me because I could dance and I wanted to show off my talents as much as possible. I made friends with a girl my age called Carla who was the *barista* in the local café. It was the neighbourhood's equivalent of The Rovers Return and she was the belle of the bar as she made espressos and poured beer (nobody in the bar cared how young she was – it was a Saturday job for her). She was beautiful with her gorgeous eyes, long hair and a taste for mini skirts that went all the way up to her crack. Every red-blooded boy wanted to be with her, so I suppose she was wasted on me, but we looked good together and we became best mates.

Our thing in those days was to go to an under-18s club in Ferrara. It was free to get in and it always took place on a Sunday afternoon. I loved it because I could express myself on the dance floor without anyone taking the mickey out of me. I felt safe. And when Carla and I moved together, we exploded like two sticks of dynamite. Crowds would gather around us as we writhed to a live band which played cover versions of The Stones and The Beatles intertwined with old ballroom classics, which was everybody's chance to have a bit of a snog. Everybody apart from me. I would still get into the vibe, making shapes and creating different moves. People would stare at me, but unlike the stares in the playground, these looks were full of happiness; people would point and laugh, but they weren't like the bullies at school. They were nudging their friends and saying how good a mover I was, and my confidence was going up, up, up like a rocket.

Did Carla know I was gay? Maybe. She could probably sense that I wasn't going to try it on with her, so she might have felt safe with me. But it didn't seem to matter. We were young at the same time, pretty at the same time, and she was suddenly my best friend. The only hitch was that Carla was forever being hassled by good-looking guys who wanted a roll in the hay with her.

Of course, that attention caused problems for me. A lot of the boys in the club couldn't work out why I was so popular with some-body as beautiful as Carla, and the rougher elements of Ferrara's youth soon became jealous. There were remarks and threats. One Sunday I was even pinned to a wall when Carla and her friends left for the afternoon. I was outside getting on my bike when three delinquents dressed in leather jackets took hold of me and shoved me into the brickwork. The ring leader was an incredibly good-looking person for a thug, but definitely not someone to be messed with: word was on the street that he had been to juvenile prison for robbery. He grabbed my throat and pushed a glass to my face.

'I'm going to cut you open, Bruno,' he snarled, his lip curling into a hateful sneer.

Well, I don't mind telling you that I nearly wet myself with terror. I could see the hate in his eyes. He was trembling with rage. I knew I was in trouble because I had seen this particular dance before, outside the bars in Ferrara's town centre, late at night, and it was always bloody. I could tell that my assailant was a rampant, Italian bull with lust in his loins for a mate. I was the obstacle standing in the way of him and a bit of how's-your-father with Carla.

'How are you with her?' he hissed, the glass pressing harder into my flesh. 'What makes you so special?'

I thought, 'Hmm, swearing like Uncle Silvano is not going to work here, I'll have to try another tack...'

In a mad rush of blood to the brain I decided to crack a joke. It was a desperate attempt to save my skin, or at the very least, my good looks.

'Well,' I stammered, doing my best not to burst into tears. 'You know, if you want to have it off with her, I can arrange it for you.'

The murderous stare softened. A smile began to break across those stubbled, psychopathic features. He changed from a shark to a dolphin. And as he laughed, the glass across my face was lowered and he released the grip on my throat.

'Oh well, Bruno,' he said, his henchmen backing down, too. 'If that's all it takes...'

I was free, and respected for my sense of humour all of a sudden. Within days, word got around that I was a bit of a character and because of Carla's incredibly long legs, I met some of the coolest cats in the town. On a Sunday afternoon I would often hang with Ferrara's top boys, all of whom wanted to bed her.

This was a small mercy, because at home I was going absolutely, flippin' mental, what with the arguing and the constant disagreements. In the end my wishes to attend art school were completely ignored and at fourteen my parents forced me into the *instituto tecnico commerciale* or the *Ragioneria* as it was also known, which sounded, on paper, like a terrible affliction one might pick up on a Club 18–30 holiday. Once I was there, I undertook classes which would supposedly help me to become an accountant. *An accountant?* Can you imagine it? I hated the place from the outset, and I went even more ballistic when I learned that I wouldn't be able to learn English as part of the curriculum.

I was devastated. The English style was really appreciated in Italy. London felt exotic and faraway, like all the places I had studied on my maps at home. Through magazines and the radio, I knew of the music and the fashion. The first single I ever bought was years earlier, a cover of The Rolling Stones' 'Paint It Black', sung in Italian by the singer Caterina Caselli, and I played it on a crazy little machine called a *mangiadischi* which only played singles. I even fantasised about visiting London one day, where I could waltz down Carnaby Street to buy a *bellissimo* pair of shoes and dance in the fancy clubs. Having to learn German instead felt like a prison sentence.

At home there were more rows, more screaming arguments, more tantrums. I told my parents that I hated them, that I wanted to run away, but what was I going to do? I couldn't leave their care because the *polizia* would have dragged me home. Furthermore my parents were feeding me and stitching my turquoise trousers together, so I had to stay.

Thankfully my misery at the *Ragioneria* was lightened somewhat by the introduction to another friend – Lia, a stunning redhead with an hourglass figure and incredible eyes. She was a catwalk model-in-waiting, funny, a comedienne, and as we talked we shared the same dreams and fantasies of one day escaping Ferrara and moving to an exotic and faraway city. Very quickly we made a large circle of friends who I would meet in the town bars at weekends. There was the stylish, playboy hangout, Boni, where the rich kids would arrive in their Jaguars (which were considered the thing back then), BMWs and sleek motorcycles. Down the street there was Nazionale, which attracted an edgier crowd – the students, the revolutionaries, the Che Guevara lot.

I fell in quite happily with both, but I really found there was more enjoyment to be had by hanging out with the Nazionale's scruffier clientele because they were forever organising protests and encouraging the students at the *Ragioneria* to down their pens and strike. At the time there was a lot of student unrest in Europe. Trouble had started in Paris and was sweeping across the continent, not that I could have told you what was going on at the time because I didn't give a hoot. My motivation was getting out of German studies and I was more than happy to shout, 'Strike!' whenever the mood, or the workload, took me. Half the time, I didn't know what I was striking about, but by then I wasn't going to school for political discovery, I went there to smoke cigarettes and look cool.

I must admit that being a militant communist for a brief period gave me my first taste of fame. I found I could command audiences with my rousing speeches (despite a lack of passion, I loved playing to a crowd) and people were forever stopping me in the street to say hello. The experience was enlightening and thrilling. It also gave me my first taste of drugs when Il Che, a long-haired boy in class who looked slightly like the infamous Cuban revolutionary, passed me a lighted joint. I'd smelt his strange roll-ups as they were passed around at student meetings for quite a while, but I honestly didn't know what they were. Like most Italians, I'd started smoking at the age of fourteen, but drugs were completely alien to me. Still, if I thought this funny smelling cigarette could add another layer of sophistication to my image then I was going to bloody well try it, even if it did reek of patchouli, the strong-scented oil that everyone used to wear at the time.

'What's that?' I asked Il Che as he waved the smoke under my nose.

'It's a joint, Bruno, maaan,' he said. 'Take a hit.'

I puffed away on this thing like it was a Gauloises cigarette and after a few drags it felt as if someone had smacked me over the head with a frying pan. I was out of it. I couldn't talk, I couldn't move, and the room had started to spin. It was like one of those scenes in a Tom and Jerry cartoon when the cat runs into a wall. I was slumped on the floor with tweety birds and stars spinning around my head. All the energy had drained from me.

'It's cool isn't it, Bruno?' breathed Il Che, thinking he'd turned another student over to his smelly cause.

If I'd had any energy left in my body I would have told him where to stick his joint because I hated it.

'What is the point of this?' I thought. 'What is the point of sitting around saying, "Yeah man, cool man." What the heck does all of this flippin' mean?'

And the eating? Oh my goodness, I was stuffing my face with bread and pasta for hours afterwards, but nothing seemed to satisfy my appetite. It was then I realised that getting overweight and talking stupid through marijuana was not for me. Not if I wanted to carry on dancing and squeezing myself into those sexy, tight trousers. I knew that to hang with the top dogs of Ferrara and survive, I would have to look good, baby.

CHAPTER 3

REBEL WITHOUT A CAUSE

After those brief but eventful duets with militant communism and wacky baccy, it was a relief to my sanity and senses when Ferrara opened its first discotheque. I was in raptures. No longer would I have to sit around breathing in the smoke from those weird-smelling roll-ups. My days of painting political slogans onto placards for causes that made no sense to me were over. Instead I could dance the weekend away while showing off my increasingly extravagant sense of rhythm.

The club had been named My Dream and was located near the *stazione centrale*. From the second I stepped through the front doors I loved its salubrious vibe. It was a basement club, and the dance floor lit up with a rainbow of colours – I had never seen anything like it in my life. The decor was all velvet and mirrors. In those days it felt very, very trendy. The DJ was one of the town playboys, a man named Filiberto who had fantastic shoulder-length hair, in a Mick Jagger style. He dressed immaculately in tailored shirts, figure-hugging trousers and a pair of wonderful, handmade shoes from the town of Bologna, where a shoemaker called Franco used to make boots for the young studs of the region. His eye-catching appearance set the tone, and in next to no time, the My Dream club was the hottest joint in town.

In a strange way I set the tone too, because I came alive whenever Filiberto flipped a record onto the turntable. The year was 1972. The British Invasion was taking place, so David Bowie was very hip; Elton John and Roxy Music were also becoming big hits. Those acts were like a laser bolt from another generation. Although I had no training in modern dance, I found I could move naturally to its rhythms, just like I had shown on those Sunday afternoons when I danced in the clubs with Carla. This time, Lia was my partner in crime and as the crowds gathered and sashayed around us, I threw her – and myself – across the dance floor.

I loved the limelight. Whenever it seemed as if Lia was drawing too much attention to herself, I would nudge her to one side and hog the floor on my own, grooving wildly in my frilly shirts and way-too-tight pants. It wasn't long before the town stud took notice of our wild routines and like a ravenous lion eyeing his prey, he began to drool from the sidelines. Not at my gyrating body, I'd hasten to add, but at Lia with her striking red hair and curves in all the right places as she rippled and writhed under the spotlights.

The lucky, lucky girl. His name was Paolo and he was a hybrid of George Clooney and Marcello Mastroianni; he smouldered. But it turned out that there were brains to match his beauty. When Paolo opened his mouth, he was witty; he drove a Jag and was considered the height of sophistication because he'd been to Rome. This boy was the alpha male in a pack of town Romeos that included DJ Filiberto and their two friends, Donnato and Aroldo. His status as a top dog also meant that he could conquer just about any Ferrara woman he wanted. On this occasion Lia was on the menu, and she, like any woman, succumbed to his sultry charms.

The pair of them began to dance together at the club, and as they became closer and closer over the following weeks, Paolo and his friends took me under their wing. They liked me, even though I was most definitely not a macho Italian male (and just about everyone in the club knew that I was gay); they appreciated my sense of humour and loved the fact that I was a great dancer. With their support, my levels of self-belief grew even more.

Not that my confidence had ever been in doubt. Despite the warring at home, I was very sure of myself. So much so that I even entered a singing competition in a desperate attempt to get noticed by somebody, anybody, who could transport me away from Ferrara and into a world occupied by the Kessler Twins. I wasn't the only one. Plenty of other people were chasing the same dream, and in Italy it was common for a town or village to hold a music competition in the summer where all the local wannabes could put on a show. The hope was that the invited talent scouts would spot one lucky starlet and whisk them away to Hollywood, or Carnaby Street, or *Studio Uno*. Of course, it was a rip off. People paid a fortune to enter, but there were never any talent scouts in the place. Still, it made for a lovely day out for everyone in the town, even if there was the strong suspicion that the competitors were being conned.

Undeterred by the whisperings and mutterings that accompanied these competitions, I paid my entrance fee to an event which was being held several miles away from Ferrara. It wasn't cheap and I funded my ticket with the money I'd made from the sale of my flowery paintings and Jackson Pollock-style masterpieces. The extra cash I had left over was then invested in singing lessons with the local tutor Signorina Gioseppina Guastaroba, a reputable vocal coach from the town. (Guastaroba when translated actually means 'rotten gear'. I should have known.)

Now, for those of you not schooled in Italian titles, a *Signorina* is somebody who isn't married. In this case, Signorina Gioseppina Guastaroba was about as likely to marry as me because she was fifty and a lesbian. Weirdly, nobody in Ferrara ever mentioned anything about her sexuality, even though she dressed like a man. Her regular outfit was a masculine suit with flat shoes and a severe hairstyle which she would oil into a parting. When I first saw her, I thought she looked like Rosa Klebb (the lesbian spy with the knife in her shoe) from the James Bond movie *From Russia With Love*. The only discernible difference was that she was much, much, uglier.

Signorina Gioseppina Guastaroba's biggest claim to fame was that she had once tutored a singing sensation from Ferrara called Milva, who would go on to release dozens of albums. She still performs today. Everyone in Italy loved Milva, so I was thrilled at being coached by the woman who had honed her style. After five lessons, which involved me practising several totally inappropriate songs by another famous Italian singer of the time, Mina (who was a soprano; I would later discover that I could sing really well, but only as a baritone), I felt ready. I then had to beg my poor grandmother to drive me several miles to the village where the competition was being held.

Much to the surprise of everybody at home, I came third, though I'm sure my trousers had something to do with the result because my mother had made me another pair of polyester 'Zeppelin Pants' for the event which arrived in an aggressive shade of lemon sherbet. Certainly my bronze medal wouldn't have had anything to do with my actual performance. I must have sounded awful, what with my baritone voice straining to perform a soprano song first aired by the Italian singing sensation Mina.

I think I was more thrilled at seeing my grandmother's face as I sang. She looked so happy. I loved her very much and would always cycle to our old house to see the other side of our family. She often gave me money when I left, usually without telling my grandfather. She felt so guilty that I wasn't living under their care anymore. My cousin – Uncle Silvano's son Massimo – was in the house and he received much more attention than me. Sadly, there was still a lot of simmering tension between my father and his brother, and they would rarely speak. Whenever his name came up in conversation at home, my father would spend hours slagging him off.

Anyway, it was because of my experience in the singing competition that I felt confident enough to enter a play organised by the *Ragioneria* in 1973 when I was seventeen years old. The people of Ferrara liked to put on shows every year as part of a project to extend the town's cultural heritage and these performances were always carried out in local dialect. More exciting was the fact that the event was always held in the *Teatro Comunale di Ferrara*, an incredibly stunning and beautiful renaissance theatre. When my college announced that they were looking for actors, I applied immediately and auditioned for a role as a mother-in-law.

The character in question was a screaming, horrible battle-axe

– a bit like Pat Butcher from *EastEnders*. I had no idea that I could pull off a comedy performance at the time, but having convinced the producer – who was adamant the role should be played by one of the girls in the college – that I was worthy of the part, I threw myself into the script.

Unbeknown to the organisers, I had a show-stopping trick up my sleeve and when opening night arrived, I walked onstage dressed in my grandmother's clothes. Every piece of fabric had been stuffed with cushions, which gave the impression that I was fat. The grotty ensemble was topped off with a dark wig which was streaked with shocking white patches. I looked like Cruella De Vil on doughnuts. As I waddled onto the stage for the first time, my stomach somersaulting with nerves, the whole place fell about laughing. The *Teatro Comunale di Ferrara* was packed to the rafters with 1,500 people, including my parents who were giggling hysterically, and the sound of the audience screaming and applauding at my act was so intoxicating that it felt like a drug, and one that was much more pleasant than the joint I had smoked in college.

'This is it!' I thought. 'There is nothing else that could possibly compare to this.'

For several days afterwards I enjoyed an adrenalin rush that was both unexpected and indescribable. The adulation of that evening was so addictive that it kept me awake at night. I craved more. And I knew right then that the stage had me. I'd do anything to perform and nothing could stand in my way. One weekend I told my parents I was staying with Lia. Instead I hopped on a train to Rome with the intention of hanging around the world-famous *Cinecittà* Studios – or Cinema City – where La Liz's movie *Cleopatra* had been filmed in 1963. *Cinecittà* was the Pinewood Studios of

Italy and I was convinced that with a locally acclaimed performance as a mother-in-law under my belt, I was sure to be spotted by an eagle-eyed director.

How mental was I? It took me eight hours to get to *Cinecittà* and by the time I'd arrived at the imposing gates flanked by security guards, it was dark. Even more annoyingly, there wasn't a soul around to notice my unquestionable talent because it was the dead of night, so I hung around for five minutes before wandering forlornly back to the station where I caught the overnight train to Ferrara. Once home, I concocted a fabulous lie about how Lia and I had studied all weekend and that the reason I hadn't called was because her phone line had been broken.

I was just as determined when it came to dancing in the My Dream club. Around the same time, when I was seventeen years old, I bought a bright red scooter, a Vespa that growled like an angry puppy whenever I pulled at the throttle, and I would cruise around town on a Saturday night with Paolo and the other Ferrara top dogs. I loved to dress in a flame red outfit: a bright pair of red trousers that looked sprayed on (they were that tight) and a bold, blood-red t-shirt that would have probably glowed in the dark; I always looked hot. Given that I was a young and fearless individual, I would often drive like a lunatic on my bike and my mother was forever begging me to wear a crash helmet.

'But Mother, come on,' I would always argue. 'Why would I want to mess up my hair?'

Of course, one night, the inevitable happened and as I zipped along the road that led to the My Dream club at a crazy speed, I was clipped by a car and hurled into a nearby ditch. I landed hard on my shoulder and as I fell, I heard a sickening snap, like a twig being broken in two, but because the adrenalin was pumping around my body I couldn't feel any pain, so I picked up my scooter and sped on to my destination. I only realised I was in trouble when I limped through the doors of the club. Paolo and the gang were looking at me, aghast.

'Bruno, your shoulder is dropping off,' Aroldo cried, running to my side. 'What's happened?'

The pain hit me in a rush. Up until that moment, I'd refused to accept that anything was wrong, I felt bullet proof and in my head the scooter crash had been a minor incident. But as the reality of what happened hit home, an agonising, blinding sensation seemed to tear at every nerve in my body. I passed out and was rushed to the local hospital. X-rays that night would reveal that I'd broken my shoulder in the fall. It probably won't come as a surprise to learn that I haven't been on a motorbike since.

☆

The buzz of performing in front of an audience wasn't the only exciting discovery that year. I also ventured into my first gay club, completely and blissfully by accident. The adventure, like so many in life, started with a shopping trip. Having been enthralled by Filiberto's wonderful, handmade shoes at My Dream, I saved enough money from my paintings (not to mention my grand-mother's hand outs) to buy a pair of my own. I decided to travel to Bologna, where Franco the shoemaker ran his fancy boutique and I lost myself among the fine leather creations on display. After what seemed like hours of debating, I ordered a stunning blue pair of Chelsea boots, just like the ones The Beatles used to wear.

In those days the shoes were made to order. That meant the customers would have to put a deposit down before their leathers could be stitched together. I didn't mind waiting a few weeks because I knew my Chelsea boots were going to be exquisitely made and after paying the money I decided to explore Bologna. As I walked around the town, wandering past the shops and cafés, my mind went into overdrive. Bologna was one of the most beautiful towns in Italy, and it was renowned for its miles of *porticos* – the pavements which were covered so people could walk around in the winter without fear of getting wet in the rain; it was always cool and shaded in the summer. The piazzas and cobbled streets were incredibly picturesque and there were fabulously dressed men everywhere. I noticed that a rather a large gang of them were hanging around a bar in the town centre.

'Oh, there are a lot of colourful people,' I thought. 'I wonder what they're up to?'

I walked inside the taverna and to my surprise it was a gay bar. There was music playing, people were having drinks and everybody seemed to be having a great time. Even though it was the middle of a beautifully sunny day the windows had been blacked out, just in case any of the passing locals took offence. But there was no secrecy or paranoia among the clientele inside. Everybody seemed very happy and incredibly friendly, so I decided to stay.

I ordered a coffee and immediately felt like a duck taking to the water; it made Ferrara seem like a sexual desert. I had been stumbling around, living off scraps for years, and suddenly I had wandered into a gay oasis. A whole new scene had opened up for me and I felt invigorated. It wasn't long before I was going back, again and again, long after my shoes had been collected. During the first couple of visits I would go in for coffee afternoons. As I became more emboldened I began staying for wine in the evenings.

And then the snogging began.

Well, to be able to do that in public was like a shock to the system. I would never have dared to kiss another man in the open at home. Suddenly I was able to live in a world where everything was open and without taboo. Well, not quite everything. A lot of the men I ended up meeting were actually married and had families. They would have been run out of town had their wives discovered their secret lives. Still, it didn't stop me from making plenty of friends in Bologna and together we discovered the gay hangouts of the town and beyond. We went to Riccione, a seaside resort south of Ferrara and one of the first towns to have a proper gay nightclub, which was called *La Villa Delle Rose* – The Villa of the Roses. We even travelled to places as far away as Rome to drink in the gay bars there. It took a lot of effort and travel money to be a gay man in those days, but unsurprisingly I was up for the adventure. If only my poor grandmother knew how her pocket money was being spent.

I think my wanderlust came about because I was reaching a massive turning point in my life. I was just about to turn eighteen and I had become increasingly determined to stick to the pact that I'd made with myself when my parents prevented me from going to art college. I felt like I had conquered Ferrara and that I needed a bigger adventure. Travelling around Italy with my new friends had taught me there was a wider, brighter world to explore and I was determined to enter it.

Luckily, Lia wanted to explore the world with me too, or so she said. When we graduated from the *Ragioneria*, the pair of us even made a fantastically ambitious plan to run away to London and Carnaby Street where we would undoubtedly meet David Bowie. I loved his music because of what he represented: his sexuality was irrelevant; Bowie was being himself and had been celebrated for his image. I simply had to get to London to befriend him.

After a couple of weeks of plotting, however, I could sense that Lia's enthusiasm for our escape was waning. She stopped visiting our usual hangouts for coffee. She didn't call me to chat or to fantasise about London. I soon found out that she had met another man in the My Dream club and had fallen in love. Well, I was devastated, not just because I knew her new fella and he was a tosser, but because I had been jilted and I was heartbroken. Our changing friendship felt like a betrayal, and like so many painful divorces, I never spoke to her again.

But darling, as you may have guessed, I like to move it. It wasn't long before I was hanging out with two new friends, Monica and Chinzia, a pair of gorgeous girls from the club. Chinzia and I decided one weekend to travel to the cliff-top village of Positano on the Amalfi coast. The pair of us had heard that a film festival was being held there, hosted by the wonderful Franco Zeffirelli – the famous Italian film director who made *Jesus of Nazareth* and *Romeo and Juliet*. Of course, we had to go! The event also promised appearances by massive movie stars such as Laurence Olivier and Liza Minnelli and word reached us in Ferrara that the organisers were going to build a huge stage in the harbour where they could screen films and perform plays.

Even if Franco Zeffirelli hadn't been holding a film festival there, Positano was a place I'd always wanted to visit. Its beaches were portraits of romantic beauty. Small fishing boats were dotted around the bay and many of the crumbling houses in the village were cut into the cliffs that looked out to the Mediterranean Sea. The dome of the local church and an old fort dominated the skyline, and in summer the place was a riot of vibrant colours. At dusk the rusty sun turned the town a beautiful orange. By day, the wild flowers that grew there looked fantastic in bright shades of red and pink.

It was the sort of village where one could imagine a movie hero cruising the streets in his Aston Martin, searching out a beautiful woman or three (the Jude Law film *The Talented Mr Ripley* was filmed there). The author John Steinbeck even wrote an essay on the former fishing commune. In it he proclaimed that 'Positano bites deep. It is a dream place that isn't quite real when you are there and becomes beckoningly real after you have gone.'

I knew it was a fantastic hangout for the summer, and along with Chinzia we travelled south by car through Naples in a Volkswagen Beetle, not stopping until we'd booked into a small shack for £2.50 a night. For that money, our accommodation was unsurprisingly down-at-heel, not that we cared. Within minutes of walking around the town we were approached by a French guy called Alban, who claimed to be a dancer from a French company due to perform at the event.

'Would you like to see our musical revue tonight called La Grande Eugene?' he said. 'It's a huge hit from Paris and everyone's raving about it.'

Well, we were naturally bowled over by the invite and nodded our heads in agreement. He handed us some tickets and told us we were to find him later in the theatre, which all seemed a bit weird to me, but in my naive head I assumed that it was simply another way of socialising, one I hadn't yet experienced in Ferrara.

Anyway, when we saw the show later that evening I was beside myself. La Grande Eugene was a satirical masterpiece directed by the brilliant Frantz Salieri, full of mime and dancing. The script included several pastiche performances which took inspiration from the musicals of the time, such as *Jesus Christ Superstar*, and singers such as Nina Simone and Josephine Baker. What I loved most about the show was that its three leading actors were men pretending to be fictional women, *impersonating other women*. It was double layered, and the main roles were surrounded by a troupe of handsome young dancers. I was mesmerised. I had never seen anything quite like it in my life.

After the performance Alban, our friend from the company, tapped me on the shoulder.

'There is a lunch tomorrow at the Zeffirelli mansion,' he said. 'Would you like to be my guest?'

I wasn't stupid. I'd been around the block a bit, despite my tender age, and I knew he wanted to bed me. So I readily agreed and when I arrived at Franco Zeffirelli's house the next day I could hardly breathe for wonderment. His home was a fantastic building that had been cut into the cliffs. It was called *Tre Ville* – which when translated meant 'The Three Houses' – because it was so big. Nothing from my limited cultural experiences in Ferrara, Bologna or Rome had prepared me for its grandeur.

It was huge, like something from another world. The house had ornate statues and fountains. Chandeliers hung from the ceilings.

Vast windows overlooked the dramatic Mediterranean skyline and the crashing waves below. For a moment I felt as if I was hallucinating. I couldn't speak.

Only ten people had been invited to the banquet and only one of them – me – came from Ferrara, with its coarse dialect and limited world view. Naturally I became incredibly self aware as I made my introductions and I didn't know what to do with myself. When I looked down at my place at the table and saw how many flippin' knives and forks and spoons were laid out before me, not to mention the other pieces of cutlery that I had never seen before in my life, well, I didn't know what to do. Course after course of fantastic foods – soups, seafood platters, salads, pasta dishes, *antipasto*, meats – were served to us, and every time a new dish arrived, I took my cue from the other diners around me, selecting the appropriate cutlery only when I was 100 per cent sure that I wasn't going to make a fool out of myself.

Eventually, the man himself, Franco Zeffirelli – the Maestro – arrived to meet his guests. He swanned into the room halfway through the fourteenth course, dressed in a kaftan. A beautiful blonde Adonis joined him at his side and I was overwhelmed with excitement. Here was the orchestrator of this fabulous event. I felt amazed at how beautiful the house was and how beautiful the people were. I couldn't comprehend the fantastical nature of Zeffirelli's life.

'Oh my god,' I thought. 'This is the world.'

It was a whole new dimension of culture. I was blown away by it all and as I chewed my food and fiddled with my cutlery and stared, wide-eyed, at the wealth and the beauty around me, the enormity of Zeffirelli's life dawned on me, and I wanted it more than ever. The guests at the table dropped names and told amazing stories. At first I loved it, but then it made me realise just how ignorant I had been. Suddenly, I got a sense of how much hard work I would have to do if I was going to live a wonderful life like the great Franco Zeffirelli. With one lunch, he had shown me how small a part I currently played in the universe. The funny thing was, I didn't want his material wealth or the fame, or even his money, though it would have been nice. Instead I wanted to be active in his world – the art world. I wanted to exploit my creative potential. I also knew I would have to work bloody hard to get there, but at least I had a purpose.

As if sensing the epiphany within me, Alban – the man who had invited me to the Zeffirelli mansion in the first place – whispered in my ear.

'La Grande Eugene is opening in Milan in September, this is my number,' he said, thrusting a piece of paper into my hand. 'Come and see me.'

I tucked the note into my pocket as if it were a key to a bank vault that contained diamonds and dozens of pairs of handmade shoes from Bologna. I knew right then that it was my one-way ticket out of Ferrara.

It was like being struck by lightning.

CHAPTER 4

STAGE DOOR

How would you feel if you were to arrive at a party and receive, for the first time in your life, a glass of bubbling, seductive, sensuous champagne? And not just any old champagne, but a flute of perfectly chilled Shipwrecked 1907 Heidsieck, which sells for $275,000 a bottle and feels lighter and more heavenly than a kiss on the smackers from Aphrodite herself. I'd imagine sipping it would be *bellissimo*, wonderful, like a wild awakening to the taste buds.

Then imagine a horrific turn of events; that after sampling such a divine fizz, the host takes your drink, apologises for making a terrible mistake and hands over a glass of Asti flippin' Spumante instead. How would you feel? Not too happy about it at all, most bloody likely. And that's what it was like for me when I left Franco Zeffirelli's *Tre Ville* and returned home to Ferrara. For a brief moment I had gorged upon the best metaphorical champagne money could buy, I had tasted the high life, and I wanted more. But in Ferrara the champagne bottle was empty and returning home meant that I had to slurp from the dregs.

It was a slap to the chops, not to mention the ego. The truth was, I hadn't been starstruck by Zeffirelli's soirée, but my adventure in Positano was both humbling and inspiring at the same time, and almost immediately a voice inside my head started to scream and shout, 'Bruno, you have to get out there! You have to leave your friends and family and start again. You have to see the world.'

I knew it would be risky. Ferrara was a very safe environment and I could understand why people would want to live their whole lives in a town like that. The daily routine was simple and the area was picturesque. There was comfort to be found in a working existence within the town because change and grand upheaval was unheard of. In fact, it wouldn't surprise me if my school and college friends from the 50s, 60s and 70s were still hanging out in the bars and cafés in the Piazza Trento flippin' Trieste now. For all I know, some of them could be arguing over the Ferraris, Maseratis and Lamborghinis as we speak.

In my head I knew that I wouldn't grow as a person if I remained in Ferrara; I feared that I might die inside. And so I took a jump of faith, the *grande jeté* that, with hindsight, was the first step towards freedom and my seat alongside Craig Revel Horwood's Titanic-sized booty on the *Strictly Come Dancing* panel. As September approached I looked at the phone number that Alban had given me and thought, 'Oh screw it! Bruno, you are getting on a train to Milan!'

My plan was clear: I was going for three days only, and I was going to have plenty of fun and games while I was there. When I called Alban he sounded excited at the news of my plan and invited me to meet him at the opening night of La Grande Eugene, and what a treat it was. Let me tell you, the open-air event in Positano did not do the show justice in the slightest. When I had seen it a few months earlier, it had been held in an outdoor theatre by the sea and the cast had performed a scaled-down version. This time, La Grande Eugene was being held in the *Milano Teatro Manzoni*, the premier theatre in Italy, and it was a feast for the eyes. Everything looked elegant and beautiful, the performances were electric. It was the best thing I had seen. At the tender age of eighteen I felt as if I had been wired for sound.

One of the stars of the show was a very pretty boy who played the Messiah in a satirical version of the Andrew Lloyd Webber musical *Jesus Christ Superstar*. He was illuminated by glitter balls throughout the entire performance and wore a dress made from shards of broken mirrors. He looked incredible. I was spellbound.

As the show came to an end, Alban rushed over to greet me.

'Bruno, I have a surprise for you,' he whispered. 'I have arranged it so I can take you backstage to meet everyone.'

I was thrilled. I swanned back to the artists' area and told the cast how great I thought the show was. I regaled the production crew with my thoughts on lighting and staging, even though my only real experience of performance was a minor role as the mother-in-law in a play at the *Teatro Comunale di Ferrara*. I thought I was in my element, though in reality, everyone around me must have thought I was a right pillock.

My arrival backstage was quickly forgotten when all of a sudden, a loud kerfuffle broke out in one of the dressing rooms. It was a star of the show, Jesus himself, and the director of La Grande Eugene, Frantz Salieri. The pair of them were having a full-scale ding-dong over god knows what.

'I don't care about La Grande Eugene anymore!' screamed the boy, still in his boots (which looked clunky and impractical for a messiah), tears and make-up running down his face. 'Screw you all, I'm going home to Paris!'

Well, there were audible gasps from the rest of the cast. Jesus was storming from the building in a diva strop and as everyone looked at one another in disbelief, the enormity of what had happened seemed to settle upon the room: one of La Grande Eugene's leading figures had quit the show in the middle of their Milan run. It was a disaster! I couldn't believe what I was seeing, but events were about to take an even more dramatic turn because Frantz Salieri, still raging, was now staring at me. He stepped back and pointed a trembling finger in my direction.

'You!' he shouted, triumphantly. 'You! You could be his double! You're identical to him. What can you do?'

Salieri looked terrifying. His hair was thick and grey, it was long and wild too, a bit like the murderous cult leader, Charles Manson. His beard was unkempt and the frilly shirt he was wearing had been undone to the midriff which exposed a jungle of chest hair. I stammered. I knew I could dance – I had proved that I was a natural in the My Dream club, but I hadn't been to ballet school or undergone any proper training. I could also sing, providing I picked the right songs, and I knew I could act because I'd starred in plays dressed in my grandmother's clothing. But something as huge and renowned as La Grande Eugene was out of my comfort zone.

'Er, well, Mr Salieri . . .' I stammered.

The director was in no mood to wait for a verbal summary of my resumé.

'Can you dance?' he snapped.

I didn't miss a beat. 'Oh yes!' I said, realising that I was looking an angry gift horse in the mouth.

He clicked his fingers and a wardrobe assistant appeared from nowhere carrying what looked like a big bag of Accessorize mirrors in his hands. It was the Jesus Christ costume, as worn by the diva sensation who had spectacularly quit the show a few minutes earlier.

'Try this on,' said, Salieri.

My head was spinning. Without thinking, I stripped on the spot and climbed into the robes, which were still wet with Jesus's tears. To my surprise, the whole outfit fitted perfectly. Well, apart from the cumbersome leather boots, which were so tight that my toes felt as if they were being crushed by a cold, steel vice. Beads of sweat started to break out on my forehead with the pain, but as I winced, a voice in my head yelled, 'Whatever you do, Bruno, don't cry about the boots! Don't blow your big chance by complaining. You're not at home now . . .'

Salieri stepped back and eyed me aggressively. His arms were folded, a finger was placed on his pursed lips as he ummed and ahhed and tutted and hissed. Minutes seemed to pass – though it was probably only a matter of seconds – before he clapped his giant hands loudly, like a grumpy French genie granting a wish. *The director had made a decision!*

'You! Come to rehearsals tomorrow at 10 a.m. I want you to audition . . . *for me.*'

There was another loud intake of breath from the cast members who had gathered around the scene. Salieri turned on his heels with a flourish and left the room. My mind was in a spin, I felt light-headed. I didn't have a clue what was going on and neither did Alban, who was shaking his head in disbelief. I had wandered backstage with the sole intention of mixing with some of the most brilliant performers I had seen to date. Instead I had been offered an audition for one of Europe's hottest musicals. In hindsight, I had just experienced what some people would describe as a 'lucky break'. Though nothing could prepare me for the back-breaking work that lay ahead.

Flippin' hell, the next morning I was beside myself with fear. After a night of tossing and turning, I woke around six a.m. and began fretting about how I was going to try out for a show that I had barely seen twice. This was not some small play after all, this was La Grande Eugene, one of the most talked-about productions on the continent. I could sense that my 10 a.m. meeting might be a life-changing moment. I also knew that there was a good chance my audition might end in embarrassment and disaster, especially in the boots Salieri had given me to perform in. Every time I laced them up, the tight leather crushed and buckled my toes. My ankles were sure to be sore and bleeding after a few minutes of dancing.

I tried to calm myself: 'Bruno, you're doing this!' I shouted in my head, but inside I was a bag of nerves.

Thankfully, Alban had promised to hold my hand throughout the terrifying experience (not literally, that would have got in the way), and having watched me as I smoked and paced around his Milan digs at the crack of dawn, he finally took pity on me.

'Right, come on then, we're going to the theatre,' he said. 'I'll teach you the scenes.'

Luckily for me, Alban was not just a dancer with the show, he was La Grande Eugene's ballet master and that morning he taught me the moves I would have to perfect were I to star in the show's extravagant finale, the pastiche of *Jesus Christ Superstar*. The *Milano Teatro Manzoni* was empty and silent when we arrived. I looked up at the cavernous hall with its grand balconies and ornate ceiling and felt sick with nerves. But there was no time for stage fright. Under Alban's instruction I twirled and moved in the Jesus suit. The broken mirrors that had been glued to the fabric weighed a bloody tonne. Combined with my murderous boots, I knew that a long stint in La Grande Eugene would be the death of me because my performance involved a hell of a lot of running around from what I could tell.

That wasn't the half of it. According to the script, the character of Herod and several of his soldiers had to attack Jesus with their fists.

'Hmm,' I thought. 'That doesn't sound like a lot of fun.'

How right I was. As Alban played the varying roles in our practice sessions, he battered me black and blue with a series of blows and I was thrown around like a sack of potatoes. Every bump caused me to cry out in agony. Alban explained that I would eventually learn how to take the blows properly without feeling any pain, but part of me had a sneaking suspicion he might have felt jealous about the fact that I had swanned backstage for the first time and landed an audition for a part that plenty of people would have killed for.

Having crushed my toes, bruised my body black and blue and sweated buckets, Salieri finally arrived for my grand audition. His hair looked even wilder than when I'd first seen him and his eyes bored into my soul as I took to the stage. Thankfully, Alban's heavy-handed treatment worked and I pulled off my dance routines perfectly, gritting my teeth as the weight of several tonnes of glass and fabric threatened to buckle my spine.

'Do you want to be in the show?' shouted Salieri from the darkness of the seats, as I stood there panting and sweating and wanting to break down in tears with the pain.

'Yes,' I stammered, in a state of disbelief.

'Well Bruno, you start this evening,' he said. 'We'll give you one number to learn for tonight. And after that Alban will teach you a new number every morning. That number will be introduced into the show the same evening.'

There was no question about whether I could cope with the pressure; I had no time to think about my predecessor who was probably drinking himself into oblivion at that very moment. I was thrust into rehearsals almost immediately. And I mean that literally. Having been allowed a few minutes' rest and a glass of water, I began learning my first number, the scene that myself and Alban had already worked on that morning. My feet were killing me and my body was throbbing from King Herod's haymakers, though with hindsight, a manic day of rehearsals was probably the best thing for me. Because I'd been working all day and was crippled with pain, I didn't have the time for any first-night nerves as stage time approached.

When the curtain came up for my debut scene later that night, the only thing that was flying around my mind was a sense of disbelief. I could not believe that this was happening to me. I had met Alban by chance, I had decided to call him as a way of escaping Ferrara; through sheer chance I'd stumbled backstage via an unexpected invite and suddenly Lady Luck was giving me a part in a major theatrical production. If there had been a National Lottery in those days, I would have bought a ticket that same day. I decided right there that fate was working out a path for me and I was determined to travel down it.

I admit it, there were a few brief moments that night when I did worry about what had happened to my predecessor, the diva who had thrown a strop the day previously. I knew he was talented, I could tell he was respected, but whatever his reasons were for quitting the show — whether it was his ego or an unhappiness at something that was going on — they had presented me with an opportunity. I wasn't going to spend hours worrying about his mistake so I threw myself into the action without fear. When I took to the stage, the audience gasped at my fantastic outfit. With my long hair and make-up, I looked like a rock star. Every step I made was greeted with a round of applause and it set my heart racing. My skin began to tingle. The hairs on the back of my neck stood up. The adrenalin rush that had taken hold of me for the first time in the *Teatro Comunale di Ferrara* returned and I felt as if I was making my escape into the big, wide world. I went to bed that night feeling like a whole other person.

As the days passed, more and more scenes were given to me. I had to dress up as a male hooker in a black leather corset for one number, complete with the dreaded shiny, black boots. In another scene, I wore a wig made of beautiful real hair and was made up to look like a girl. Even more exciting was the news that for the privilege of performing, I was being paid approximately £100 a week, which was a lot of money back then, especially for a boy like me. All of a sudden I was able to pay my way.

I called my mother excitedly.

'I'm not coming home,' I told her boldly. 'I've got a part in La Grande Eugene and I'm the star of the show.'

I could hear her tears and sobbing at the other end of the line. It broke my heart.

'Oh why, Bruno?' she cried. 'Why?'

I tried to calm her down. 'But mama, I'm earning £100 a week, it's great, and I'll send some money home for you to look after.'

The tears and sniffing at the other end of the line came to an abrupt halt.

'Oh, OK, Bruno,' she said. 'I'm sure it's just a phase you're going through. You'll come home soon.'

The thing was, it most definitely was not a phase. Despite my bleeding toes and broken back, I was loving every second of my role in La Grande Eugene. The show began to tour all over Italy and it soon became a major sensation. We picked up rave reviews in the national press and sold out theatres up and down the country. Everywhere we went, the cast became overnight stars and local celebrities would come to watch the production whenever we performed in their town. In Rome, Ursula Andress, the world-famous bombshell actress from the James Bond movie *Dr No* even bought a front-row ticket. It was mind-blowing.

Then one day, somebody spoke the magic words, the sentence

I had dreamed of hearing from the day I first stuck a map to my bedroom wall in Ferrara.

'Bruno, pack your bags,' it said. 'We're going back to Paris to rehearse.'

☆

Picture the scene: the brief Italian tour of autumn 1974 was a whirlwind, a blur, like living the dream. Most of the time I wasn't even aware of what was going on around me because everything was so new. I spent my days and nights working purely on theatrical instinct, listening to what other people were asking me to do. I was learning something new every day, it was a fantasy world made true, but it felt quite easy because I was still in Italy. I was still at home.

Going to Paris was something completely different, like stepping into another world. When we arrived by train, the city had the appearance of a jewel. It was stunning. It had incredible beauty and was almost dazzling in glamour. The roads, the cafés, the cobbled streets: everything seemed to be drizzled in romance. I immediately felt that this city was the place for me, but I was soon to experience my first lesson in local life because after some chopping and changing in the cast, several lead roles and dancers were changed for a new batch of local actors and it was only then that I learned what being an outsider in the city was all about. This new gang from Paris took one look at me and thought, 'Who the flippin' heck is this?' and I became a target.

I was the youngest cast member (my nickname was *La Petit* – the little one – because of my age) in a show that had swept across Italy and was now threatening to take the European art world by storm. What I hadn't been prepared for – what no map had taught me – was that a lot of Parisians often regarded outsiders like a piece of dirt. To them I was worthless, like a lump of dog *merde* on the sole of a very expensive Christian Dior shoe. It didn't matter what I had achieved in such a short space of time. Compared to them I was a nineteen-year-old child from the sticks. They viewed me as a nothing, a no mark, as worthless as a toad.

When I walked past them they would huddle together and make sly comments and jokes, but the insults never got to me. In fact, they only motivated me even further.

'Screw it,' I thought whenever I heard a cutting remark. 'I'll get even better and that'll upset them even more.'

Whatever anyone else in the cast thought, I knew that the applause wasn't lying. The public hadn't been motivated by anything other than the performance they had been watching and whether it had been worth the entrance fee. When the clapping and the cheering rang out after the show had finished, which it did every night, it always felt like a genuine reaction. I lapped it up.

It was also apparent to me that the new cast were armed with an incredible background in dance and that I had learned nothing in the way of proper technique during my brief stint with La Grande Eugene. Sure, I had picked up some moves in rehearsals, but when it came to performing the classics such as ballet, I was completely lost. I hadn't even attended a lesson before.

'Get your act together, Bruno,' I thought. 'You have to compete with these people if they are to respect you.'

On a whim I joined the local ballet school, which proved to be an eye opener because it was full of professionals from the Paris bloody Opera House and I looked like a flippin' hog in the middle of a line of racehorses. However, rather than being dissuaded by the fact that I would have to work ten times harder than everybody else, the initiation gave me motivation. I threw myself into classes with an eagerness to learn anything and everything. I was determined to be the best that I could be.

Luckily, I had a number of friends from the cast and crew of the show, and myself and one of the choreographers, a new addition to the production team called Alain Dehay, moved into a lovely apartment in the Parisian district of Pigalle. I loved Alain, he was unlike the other new arrivals and he was a wonderful friend and a beautiful dancer. He recognised me as the rough diamond in the production and he took me under his wing. Alain had short curly hair and an aquiline nose. He was very witty and he knew everything there was to know about dance. Anyway, when we arrived we were told that the building had once been a brothel, but the pair of us loved it. Wow, what a place! The interior was crumbling and the building was clearly a fading glory, but the house was full of mosaics and tainted glass. Every room had a theme: some of them were oriental, others carried an exotic vibe such as the Egyptian room which featured a mural of sphinxes and hieroglyphics. The main living room, which was where the girls used to meet their clients when the brothel was in business at the turn of the twentieth century, was decorated with motifs from Indo China. I felt like I was living in a film set, even though I was sleeping on the floor to save money because the rent in Paris was so expensive.

Almost immediately, I fell in love with the Parisian nightlife, in particular one club called Le Set, which was very much the precursor to Studio 54, the legendary New York super-club from the late 1970s and early 80s and a hangout for rock stars, transvestites and party animals. Le Set was nowhere near as hedonistic as Studio 54, but it did carry an air of mystique. A bouncer guarded the door and chose the club's clientele by picking them out from the queue (you had to look like somebody to get in). Inside, the room was divided over two floors, a restaurant and a dance floor. All the beautiful people would go there to eat and then dance the night away.

Talk about going from feast to famine. In Ferrara, the closest thing we had to a celebrity was the vocal coach, Ms Rotten Goods herself, Signorina Gioseppina Guastaroba. In Le Set, I watched as the beautiful model Jerry Hall and the rock star Grace Jones danced side by side. One night, the French actress Catherine Deneuve sat down for dinner at the table next to mine. My darling, everybody looked glamorous, but what struck me was the sense of sexual freedom in Le Set. It wasn't a gay or straight joint – people were simply finding a new kind of sexual liberation and the boundaries between gender were starting to blur in front of my very eyes.

It was incredibly liberating. I threw myself into the club scene and I loved dressing up for Le Set. One night I even left the house in an Indian maharaja outfit. I had discovered yards and yards of satin lying around our converted brothel. It had been left there by the previous owners and I wanted to make the most of the material because in those days I couldn't afford a Christian Dior sarong.

With the skills picked up from my mother's work as a seamstress I made a party costume that resembled a cross between a sari and an Indian slave costume.

The fact that it looked ridiculous didn't matter to me, because once I'd convinced Le Set's bouncers that I was cool enough to enter the club, I was soon receiving plenty of attention, most thrillingly from an incredibly good-looking American man who was in his twenties and clearly a model. At first there was lots of smiling between us, but very little in the way of conversation. I couldn't speak much in the way of English and he knew nothing of the Italian language, but I persevered and we eventually became quite touchy-feely, if you know what I mean.

As the night progressed, his words became more and more slurred and his eyes started to roll around, but at two or three in the morning, he gathered his senses enough to utter the words, 'Come with me, Bruno.' And I had absolutely no problem translating what this Adonis had in mind, so I hopped into a cab to his apartment. When we finally arrived and he started to undress, well, my eyes nearly popped out of my head. He was the eighth wonder of the flippin' world.

'This is going to be a night to remember,' I thought. But as I slipped out of my sari, my beau staggered from one side of the bedroom to the other, where he tripped over a table and landed face down on the floor and proceeded to pass out for the night. 'Mr Big' was so out of his face that it didn't take long for me to realise that he was on something a lot stronger than booze. He must have been taking drugs of some kind and I was furious with myself for not spotting it earlier.

My embarrassment didn't end there, however. Because he lived in the middle of nowhere and it was the dead of night, I had to wait until the morning before I could sneak out of the front door and cross the city via the subway. Ordinarily this wouldn't have been a problem, but if you remember I was wearing a sari, and not a very well made one at that. As I walked down the street, avoiding the stares of passing commuters leaving their houses for the morning, the cloth hiding my modesty began falling apart at the seams. To prevent complete humiliation and an arrest for public indecency, I had to hold the fabric together like a towel. And that, my darling, is when I hit the Parisian rush hour looking like a demented person.

Oh, the drama. There were stares, people were pointing. Old ladies looked away in disgust. When I finally got home to the flat, my friends were already awake. They were desperate to know what I'd been up to. I knew I couldn't have told them the truth about my lover's pathetic end to the evening because it would have meant months and months of ridicule, so I concocted a night of passion that left them salivating. They swallowed my story and I realised I'd truly settled into the Parisian way of life: *mon cherie*, I'd finally worked out how to score points.

☆

La Grande Eugene was completely homoerotic for the time. Three of the leading roles were played by men who performed as women; some of the guys in the show were highly respected actors, others were raving queens, and as you could imagine, some of them could be incredibly bitchy. Drama seemed to follow them wherever they went. When a couple of the cast moved into the spare room in our apartment in Paris, I was struck straightaway by the fact that they were forever having guy trouble.

From what I could tell, the biggest problem was that these boys always seemed to fall for straight men. That resulted in a lot of broken hearts because they didn't have a cat in hell's chance of building a relationship. One evening, a big fat boy called José from the apartment became very distraught at yet another break-up and he threatened to commit suicide as the rest of us were about to leave for Le Set.

What a scene. There was lots of howling and wailing about how he was going to stick his head in the oven and kill himself. Not that we cared. We were happy to leave him to it because the house bills had been left unpaid and the gas had been cut off that morning. He was unaware of our meagre financial state. When we arrived home at five in the morning, José was very much alive and fast asleep on the kitchen floor, his head still in the oven. The sight of his fat back-side in the air was enough to send us into hysterics and as he stirred from his peaceful slumber, the wailing and blubbering began again.

'Oh, I wanted to die,' he screamed, banging his head on the oven, causing the kitchen top to wobble wildly, such was his hefty size.

'Well pay the bill,' one of the other queens hissed savagely. 'Then get a match.'

Those catty boys had some seriously sharp claws.

☆

In spring 1975, the show eventually moved to Munich and the adventures continued because La Grande Eugene was a smash wherever it went. People were going crazy; the performances received fantastic reviews and the theatre was packed every night. One evening, as I was taking my make-up off in the dressing rooms and hauling myself out of the glass robe that weighed a hundred tonnes, the famous movie star Helmut Berger appeared behind me in the mirror. I recognised him immediately because he was the Brad Pitt of his generation. Well, in Germany at least. It took me a while before I managed to catch my breath.

'I can't tell you how much I loved the show,' he said, resting his hands on my shoulders. 'It was wonderful.'

I was absolutely speechless. When I had first travelled to Milan all those months ago, I had never expected any attention. The adulation, the money, the lifestyle: it was all a novelty. Whenever I received my pay packet, the first thought in my head was always, 'Well, this is good, I would have done that work for free!' And the money was forever being sent back to my mother. But bless her, rather than spending it, she cared for my cash and opened a special bank account in my name because our peasant background had taught us that the next rainy day might be just around the corner. The Toniolis always had to be prepared for the worst.

Anyway, the fabulously handsome Helmut Berger invited the entire cast of La Grand Eugene to Munich's swankiest hangout, the Why Not? club, where there was a party every Saturday night. I knew I just had to make an impression when I walked through the front doors for the first time, because the club would be a *Who's Who* of local celebrity. Luckily, my wardrobe was packed with fancy outfits, many of which I had made myself. Despite my sari disaster in Paris, I still carried a creative streak with clothing and was always stitching a shirt together or making a pair of tight trousers in my spare time. That night I pulled out my finest threads: a very figure-hugging pair of flares and an embroidered waistcoat that I had fashioned myself from silk. At the time, I had a real Mick Jagger look about my hair, which was very long, and because Munich was so cold, I topped the outfit off with a fur coat I had picked up in Paris.

Anyway, when I arrived at the club, I was swept away by the mood in the room. There was champagne everywhere. The whole place was brimming with Munich's beautiful people and all of them seemed to be toasting La Grande Eugene. I was in a whirlwind of adulation. But as I drank my second glass of bubbly, something unusual happened. The room started to swirl, the colours from the lights became dazzling and psychedelic. My senses seemed to explode. It didn't take long for me to realise that my drink had been spiked with LSD.

Wow! There was a bang in my head. The only thing I could compare it to was the colourful spectrum of light that appeared whenever the Starship Enterprise went into warp speed on the sci-fi programme *Star Trek*. I had no idea what the hell was going on, I thought I was Roger Daltrey and when I looked down at myself, I was bathed in gold. It was at that point that I started dancing on the tables like a lunatic. In my head I thought I was flying, swinging from the chandeliers like a rock god, but the reality was I was jumping from table to table knocking glasses over, sending the other guests scrambling for safety . . .

. . . Everything changed in an instant.

I was outside, the buildings were looming over me, caving in, bending. My world started to distort. There was daylight and I realised that, somehow, I was in a ski resort. A ski resort! How the bloody hell did I get to a ski resort? I was two hours out of Munich, up to my shins in snow, and shivering in my fur coat with no idea how I had arrived there. It was madness.

When I finally made my way back to the hotel where the cast was staying at the time, it was hours later and I was in bits. I thought large chunks of hair were growing out of my face. My eyes looked huge and I felt very, very ill. Because I had such a fantastically active imagination, the LSD had pushed me into a huge high, but the low – the comedown – felt crushing. Alain gave me two valium tablets to bring me down, then, to take my mind off the awful episode, I walked to the nearest cinema where I watched the Barbara Streisand movie *Hello Dolly* twice in a row. And as I sat there, still wrapped in my fur coat, I cried and cried and cried for hours. The experience was enough to put me off hallucinogenics forever. But I was soon to discover that something far more mind-bending was just around the corner.

CHAPTER 5

ALL IN A NIGHT'S WORK

Now I don't want you thinking my brushes with fame, the undersized boots, and a brain-melting acid trip were merely the results of good fortune. Oh no, there was plenty of gumption needed along the way; some elbow grease, a little bit of *oomph*. Despite finding the time to make my own sari – not to mention the occasional waistcoat for all those glamorous parties at Le Set and the Why Not? Club – I actually worked my flippin' socks off during my spare time away from La Grande Eugene. The shows were gruelling, the schedule was tough, but whenever I wasn't perform-ing, I would spend my time practising, practising, practising. Then I would practise some more. I was like a man possessed.

As I started working with the show in Paris and then Munich in 1975, the ballet lessons became more and more intense. Were they tough, I hear you ask? Well, yes they bloody well were. When I started the classes I found ballet was very different to anything I had experienced before and far more complicated than the dancing I had done in Ferrara. Every new position felt alien and uncomfortable, and after my first class I could barely move, though that was my own fault. In my infinite wisdom I had enrolled in a group that was a grade higher than the beginner's level, the level I should have been working from. What a mistake that was. I had a job to keep up with everybody in the group – the kids from Paris bloody Opera House – even though I was nineteen years old, supple and very, very fit, because those kids had started learning when they were ten years of age. At times I thought my legs were going to explode from the sheer force of the different movements I was having to perform, over and over and over.

The funny thing was, I loved it, despite the aches and cracking joints that dogged me as I walked home to my apartment in Pigalle, or our Munich hotel. Whenever I felt a passion for something, any pain or hard work usually faded into the background. Ballet was no different. I soon found that my body could respond to the training. The more I practised, the more quickly I recovered from the physical exertions. Even better, I had a natural aptitude for ballet and I seemed to pick up the moves and techniques instinctively, though I quickly realised I was never going to be Rudolph Nureyev.

I was also challenging myself mentally. From the minute I started working with La Grande Eugene, I wanted to prove that my appointment wasn't a fluke, that there was more to my game than some passing resemblance to a star of the show. Sure, I had been thrown in at the deep end by the director Frantz Salieri, but I had found the bravery to face up to the dance routines presented to me. Most of the time I had to improvise various moves in rehearsals

(I would learn the proper techniques as soon as I was able), but I always delivered whenever the audiences arrived, and no punter ever complained about my lack of experience because my natural ability meant that I could carry everything off with grace and style.

I suppose there's no better school of learning than practising something for real; there's no way of theorising about how something works until a person actually does it properly. Luckily, the dancer's instinct was in me. I knew that I could learn the different techniques required in La Grande Eugene, whether that be acting, singing or dancing. But the really important skills – delivery and a sense of timing – came from a sixth sense which I was able to draw on when required. La Grande Eugene brought that sixth sense to life and I thrived on it.

It also helped that the people I was working with were proper professionals; I was constantly learning. Just by turning up every day and watching the other dancers perform gave me a chance to absorb new skills and techniques. I didn't waste a second when I was in the theatre. If I wasn't working myself, I was always asking questions of others. I would get the other dancers to show me new techniques because I knew that by learning and practising, I would improve. I was probably a right pain in the bum for everyone around me.

Thinking about it now, I had probably taken more from my working class upbringing in Ferrara than I realised. The desire for self-improvement and hard work came from my parents and my grandparents. It was driving me on in the same way that it had pushed them on to work harder. I was taking pride in my profession much in the same way as my father had looked upon the cars in his workshop, or the satisfaction my mother took from her seamstress work. The difference with my life and theirs was that I had managed to follow my dream. I knew that if I knuckled down even more, then more successes would surely follow.

☆

It was only natural that I would want my parents to share in my new life, to see what I had become. I wanted them to understand that I wasn't living with my head in the clouds (well, apart from the unfortunate LSD incident, which I never discussed with them), so as soon as I felt comfortable, in spring 1975, I invited them over to see the show in Munich, where I got them the best seats in the house.

They were delighted at the invite, though I suspect that they still viewed my work with La Grande Eugene as a phase, a fleeting fancy. They probably assumed that I would eventually become bored and lonely and then return to Ferrara, but they were wrong. There was no real sense of homesickness because I could be me all of the time with La Grande Eugene. It was the first period in my life where I felt complete freedom. At the gay bars in Bologna or Rome I felt free, but that sensation only lasted until I had to go home. With the dance company I didn't have to pretend to anybody about who I was, I didn't have to hide the fact that I was gay to a stranger who might take offence. When I was onstage, I was being Bruno Tonioli, 100 per cent, 10 out of 10, baby.

When Mother and Father travelled to Munich by train I think it must have been their longest adventure from Ferrara at the time.

The furthest they had travelled prior to their German excursion was a two-day drive to the seaside resort of Alghero in Sardinia. Flippin' heck, Munich must have felt like the other side of the world to them. When they took their seats in the theatre their weekend became even more alien because they were then treated to one of the most homoerotic performances on the planet. But talk about the power of the stage! When they heard the applause and became entrapped by the movement and the action in front of them, Mother and Father fell in love with La Grande Eugene. It mesmerised them, much like it had mesmerised me in Positano and Milan.

Still, I think that was the moment that the lights probably went on for them about my sexuality. My father, I could tell, was a bit startled when I saw him afterwards. He kept looking at me strangely, as if he was seeing the real me for the first time. I'm not surprised La Grande Eugene had been a culture shock for him. I spent half the show rolling around, semi-naked, in a mainly male company. It must have been blindingly obvious that I was gay, what with my flamboyant sense of timing, a mirror dress and some incredibly camp friends. It was such a dazzling world for them that I could sense they were freaked out by it, but not in a bad way.

The next day, I took them to the station because the show was moving on to Berlin and I was leaving town once more. It was then that they realised my love for the theatre was more than a passing phase. It was my passion. They knew they had lost me to the stage forever and the understanding was bittersweet. I could see they were sad, but also that they seemed happy for me. The funny thing was, they never mentioned anything about my sexuality, even though it would have been the perfect opportunity. They wouldn't mention it in conversation for the rest of their lives, bless them.

☆

Living out of a suitcase, darling? I loved it. La Grande Eugene embarked on a big tour of Germany where we performed in Frankfurt, Hamburg, Cologne and Berlin.

By travelling around Germany, I was in heaven, despite my reluctance to learn the language in the *Ragioneria*. I loved geography and I loved exploring because I wanted to learn so much from the world's different cultures. I took up German again and visited the Ludwig castles in Bavaria and saw places that I'd only ever read about when I studied World War II in history lessons at school. I loved looking at the old churches in Berlin, the bomb sites, the faded glory of a once powerful nation.

In Berlin, a city of divine decadence, the show was a huge hit and one of our biggest fans was a famous drag queen and club owner called Romy Haag. She used to come to the show nearly every night. Romy was a legend in the city and a statuesque transsexual. She would often arrive with a coterie of trannies and anyone who was sitting behind them would miss the entire show because they weren't able to see over their wigs.

Oh, but Hamburg was filthy. It had the grubbiest red light district in all of Europe and our hotel was positioned on the infamous Reeperbahn, a parade of sex shops and brothels, which naturally we loved. One night the entire cast went into an adult cinema. It had lots of neon lights flashing outside and the letters 'XXX' written all over the window, which meant nothing to me. I didn't have a clue what they stood for. It didn't take long for me to find out because I couldn't believe my eyes once I had got to my seat with a box of popcorn. I had never seen a pornographic movie before. It was certainly nothing like the films I had watched when I used to visit the cinema in Ferrara. Oh my god, *OMG!*, when a man's bits flashed up on the screen for the first time I went into shock.

It wasn't just the cinemas that were racy in Hamburg, the world of performance was steamy, too. For most audiences in Europe, La Grande Eugene was considered an adult production, what with the drag queens and partial nudity among the cast, me mostly. In Hamburg, however, we were thought of as being tame. The visiting clientele expected flesh and frolics whenever they visited a Reeperbahn production, and so the owners of the theatre where La Grande Eugene was being held confronted me a few hours before our first performance was due to start. They wanted me to do the show stark flippin' naked.

The funny thing was, my costume was hardly conservative. When I wasn't dressed as a male hooker or wearing a dress made from broken mirrors, my 'look' comprised a see-through catsuit with a flesh-coloured g-string. 'Little Bruno' was not on view, but my outfit left very little to the imagination. Weirdly, I had no problems with nudity – I would have done it – but in my mind, it didn't suit the character I was playing. He was supposed to carry an air of mystery. The audience was supposed to feel uncertainty as to whether I was a man or a woman. So I put my foot down and knocked on the hotel room door of Frantz Salieri.

At first, he seemed startled that *La Petit* was making a song and a dance about a costume alteration, but he listened to my theories on the character and after much staring and tutting and ruffling of the wild hair, he agreed with me.

'Bruno, you're right,' he said. 'It wouldn't work.'

I breathed a deep sigh of relief. My instincts had been spot on, and I had stuck up for my beliefs, probably for the first time in my career. My inexorable rise continued. My kit stayed on.

☆

Where was I? How did I get here? How the flippin' heck had all of this happened? These were the questions that I asked myself every single day. The truth was, I didn't know what was going on. It was as if all the prayers I had once made as I sat lonely and despondent in my Ferrara home were being answered at once. I was starring in a top show, I was seeing the world. I had escaped the humdrum of northern Italian life and I could be me. I wasn't sure whether I was incredibly lucky or making my own luck by working so hard, but I decided that I was going to take every opportunity that life chucked at me, however weird or wonderful it might be.

Then along came London. The city I'd dreamt of visiting more than any other, what with its fantastic culture, its wild clubs and the fabulous shops. The Rolling Stones, Elton John and The Who; Carnaby Street and Covent Garden. David bloody Bowie. When I heard that La Grande Eugene was due to open there in May 1976 I was beside myself with excitement. We had been booked to play at the Roundhouse in Camden which meant I would be wandering the city for a couple of months at least. What a trip!

When I arrived in England, everything was so big. I saw the

Top left: My first steps in ballroom dancing with Mum and Dad.

Top right: Good Catholic boys. Outside church with my cousin Massimo.

Bottom left: Moustache apart, can you spot the resemblance? Dad posing in front of a Bruno masterpiece. Flowers were my speciality.

Bottom right: Under restraint on the beach with my parents. Stolen clogs not in shot.

Top left: Teenager with an attitude. Pretty boy, though.

Above: Mum and Dad's wedding in 1954. Ceremony styled by Francis Ford Coppola.

Top right: Looking grumpy with Mum. Probably because I was being dragged away from The Land of the Butterflies.

Bottom right and left: My parents on honeymoon in Florence. Dad had Rat Pack good looks and Mum took her cues from Barbara Stanwyck. The 'La Liz' look came later.

Above: London 1976. Trying my best impression of the TV cop show *The Professionals*.

Left: Teaching yet another class at the Covent Garden Dance Centre.

Bottom left: Again, keeping a keen eye on my students.

Bottom right: Acting mean and moody in the 1980s. I should have been in a Brat Pack movie. What a waste!

Above: Ready to go on stage for Lindsay Kemp's production of *Salome*. Siouxsie Sioux stole my look.

Below: The famous mirror dress from La Grande Eugene. By god, it weighed a ton.

Above: In full flow. Firing on all cylinders behind the camera on a commercial shoot.

Below: Posing in the 1980s with my first Paul Smith jacket and shirt. A picture of yuppiedom.

Above: 'No cameras, I want to be alone.'

Below: Singing in French with Le Ball. Alain is in the middle, Luc is on the right.

Above: The Disco Kings in all their glory. No provincial night club was safe. Funny, after our arrival on the scene, they all closed down.

Below: Posing for the famous photographer Johnny Rozsa. Feeling like a work of art (but still a work in progress).

Top left: Christmas with Oliver. A new member of the family is introduced to the world. What fabulous hair!

Top right: Auditioning for The Disco Kings in my world famous fake leather pants and stunning Cuban heels. They came all the way from Franco's shoemaking shop in Bologna.

Middle left: In my garden during the summer of 1991 with Mum and Dad.

Middle right: My parents ballroom dancing in Ferrara.

Left: Strike a pose, there's nothing to it.

Above: Demonstrating the correct lines to my dancers. It's all about the lines, baby!

Below: Long before *Fifty Shades of You-Know-What*, the softest Italian leather always works.

Above: My design skills were put to good use when I constructed my own costume and headgear for Lindsay Kemp's *Salome*. It hardly concealed my 'hidden talents'.

Below: In La Grande Eugene with my hooker boots, suspender belt and corset. It was in the contract!

Left: The red-hot choreographer in action.

Bottom left: With Arlene Phillips and Alain in Mangburry's watching one of Hot Gossip's first performances.

Below: All of me at seventeen, in all my glory.

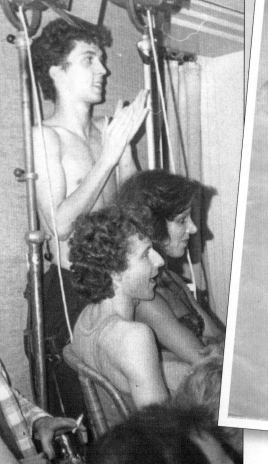

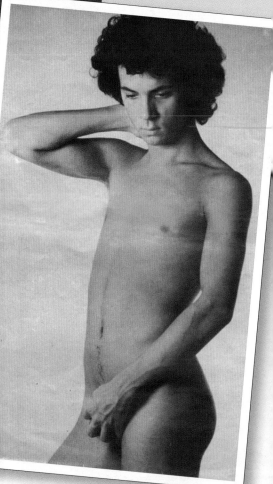

White Cliffs of Dover when we arrived by boat, and as the train made its way through the Kent countryside to the capital I was like a little kid counting down the days to Christmas.

'Are we there?' I would shout. 'Are we there yet?'

It's funny, I didn't feel as if I had caught the enormity of London when I first arrived. As we got off at the station it seemed a bit underwhelming. There were no landmarks or fantastic buildings to look at. I was greeted instead by some drab offices and a lot of grumpy looking commuters. It was only once I'd settled into my digs in Belsize Park that I really experienced the beauty of the place. Everything was so green. There were tree-lined streets and parks everywhere. I loved the architecture of the old buildings and the famous sights like St Paul's Cathedral and Tower Bridge. I could sense straightaway that it was a totally different place to Paris or any of the other cities I had visited. Paris, for example, had hit me instantly. It was an assault to the senses. London was a completely different beast. Once I got used to the place, it grew within me. It became part of me. Its pleasures, such as the Royal Opera House in Covent Garden, had to be discovered because they weren't going to give themselves up easily. The only thing I wasn't sure of was the food. Sure, I could eat some Italian dishes, but a lot of the English delicacies left me cold. I thought toad in the hole was an animal when I first heard the name. And the doner kebab. What the hell was that? The first time it was mentioned to me, I thought it was a person.

'Who's this Donna Kebab they keep talking about?' I said. 'Why are we going to meet her after the pub has shut?'

When I saw a doner kebab for the first time, I nearly passed out. And when somebody told me they had a spotted dick, I begged them to see a doctor immediately. I just didn't get it, but that wasn't surprising really, the culture was so new to me. At the time, I didn't speak any English at all, only Italian, some French and a smattering of German (which wasn't going to get me very far), so getting across town was always a problem for me because a) I couldn't ask anyone for directions and b) it was so huge. In Paris I could walk anywhere and I was often able to find my way around the place with a map. Sometimes I would stroll from my apartment in Pigalle to the Opera House and it would take me no time at all. In London, however, I was overwhelmed by the size of the city. I wasn't even able to walk from my hotel to the Roundhouse, it was so far away.

By the time work had started on the show, I was overwhelmed by London. I felt the buzz. Opening night was like a scene from a movie: the Roundhouse was packed to the rafters and there was a buzzy chatter among the audience. All the big newspaper reviewers were there, including a writer from the London *Times*, which everyone was very excited about. Applause rang out throughout the show and when the performance finished, the Roundhouse doors blew open afterwards and a rapturous audience flew into the street like old pieces of newspaper blowing around in a gale, flittering down the road with excitement at what they had witnessed. Ladies and gentlemen, La Grande Eugene was a London hit!

☆

It's funny how life can take you to some funny places. Coincidence can throw you into the path of a person or people that will forever pop up in your career. When La Grande Eugene was rehearsing in Paris, Alain became friends with a choreographer called Molly Molloy, an American lady who had trained at the New York High School of Performing Arts and the Metropolitan Opera Ballet School. She later went on to work with the famous choreographer Luigi and danced alongside Sammy Davis Jnr. She had a wonderful reputation.

Anyhow, whenever they met in Paris, Molly would always say to him, 'Alain, if ever you travel to London, you must go to the Dance Centre in Covent Garden. My friend Arlene Phillips works there and she is sure to look after you with some lessons.'

Of course, Arlene would go on to be a fellow judge alongside myself, Len Goodman and Craig Revel Horwood on *Strictly Come Dancing*, but god knows what she must have thought when Alain and I walked into her studio for the first time. I had just arrived from mainland Europe, I could barely speak a word of English and I was consistently curious about everything.

'Why are you doing that?'

'What is this you're doing?'

'Why does that foot go there?'

It must have driven her flippin' mental.

The reason I had joined up with her classes was because I was compelled to. Like Paris, Munich and everywhere else I had travelled, I needed to learn. I wanted to improve. I wanted to be schooled in other styles of dance like jazz and modern. The Covent Garden Dance School covered the lot, so when myself and Alain enrolled, I bombarded Arlene with questions in my eagerness to improve.

Whenever she tried to explain, I would pull faces at her, mainly because I didn't have a clue what she was saying. I could barely order an omelette in the local greasy spoon, let alone comprehend the finer intricacies of modern dance in a language that I had only just started to learn. It didn't help that all the other kids in my class had been working together for months. A large number of them were professional dancers from TV and West End productions. There was so much talent on show that every lesson was like a scene from the 1980s TV show *Fame* and each one of them instinctively knew what stretches to pull and when. It was second nature to them. When Arlene put the music on, they would start performing moves that they had probably done a hundred times over. Once more I was a hog among the horses.

Thank god for my enthusiasm, darling. I persevered and kept up as best I could. The other dancers in my class seemed to like me, probably because my attempts to communicate were so bad that I would get my words muddled up. After a while, they would speak to me in pidgin English during lessons, or as we gathered together during the water breaks in class. It turned out that some of them were actually the dance troupe called Hot Gossip who would later go on to work on *The Kenny Everett Video Show* and release a hit single called 'I Lost My Heart To A Starship Trooper'. At the time they were still in their infancy, but sensing an opportunity to make some friends, I invited them to La Grande Eugene, along with Arlene.

They loved it, especially the costumes and choreography. Arlene, in particular, was taken by the make-up that I would wear during the *Jesus Christ Superstar* climax to the show. The look was very heavy and dark around the eyes. I often resembled a girl who hadn't been to sleep for a week, like Posh Spice after a night out.

'We really must get that look on the girls,' she said. 'Do you think you could teach them how to do it?'

Hot Gossip were about to start a residency at the West End club Mangburry's. It was a place I'd been eager to try because I'd heard it was quite a decadent hang out. I was happy to travel with the band, so a few days later, Arlene picked me up in her battered Fiat Panda and I sat backstage at Mangburry's and slapped on bucketloads of eye liner and lippy for the girls.

In those days, Mangburry's was the place to be seen. It carried a decadent vibe and there was a cabaret show nearly every night. Showbiz talent spotters were forever waving contracts around; potential stars were often schmoozed with champagne. A buzz had built around Hot Gossip following a series of gigs, and after their show a big wig from Thames Television seemed eager to meet them.

The whole evening was a real eye opener. I could see how people could make it in show business in a city like London, but I also learned that it wouldn't come easily for anyone who wanted it. Hot Gossip and Arlene weren't being picked up that night through luck. They had spent months and months and months together, dancing and rehearsing for hours on end in the hope that something might fall their way. It was inspirational really, and it made me realise how limited my knowledge of dance had been. I had only appeared in one show. Seeing so many dancers, with so many skills and credits to their name, had blown my mind. I wanted to be as good as them.

I continued to book more classes. My schedule was off the scale. I did ballet in the morning, jazz in the afternoon and La Grande Eugene in the evening. I learned more and more English because I knew that if I was to succeed in London, I would have to be able to communicate properly. Besides, asking questions of Arlene could only get me so far. I taught myself English every week. And when I wasn't dancing, or performing, or helping Hot Gossip to apply their eyeliner, I read the London newspapers and watched English telly in order to pick up more and more of the language. It's amazing what you can learn from watching *Dr Who* – it was the first show I became hooked on because I could follow the plot without understanding a word. Oh, the universal language of the Daleks!

At that time, there was never any aim or end result. I didn't want to be famous or appear in a Hollywood film (though that would have been nice). My hope was to be as good, if not better, than the people I was seeing in my Covent Garden dance classes. I wanted to be good enough to perform in Mangburry's. My attitude was, 'If you can become good enough, Bruno, something will happen for you.' It was crazy planning I know, but as you may have guessed by now, I've never been a planner. I was simply sticking to my pact – to follow whatever path destiny had laid out for me.

I wanted to take more singing lessons; I wanted to act; I wanted to appear in shows. I wanted to do everything. I was hooked on the vibrancy and the artistry and the culture of life in London because it felt so exciting. It was something I had never experienced before, not even in Paris. Compared to London, everywhere else was provincial. On the tubes and buses, in the theatres and clubs, I was surrounded by inspiration everywhere I turned. There were so many things to be involved in. And I wanted to experience them all.

☆

There were some harsh facts to face, however. La Grande Eugene wasn't going to stay in London for long. I decided that when the show paid farewell to England for good, I would pay farewell to the show. I had rented a room in a Notting Hill flat from a wonderful actor called Eric Roberts. I loved it, and I couldn't face the thought of going back to my Pigalle apartment. I felt free in London. I was meeting wonderful, wonderful people – friends and lovers – and my main aim was to explore everything the city and its people had to offer. I was young. I was having a good time.

The only problem was my passport. I would need to get a stamp from the Italian authorities if I was to get a permanent work permit – it would allow me to stay in London. To do that I would have to return to Italy, but because I'd left the country as I turned eighteen, I knew I would be held at the border. Under the laws of the land, everyone had to spend two years in national service, which really wasn't going to suit somebody like myself and I couldn't bear to break away from my dreams of being a top dancer in the home of David Bowie and Mick Jagger.

I knew that the Italian army wouldn't enrol me if they knew I was gay – it was grounds for dismissal in those days – but so many straight people had used that excuse to evade national service that the forces had become somewhat suspicious. Married men would turn up in drag just to dodge the draft and the forces had caught on to the scam. Suddenly anyone pretending to be gay was assumed to be straight. The flippin' irony.

Fortunately, I had gathered a minor level of fame at home.

Because La Grande Eugene had been such a success in Europe, quite a lot had been written about me. The gay press, which was admittedly low key at the time, had interviewed me and some of the mainstream newspapers had shown an interest, too. I had cuttings and photographs that showed me performing in my mirror gown, as well as a picture of me as I danced around in a black leather corset during my role as a male hooker. No right-thinking soldier would have mistaken me for a cold-blooded killer.

To make sure that my interviewer got the message, I started acting like a Meryl Streep-type as soon as I walked into the office. I became a luvvie, but I didn't go crazy. I just did what a kid of twenty-one could do to convince the authorities that he was gay, when for most of my Italian-bound life I had pretended to be the exact opposite.

Miraculously it was enough.

'I completely understand,' said the officer in charge. 'You're excused.'

I didn't know whether to laugh or cry.

Sadly not everyone was as understanding. Twenty-four hours after my interview had been finalised, some terrible twot – a former friend from Bologna – called me out of the blue. He wanted money.

'I know what you did,' he hissed down the phone 'I'm going to tell your parents that you're gay unless you give me some cash.'

Well, I wasn't fussed. Even if my mother and father weren't willing to admit it to themselves that I was gay, I was happy for them to know. I couldn't have made it any more obvious if I'd tried.

'That's fine,' I said. 'Feel free to do it.'

I couldn't give a toss.

Nothing ever happened, or if it did, I never got to hear about it. I was learning that by being open about who I really was, I could be as free as a bird.

CHAPTER 6

WEST SIDE STORY

Leaving the glamorous, sparkly, heaving bosom of a famous production was scary, but it was something I had to do, if only for my own self-fulfilment. I knew I had a form of talent, a *something*. Well, why else would all those people in Milan, Munich, Paris and Hamburg have paid to see me strut around in a dress made from broken mirrors? Adulation wasn't enough, though. London had opened my eyes to the wealth of incredible ability that was literally fighting for survival in the world and I had to be as good, if not better, than all of them. But how?

By taking a trip to New York, my darling. That's how.

There had been rumours that La Grande Eugene would one day make it to the Big Apple, mainly because of the wonderful reviews it had received during its time in London. Through the grapevine I'd heard that an unnamed but big-time New York producer had even started brokering a deal with Frantz Salieri. Perhaps the success of the show in Italy, France, Germany and England had gone to his head as Frantz started making demands soon afterwards.

'The show will only play on Broadway if it runs at the Ziegfeld Theatre!' he proclaimed somewhat boldly and pompously.

Now, everybody knew that this was impossible. The Ziegfeld was, by then, a cinema. It could hardly be reconverted back into one of the biggest theatres on Broadway. Besides, La Grande Eugene played to audiences of around 1,000 people which was why many critics felt it worked so well. The show carried a cabaret vibe with it and the audience had to be close to really feel the atmosphere. Performing in a theatre like the Ziegfeld wouldn't have worked because the setting was that much bigger. Unsurprisingly, the whole plan fell down the drain and at the time, I felt frustrated. I'd already explored a few cities but New York was on my hit list because I was like a junkie looking for my next fix. Instead of drugs, my high was a new city, a new adventure. Once I'd realised that I wasn't going to America with Frantz Salieri in the summer of 1976, I set myself free from La Grande Eugene.

That's when I realised that I could do whatever I liked, and so I flew to New York for dance lessons. Now, I know that it sounds like an extravagant decision, but I'd saved enough money for my plane ticket thanks to my wages from the show; a friend in Manhattan had promised to put me up while I was there, so my accommodation was free. I was also determined. I'd seen a lot of West End shows during my time in London and I could tell that the best dancers always came from New York. I wanted some of their stardust, so I hopped on a plane and crashed in the Big Apple for a month.

My aim was to learn from the best, but as soon as I landed, the atmosphere and energy of the place smashed me around the face like a hot frying pan. It was an electric eel shock to the head. The cabs honked their horns, the sidewalks frothed and steamed, and the subways teemed with crazy people. I was in my element. Immediately I enrolled in dance classes. I went to the Martha Graham School of Contemporary Dance and honestly, you have no idea: to get in I had to pass the Spanish Inquisition of auditions. There were assessments, tests and exams. Luckily, La Grande Eugene's success meant that I already had a reputation, even in somewhere as far away as New York, and I was able to enrol on a very intensive course.

That's when the pain started because I seemed to have joined the toughest, hardest dance centre this side of an SAS training camp. Flippin' heck, it was a totally different way of working. The lessons were incredibly physical and the tutors taught modern dance in a completely different style from what I had been used to in Europe. After my first session, I was a broken man because Martha Graham's techniques used contractions which started at the pelvis and went up the spine and into the neck and the head.

'Oh my god,' I thought. 'There are knives being stabbed everywhere in my flippin' back. This is agony!'

My feet were scrunched up like bits of old newspaper, my toes throbbed, my whole being trembled and I experienced intense pain in strange places – my armpits and the backs of my knees ached every single morning.

I thought that learning with the Martha Graham School of Contemporary Dance was more arduous than Chinese water torture, but because I was falling more and more in love with the movement and the discipline of the lessons, I did everything I could to improve. One week, when I decided that I needed to become bendier and more flexible in the legs, I even spent a couple of days in Central Park. I sat for hours in several different positions, just so I could stretch my muscles and become looser in the limbs. I arched and pulled, contorted, until my muscles spasmed and beads of sweat ran down my face with exertion.

And the dancers? Well, I thought the performers in London had been good, but the Americans were in a class of their own. They were doing contemporary moves that I'd never seen before. It was humbling, insane; I worked like a cart horse just to keep up with the worst performers in the group. But it wasn't just the training at the Martha Graham School of Contemporary Dance that was tough. Every other day I would visit a school on the East Side of Manhattan to learn jazz; in the evenings I would do modern in SoHo. Some days I was taking three classes in twelve hours. Honestly, I was in tears. There were mornings when I could hardly get out of bed, the pain was that much.

My agony didn't stop me from living la vida loca, however. I was in one of the most exciting places on the planet and there were plenty of adventures to write home about. One evening I went to see the musical *Chicago* – my first ever Broadway show. How exciting! It had been put together by the legendary director Bob Fosse, the mastermind behind the movie *Cabaret* in 1972. *Cabaret* had been so fabulous that I broke down when I first went to see it in Ferrara as a teenager. I was wowed by the music and enthralled by the performances, particularly Liza Minnelli, who was the star of the show.

I must have been going through a hormonal phase back then, because I enjoyed *Cabaret* so much that every day for eight days I went to watch it. It was madness, and every time the movie played, a strange thing happened: I broke down in floods of tears, even though I knew the film from the inside out. The people in the popcorn kiosk must have wondered if I was crazy as they watched me pay for a ticket again and again and again, like clockwork, every afternoon. Two hours later they would stare as I staggered away from the cinema at the end, sniffing and snorting back the tears.

Chicago had a similar effect. As the show unfolded, I sat on the balcony and wept. The whole thing – the choreography, the dancing, the music – was just fantastic, and as I allowed the sheer talent of the production to wash over me, my emotions began to go all over the shop. I started to sob. I began to sniff. I was a weeping wreck. It's fair to say that the people around me probably assumed that I was a little bit broken in the head. An old lady even handed me a box of tissues. (A word to the wise, darling, if anyone ever catches me crying these days, it's usually because I've been appreciating some form of incredible talent. Well, not all the time. When I witnessed the former snooker player Dennis Taylor performing the Cha Cha Cha on *Strictly Come Dancing*, I wept at the sheer tragedy of it all. Usually though, when I'm watching a professional perform-ance, tears are a very good sign.)

Anyway, New York to me was an incredible source of inspiration. Even walking down the street was a head spin, because there were all sorts of crazy fashions going on. The night life was just as insane and I finally went to the legendary and decadent Studio 54 night-club, which was everything I had ever experienced in London and Paris, but multiplied a million times over. When I walked in for the first time, I did a double take. There were internationally famous movie stars (who I cannot name) mixing with hookers and trannies on the dance floor. A man in Speedos began riding around the bar on a horse. Drag queens swanned about as if they owned the place. The crazy sights were like something from my Munich acid trip a year or two earlier, but this time I was completely sober. It was like living in another dimension and I thought the whole thing was absolutely fantastic. In one month, New York had completely turned my world, and my muscles, upside down.

☆

Comedown time.

Back in London, I was a nobody. A tiny goldfish in a massive lake. I had no job, I was without a show to rehearse for and I had to move into a bedsit in south-west London's Gloucester Road in order to keep the costs down. Darling, if this book were *Location, Location, Location*, Phil and Kirsty would describe my new pad as 'basic'. To make calls I would have to use a shared phone in the downstairs hallway. To pay for the gas and the electricity I would have to stick coins into a meter in a dusty cupboard under the stairs. It was grotty, like Dot Cotton's house, but I loved it because it was my place and I could make plans without having to worry about money too much.

I soon found I was able to live well on the wages I had saved from La Grande Eugene. Just like my grandmother, I could cook with a small bag of shopping and some imagination. And while there were no rabbits for me to hunt in the local park, I could quite happily live off the pasta and polenta dishes that I remembered from my childhood. All I needed was the little gas stove which sat in one corner of my room and everything was done in a pot or two, just like it had been at home in Ferrara.

Despite my ambition and desire to learn, I found that living in London would take some effort. The competition for theatre work was intense, and what followed was a period of funny gigs, self-funded projects and false dawns as I attempted to get my foot in the door somewhere, anywhere. At first, it didn't take long for me to find a job and as soon as I returned from New York, I heard that Lindsay Kemp – the amazing director – was putting on a show called *Salome* with his new company. Now, for those of you who might not have heard of him, Lindsay Kemp was a choreographer and a theatrical sensation. Anyone who was anyone took lessons from him – Kate Bush and David Bowie had asked for his help. He was a genius. I didn't think for one minute that he would be interested in an upstart like me when I tried out for *Salome*, but thankfully, Lindsay had seen La Grande Eugene and was a fan. He gave me a spot in the show and I was up and running again. The money rolled in once more and the rent was paid on time; I had enough ten pence pieces in my jar to stick into the electricity meter whenever the power ran out.

This new role did nothing to curb my enthusiasm. Just like before, I decided to throw myself into every music-related class I could find. I even took singing lessons from a man called Ian Adams, who had previously taught the likes of Elaine Paige and the opera star, Sarah Brightman. Myself, Alain – who had also left La Grande Eugene to stay in London – and another friend called Luc decided that we were suddenly cabaret singers and formed a group called Le Ball. Even more unbelievably, we managed to get regular gigs at Mangburry's, despite the fact that the entire show was sung entirely in French. My big moment in our act came whenever I performed a song called 'Marinella'. I would dress up like a French grease ball and ham up my accent, strutting around and playing to the crowd. I sounded like the policeman from the 80s TV comedy *'Allo 'Allo!*.

As you can probably tell, I thrived on unpredictability. I never knew when the next job was starting or where the next pay cheque was coming from, but I soon learned to roll with the chopping and the changing. When *Salome* finished, I moved on to the next thing. When the next thing had finished, I moved on to something else. Each job was different from the last and there was never a dull moment. For a year I pinballed from gig to gig, never stopping for breath. I seemed to enjoy not having any real sense of security or stability, something that would drive me up the flippin' wall today.

Next, I starred in a show called *Orpheus in the Underworld* where I was asked to play a character called Bacchus, the God of Wine. It was a dancing role, but the job involved my moving up the M1 because *Orpheus in the Underworld* was being produced by Opera North which was based in Leeds. I wasn't bothered. In fact I jumped at the chance and for the winter of 1977 and early 1978, I toured all over the north of the country. Because I had never been anywhere else in England apart from London, the whole relocation was an experience. Everywhere was cold and dark. It rained nearly every day, and I couldn't understand a word anyone was saying, even though I was very advanced in my English studies. The Geordies, the Scousers, the Mancs: what were they bloody going on about? Still, when I did understand what was being said, I became enamoured by the warmth of the personalities and the sense of humour that came from those areas.

Whenever I was down, which was rare, I always got myself off the scrap heap and started working towards getting another break. Moving back to Ferrara never crossed my mind. Every week I would pick up the *The Stage* newspaper – a performing arts weekly – and its pages were always stuffed with adverts for dancers, actors, singers, any sort of theatrical talent one could imagine really. One weekend, when I was journeying back from a performance in some rain-sodden corner of the north, I spotted an advert for a group called The Disco Kings. They were a dance troupe planning on making a few quid by travelling round the discotheques and nightclubs of London. The Disco Kings were cashing in on *Saturday Night Fever* mania and their 'talent' was to perform dance routines onstage to the latest disco hits of the time. Apparently, they were looking for a new male performer.

'That's me!' I thought. 'Bruno, get your fake leather pants on and get yourself to that audition.'

Clearly impressed with my trousers (and my dance moves of course), I landed the gig and what followed was a tawdry month of shaking my booty in some of the worst clubs known to man. Croydon, Bracknell, Bromley, Watford, Crawley, Woking, Romford. I was traversing the A to flippin' Z of London's provincial quarters. The clubs had names like Faces, The Blue Orchid, Jazz, and New York, New York. The clientele would drink lager and try to snog one another's faces off (and that was just the bar staff). All the while I would have to dance in a white suit which made me look like a poor man's John Travolta.

Even more depressingly, when I moved back to London from up the M1, the only place available on my small budget was in Stockwell, south London, which was about as rough a place as you could imagine in the capital at the time. Muggings were common, police sirens were always wailing up and down the high street. It wasn't a place a person would feel safe in after dark. The other guy I shared the flat with was an actor called Michael and one night his windows were smashed in with a few bricks. Michael was so poor that he couldn't afford to get them repaired. Instead, he stuck some cellophane over the shattered pane. It must have been freezing in winter.

I admit it, I had a few moments where I thought, 'Oh, screw this, it's never going to happen for you here in London.' And sometimes I thought about Paris, Milan and Munich as alternatives. Most of the time, though, I had faith in myself. Nevertheless, I could see that The Disco Kings were destined for a beheading. I decided to look for pastures new once more. The leather trousers were put to one side. I was thinking about entering a brave new world. In this case the magic of television and all the excitement and drama that came with it.

☆

I was sick and tired of scraping around for small jobs that paid very little money. Doing gigs with The Disco Kings and Le Ball was fine, but it wasn't going to help me to escape my grubby little flat in Stockwell with its cellophane windows. I knew the only way I could move to a nicer place was if I moved into a more lucrative line of work such as television, the fantastical heaven I had first fallen in love with all those years ago when I clapped eyes on the

Kessler Twins as they danced on the Italian show *Studio Uno*.

I knew it would be difficult, so rather than knocking on the doors of disinterested TV companies, as I had done when I wandered over to *Cinecittà* in Italy like a crazy person, I decided to get an agent. Razzmatazz was the name of the agency I first approached; it was run by two lovely ladies called Jenny Dunster and Jill Shirley, and I was drawn to it because the title suggested I would soon be entering a world of glamour and glitz. I told them I was a singer-dancer and they liked my style. Even more exciting was the news that they wanted to give me a record production deal. I couldn't believe it. Suddenly I was going to be a chart rival to the likes of David Bowie and Roxy Music. I was over the flippin' moon.

Well, that was the plan anyway. In late 1978, Razzmatazz hooked me up with a record producer called Lamona who reckoned I had a good singing voice. The downside was that she reckoned my accent might be too strong for English tastes, what with the fact that I sounded like a singer from the Cornetto advert. Undeterred, Lamona booked me into a studio and asked me to record a demo tape for a song that had been given to her, a track called 'River Of Love'.

Well, I couldn't believe it. There I was, living in a rotten flat in south London, desperately seeking work in television, when all of a sudden I was being thrown into the world of pop superstardom. Everything about it was exciting: the rows and rows of controls in the recording studio, the disinterested producer sat behind his desk, the headphones, which I held on to for dear life as I screamed my head off into a microphone. I felt like a proper star.

Of course, my dreams were short-lived, like so many wannabe pop singers at the time. The biggest hitch for me was that 'River Of

Love' had been written with a Tom Jones-style performer in mind. (The only lyrics I can remember are 'River, river of love . . .'. It would have had Freddie Mercury running for the hills.) It really required somebody with a serious set of pipes, but mine just weren't up to it. I threw myself into the project with the usual levels of enthusiasm, but clearly, energy was not enough to salvage this particular project. My pop career was a false start and so Razzmatazz threw me into a project not too dissimilar to The Disco Kings where I was to travel around the capital's backwater nightclubs, singing and dancing to singles from the top ten. Talk about demoralising. Every night, somebody would pick the four of us up – two boys, two girls – in a battered van and we would shake, rattle and roll in the back until we reached our godforsaken destination. Once there we would perform our cabaret act. I wasn't happy, but I guess it paid the bills.

It wasn't long before I was making another stab at the club scene, and I returned to dancing when a choreographer friend of mine, Libby – an original member of Hot Gossip – asked me if I'd like to join her dance group, Ripple & the Bodysnatchers, in early 1979. I jumped at the chance and, typically, I had to be Ripple. Well, there was no other option really, the remainder of the group were girls, but I loved the energy of the music we were dancing to. It was cutting edge and fast; the style was new wave and punk rock, the American cult band Devo featured quite heavily in our soundtrack, if I remember rightly. We cut our teeth in Mangburry's and performed whenever we could in the vain hope that somebody would sign us, like they had signed Hot Gossip a couple of years earlier, but nothing happened. Like so many of my London adventures, Ripple & the Bodysnatchers proved to be yet another a false dawn.

Suddenly, I was back to square one again and my decision to leave La Grande Eugene didn't look so smart, after all. But because of my relatively young years (I was only twenty-three) and my determination to succeed, whatever it took, I decided to grit my teeth and push on. Somehow, I sensed another lucky break was just around the corner, and it was at this stage in the story that Nigel Lythgoe reared his clever little head. Those of you who watch a lot of Saturday night television (well, it's why you've bought the book in the first place most probably, darling) will recognise his name from the TV show *Popstars* where he spent a few years working as a judge. Nigel was so horrible to contestants that the tabloid press nicknamed him 'Nasty Nigel'; the thing was, he was much more talented than the public could have possibly guessed from watching his TV appearances. As a choreographer he worked with Gene Kelly and Shirley Bassey; he even choreographed The Muppets, which would have taken some doing I can tell you.

Nigel was a brilliant choreographer working for all sorts of TV shows. At the time, there were only three channels on air – BBC One, BBC Two and ITV. While the limited airspace meant that the work on telly was well guarded, it also provided a close-knit community for dancers. Once you were in with a TV company or producer, you were in, and the work kept on coming and coming. As well as regular, choreographed programmes such as *Top of the Pops* and various kids' shows, TV companies were forever filming 'specials' – one-off screenings that, for some reason, always took place in Germany. They always needed lots of dancers for their lavish productions, and those performers often scored gigs with fashion shows and any presentation that needed a dance troupe to fill the stage. The money for these gigs was usually very, very good.

The tricky part was actually getting one's head through the door in the first place, so I would visit audition after audition in order to get a break from a TV producer or director. On one occasion, Nigel spotted my enthusiastic wriggling and booked me to dance in a group on *The Grace Kennedy Show*, which went out on air with BBC One and included luminary guests on its sofas such as *Play School* presenter Derek Griffiths. Well, talk about a change of scenery. In everything I'd ever done before, I was always the main star, the big attraction, even if the shows in question had been modest like *Orpheus in the Underworld* for Opera North. I had been Jesus Christ in La Grande Eugene, I had been a French grease ball in La Ball. I had even been Ripple in Ripple & the Bodysnatchers. But in Grace Kennedy's dancing crew, I was a bit part, an extra; part of a twenty-strong group where I was positioned at the back of the stage, somewhere behind a band or singer.

My first reaction to this discovery was one of bemusement.

'Where was my star turn?' I asked out loud, to nobody in particular on the tube home after my first shift in the studio. 'Where was my big performance?'

I wasn't stupid though. I knew complaining to Nigel would be a massive mistake because the work was so well paid, and almost from the minute I'd returned home that day, I was offered another job. Then another. And then another. The phone didn't stop ringing. I was on a roll and happy to take every bit of paid work that I could because it meant I could escape the drudgery of my Stockwell flat.

I was soon going up in the world, this time to Maida Vale where I managed to rent a place that was cosy enough to invite my parents over for their first visit to England. I took a room in the two-bedroom house from a very nice guy called Ralph who worked for the BBC, so of course, I pestered him daily to get me roles in the various programmes that were made there. But I really wanted to show my mother and father that I was OK. Had I invited them to stay with me in my Stockwell flat with the cellophane windows and scary streets, well, they probably would have had a heart attack the minute they stepped out of the tube station.

When they arrived in London, they were as excitable as I had been when I visited the city for the first time. I was pleased. They had been working very hard for so many years that they were able to enjoy themselves for once. They had enough to splash the cash a bit, and so I took them to Little Venice for dinner; we went to see all the sights and ate out every night. We had a wonderful time. They could see that I was happy and settled. I was getting more regular work and that pleased them. The only downside was that there was no doubt in anyone's mind by then that my future was in London.

I wasn't heartbroken at the thought of never returning home. It wasn't something I could do because I rarely felt like the real me when I was in Ferrara, not like I did whenever I was dancing onstage or performing on the telly; there was no way I could get TV work in Italy, not to the level of *The Grace Kennedy Show*. But it's funny, none of us got overemotional about the situation, we just accepted it for what it was, even though some of the issues affecting us were quite tricky. For example, I knew then that I was never really going to get to know my father properly, because he had never been around me when I was a kid and I was hardly able to catch up with him now I was older, not fully anyway.

Those family tensions were difficult, but my mother was quite understanding of the situation. She came from northern Italy.

Emotions weren't something that people from that area conveyed very easily. The important thing was that we all knew that our love for one another was very strong and all the arguing and shrieking that dogged my teenage years had been forgotten.

Well, nearly everything. There was one incident that I could never forgive them for, something that still bothers me to this day. It was the moment they took away my lovely dog Rin Tin Tin when I was a little boy in Ferrara. Before we go on, I'd like to warn you it's at this part of the book that you might want to reach for some hankies, my darling, because what I'm about to tell you is very upsetting. It certainly took me a couple of decades to get over the incident, and even now I struggle to comprehend the full horror of what they did to the poor, soppy mutt.

Rin Tin Tin was a sod, but a loveable sod. He was a bastard, a mixed breed, and he was a gorgeous shade of red. I remember that he always had an inquisitive look in his eye. The problem for us was that Rin Tin Tin was bloody nuts. He used to walk with me to school in the morning and wait for me at the gate until the bell rang again at three o'clock. If anybody cycled past the front of the house while we were all sitting indoors, he would race outside and bark, usually while making some desperate attempt to bite the legs of anyone unfortunate enough to cross his path. But the minute he came back into the house again he was so lovely and friendly that I forgave him for his craziness, I thought we all did.

I think the first clue that he wasn't popular came when my grandmother started hitting him with a broom if ever she saw him eating around the house. He would dribble and drool all over the place, so the clever little thing found a piece of cloth and if ever he was given food at the table – leftovers usually – he would run to the rag which he had dropped in his corner. There, he could eat messily, dribbling his dinner without fear of a bristly blow to the backside.

The tear-jerking conclusion to this tale happened when we moved homes in Ferrara.

'The dog has to go,' said my father one day, in his usual blunt and forthright manner. I started sobbing uncontrollably.

'They won't allow pets in the new house,' reasoned my mother.

We tried to get my grandparents to look after him, but because my father had fallen out with Uncle Silvano so badly, he refused and we were left with no option but to get rid of poor Rin Tin Tin. Rather than taking him to a home or having him put down, however, they drove for a hundred miles with the dog in the back of the car. When they found a suitable spot, I'm not sure where, they dumped him in the street. I could not believe it. I was devastated.

'Mama, how could you do that to a dog?' I screamed when I heard the news. But there was no going back. My parents knew that he would have followed us to wherever we went. They weren't going to take the chance that he might come back.

Rin Tin Tin's abandonment still makes me cry when I think about him today, but at least by the time my mother and father had come to visit me in London, I had buried my anger, though the thought of it still upset me. And overall I was glad that my parents could see I was contented and safe in London. When they returned to Ferrara, I kept in touch every week. On a Sunday afternoon, I would always find a phone wherever I was so I could call home. Sometimes I lied to Mum when things were tough – like if I was overworked, or short of money as I waited for a cheque to arrive – and I often told her that my career was going a lot better than it really was. She could always read between the lines though. If ever I'd had a slightly emotional conversation on the telephone, a letter would arrive the following week. Money from my special account was always stuffed inside the envelope.

CHAPTER 7

IT'S A MAD, MAD, MAD, MAD WORLD

Then along came the 80s. The fabulous, flamboyant, fantastical 80s. And baby, I had the look. I fizzed around town, a living, breathing, voguing art installation, like one of the Pirates of the Caribbean crossdressed with a dancing gladiator; I wore sparkling brooches, shirts with fancy frills, satin scarves, tight jeans and big, leather, electro-punk boots with studs and buckles. People glimpsing me as I glad-ragged through Carnaby Street and Soho would have mistaken me for an extra from a sci-fi movie. My darling, we'll call this blockbuster, *Mad Max 5: Beyond Glitterdome*.

I loved London at the start of the decade. Whenever it came to choosing my look for a night out, I could basically do whatever I flippin' well wanted because the more outrageous and creative a person was with their outfits, the better. It was wild. Everybody in the city started dressing in crazy clothes and bright make-up, and while there wasn't a set look as such, the attitude had to be just right. It was, '*Anything goes!*', and because of that mindset the city became a fabulous cauldron of frothing, bubbling imagination.

If I was to put a year on this exciting chapter in my life, it was probably around 1981, the explosion of the New Romantic movement. I was slap bang in the thick of the action, hanging out in incredibly trendy bars in London such as Club For Heroes where I used to bump into the likes of Martin Kemp from Spandau Ballet, and Steve Strange and Rusty Egan of Visage. We danced to Japan and Orchestral Manoeuvres in the Dark. Other times, I'd hand my coat over to Boy George who was working as a cloakroom attendant at the Blitz club in Covent Garden; Adam Ant had just started up and we would catch him whenever he played around town in his brilliant outfits. What a scene!

If I wasn't hanging around in the Blitz, or Club For Heroes, I could often be found in Heaven, which had opened for business in the arches under Charing Cross Station. It was the biggest gay club in Europe and, oh my god, it was huge. There were two floors decorated in flashing neon lights, glitter balls hung from the ceiling and everybody danced wildly below. It was an incredibly trendy place to be seen in and everybody who went there had an eye for style and fashion like you wouldn't believe.

Heaven was different to a lot of the super-clubs I'd been to in the past because it didn't operate a selection policy at the door. If you wanted to go in and you looked smart enough, then fine. There wasn't a spotter outside to select the local talent from the queue, the club was much more democratic, but then I suppose Heaven didn't have to worry about quality control in those days because people would travel from all over the world to its front doors. The clientele was always dressed immaculately and gay models from

America would even stop by during their Saturday night blowout, if ever they were in London for a photo shoot. My friends and I would use the place as a hunting ground for fresh talent and there was so much of the stuff that it was like shooting sparkly fish in a barrel.

It was under the neon lighting and glitter balls of Heaven that I met my first serious boyfriend, an American vision of beauty called Scott. I bumped into him as I stood at the bar. There I was, waiting to order a Campari and orange (like Joan Collins) and when I looked over he was staring into my eyes, a red and white pool ball in his hand with the number three printed in the middle. (I can remember it now because I still have the bloody thing at home.) He had been playing a game on the nearby table, but I had clearly put him off his stroke.

Bang! Time stopped, everything was happening in slow motion. It was like something from a movie, a scene from *Pretty Woman*. A lightning strike bashed me about the head and my heart felt like it was about to burst from my chest, like an alien trying to chase Sigourney Weaver down the high street. It was an instant hit of love and lust. It was crazy. Scott and I started chatting and I soon learned he was a magazine model (of course), working in London. He came from New York and he had brains to match his divine beauty – a degree in technology, no less. As we talked and talked, it was obvious there was something between us, a spark, and we started dating.

Wow, it was a whirlwind, I was head over heels in love. I thought my life had changed forever and for six months we shared an existence of absolute bliss. I was absolutely blown away by him and we did everything together, but like all whirlwinds there was a trail of devastation in the wake. In this case it was Scott's home life. He was a New Yorker, he loved the city, and while the British way of life appealed to him – it was the year of the Royal Wedding after all, there were images of Lady Diana *everywhere* – he wanted to move back to The Big Apple.

I was torn. I wanted to go with him, but my career was exploding like a firework shooting into the night (I'll come to that in a minute). There were discussions, teary arguments and sobbing embraces as we argued over whether we should move to New York, stay in London together, or go our separate ways. Oh flippin' hell, we just couldn't make the decision, but as we debated and wept and wept and wept, it became clear that something wasn't quite right.

At first I made the effort. Even though we'd only known each other for six months and we were both still very young, I wanted it to work out so I got on a plane to New York. Scott had a lovely Manhattan apartment, but the leap over the pond was too much for me. Moving from Paris to London had been one thing, but a permanent shift from London to New York was a completely different jump altogether. It was so far away! And the hoops that had to be skipped through. If it wasn't an immigration issue that was causing a headache, then it was a work permit. I didn't have the strength to deal with it all, it was too much for me, and so I went back to London on my own. I knew then that ours was a relationship that would be impossible to maintain.

I was heartbroken, Scott was heartbroken. I loved him and he loved me, but forces beyond our control were ensuring that it wasn't going to work out for us. The story was almost like something from a pop hit at the time (Yazoo's 'Don't Go', maybe) and it hurt like hell. He was the first person I had truly let into my life, I had shown him the real me, but our love just wasn't going to last the distance, which felt like a knife to the heart.

Like all broken relationships, there were positives, though. When I think about Scott now I see that he helped me to mature in those six months. I was a boy when I met Scott; I left him a man. Some people get that when they're seventeen or eighteen, but it happened to me at the age of twenty-five. I was a lot older and Scott flipped a switch in my head that forced me to grow up. It was a rite of passage.

The funny thing was, the pain of our failed relationship helped to push me on in my career. From the minute I touched down in London again, the heartache sharpened my focus on life. Thanks to Scott I was ready to push on to the next adventure, the next challenge. Once I'd gone through the inevitable tear-filled nights and a marathon of heart-wrenching recordings by the opera singer Maria Callas, that is.

☆

How I came to be strutting about London's hottest night spots is a whole other tale. And if my story, my life, comes across as being a somewhat disorientating, dizzying, heart-racing experience at this point in the book, well that's because it was, my darling. You should have been me for five minutes. Bloody hell! I was all over the shop in the head.

My advice to you is this, if the Bruno Tonioli adventure gets too much, well, sip a deliciously chilled white wine as you turn the pages. Maybe suck on a ciggie. I find it helps to soothe the palpitations of an adrenalin-charged experience. Just thank the stars you're not reading a literary work by Craig Revel Horwood. You'd be snoring soundly by now.

Anyway, we'll go back in time, like Dr Who, to the story of how my presence on the London club scene came to be: it was 1980, I was at the Covent Garden Dance Centre with Alain all the time, who had started working with the girls from Hot Gossip as well as teaching his own classes because Arlene really liked his style. Hot Gossip had started to make a name for themselves by appearing on *The Kenny Everett Video Show*, and Alain and Arlene were rushed off their feet. (For those of you who don't know, Kenny was one of the best comedians around at the time – very chaotic and racy, and very gay.) Because I was so familiar with the set-up, Alain asked me if I'd like to take the pressure off him by teaching some classes of my own.

Would I? Of course I bloody well would! I was beside myself with excitement. What a pleasure, and after the initial lesson or two I found that teaching came naturally to me. I wasn't shy, so I knew how to hold an audience and my English was improving by the week, which meant I never had any trouble getting my point across. I also liked telling people what to do. At the time, I had no idea whether I wanted to be a part-time tutor or if this was going to be a long-term career choice, but what I did know was that it was providing a nice balance to all the TV work that was cropping up at the time.

At first I taught jazz (I had been to so many of Arlene's classes that I knew the drills off by heart) and one of the perks of the job was that I got to know the kids from the Royal Ballet. We were working next door to the Royal Opera House in Covent Garden and they were forever popping in and out, which meant that they would always give us the nod whenever a new ballet was about to open for business. With each tip off, Alain and I rushed next door to buy the best seats for the show. Well, the best ones we could afford anyway.

I saw some fantastic performances during that time and I realised that ballet, like opera, when it's done properly, beautifully, at the highest level, could change my mood for days, weeks even. It was impossible for me to be unaffected by it. The only problem for me was that whenever I saw a beautiful opera, or a mind-blowing ballet performance, the same thing happened. That's right, tears. Just as I had broken down when I watched *Chicago* on Broadway, so I would again and again: a grown man sobbing uncontrollably in a hushed theatre, blowing his hooter noisily into a box of Kleenex.

So ... back to the classes. To my surprise, they became ridiculously popular, a hit. So popular in fact that I had to add more and more, just to satisfy the demand. My clientele was broad. There were lots of models in the groups who wanted to sharpen their movement for catwalk shows and any performances that required some kind of dancing. Elsewhere, I was teaching dancers at intermediate level and people who wanted to learn for fitness. There were even kids' classes in the afternoon. Sessions were filled to the brim and the money rolled in, but it was exhausting work. I was up at the crack of dawn every morning and falling into bed in the early hours, every single night. I was physically shot, but it was nothing I wasn't used to. Not after my adventures in New York, anyway.

While all this was going on I decided to keep my hand in with the theatre work, just to fill my last spare seconds. I did *Joseph and the Amazing Technicolor Dreamcoat* because everybody did *Joseph and the Amazing Technicolor Dreamcoat*, though not everybody did it at the Fairfield flippin' Hall in Croydon, which was nice, but no offence, hardly the height of glamour. During the performance I used to sing in a French accent which got everybody rolling around in the aisles and to this day I'm still not sure whether that was a good thing or a bad thing. Still, it stole the show every night and it quickly scored me some serious attention. It wasn't long before a director approached me and asked me to try out for a part in a TV biopic of the performer Jimmy Jewel which he was putting together with an all-star cast.

Well, this was fabulous news. A marvellous development. It turned out that he needed a character with a Latin accent, which meant that I could hardly fail – it would be like asking Len Goodman to replace Richard Wilson as Victor Meldrew in *One Foot in the Grave*. Very little acting would be required. (Of course, I'm kidding about Len. Victor Meldrew was Mother Teresa compared to him.)

I auditioned for the part and, blow me, they only gave me the gig. I was over the moon, delighted. It was to be my first speaking role on the telly. I went to rehearsals and everything went swimmingly. I even became friends with the TV comedienne Pamela Stephenson who had picked up a major role in the show. At the time she was very famous through her position on the BBC Two comedy sketch show, *Not the Nine O'Clock News*, which starred Mel Smith, Griff Rhys-Jones and Mr Bean himself, Rowan Atkinson.

So, with my TV debut shaping up promisingly, what could possibly happen to pull the wheels off the applecart in the week before filming was due to start? A bloody actors' strike, that's what. The acting union Equity had decided in their wisdom that they were going to down tools over some issue or another and the whole show was cancelled in the process. Typical! I was devastated. Though my mood improved when Pamela asked me if I would give her some dancing lessons at the centre, probably out of pity for my bad luck.

I wasn't sure. Surely she could have got someone from the BBC to help her?

'You'll be doing me a favour, Bruno,' she said. 'I want to work with someone I know. We're doing a second series of *Not the Nine O'Clock News* and I'm writing some sketches that'll need some dance numbers in them. I could really do with a bit of help.'

When it was put to me like that, I could hardly turn down my first celebrity client. I was also getting a real sense that, somehow, I'd be making my own luck if I took the job on. I was working so hard that something good was bound to happen, I could feel it in my bones. And besides, Pamela was bound to have some fantastic contacts at the Beeb – there might be another acting part in it for me somewhere down the line. After a few phone calls and some chopping and changing of the diary, I booked her in for a few sessions. In the end it was great fun, we hit it off like a house on fire, and after only a few weeks, Pamela made me another proposition, though this one was far more exciting.

'Look, the show are planning to do a musical number with the boys,' she said. 'I won't be involved, it's just the guys and some dancing girls, but they're not sure what to do and they're looking for some ideas. I think you should apply to do the choreography. Interested?'

125

At that time, *Not the Nine O'Clock News* was a smash, incredibly popular, and I was a bit unsure of what they could possibly want me to add to the already brilliant formula, especially given that I hadn't done any TV choreography before in my life. Still, I went to the BBC and met with the producer John Lloyd (who later went on to produce *Blackadder*) and an idea came to me for a satirical sketch that worked along the themes they were looking at. It was called 'The Nancy Boys', and it was supposed to be a mickey take of some of the sexy dance groups that were always appearing on telly at the time, like Hot Gossip. The sketch featured dancing girls who gyrated around in skimpy skirts, stockings, suspenders and chains. But I also wanted the scene to include Mel, Griff and Rowan; their reaction to what was going on around them was the main thrust of the gag. I knew the show and I knew the guys were great comedians, but I also knew that they couldn't dance, so my hunch was that it would be very, very funny. John loved the idea and I went into the studio to work with three of the finest comedy actors of the time.

Talk about a duck taking to the water! I think because I was a frustrated actor myself, I was able to talk to the cast in a way that they liked; I had an instinct for what they could or couldn't do just by watching their body language when they weren't performing in front of the cameras. Rowan, for example, was a genius. He was somebody who could make the audience laugh just by raising an eyebrow, a trick I knew would work very well for a sketch like 'The Nancy Boys'. The strange thing was, when I first met him, I thought he was so normal – he was polite, friendly, a bit reserved even. It was only when the cameras were switched on that he came alive. He was an artist, and his whole body and mind was a tool for comedy. It was incredible to see and with hindsight I think he's one of the most incredibly talented people I've ever worked with. He's certainly up there with Steve Coogan, who was another comedy mastermind, but we'll get to him in a few chapters' time.

Anyway, when I choreographed 'The Nancy Boys', the look of the sketch was very much 'in the moment' (as they would say on a TV set). The backdrop buzzed with neon strips and pulsing graphics, the song 'Atomic' by the pop band Blondie formed the soundtrack and Mel, Rowan and Griff danced around in leather jackets, dog collars and leather trousers which were decorated with zips and safety pins. It looked hilarious. Even better for me, as the cameras started to roll and the trio got into their characters, John Lloyd could see there was some serious magic taking place.

I could sense something was happening, too. It was weird, almost immediately I felt at home in a TV studio. In the same way that I had spent my time offstage at La Grande Eugene, studying and observing everything that went on in an attempt to learn as much as I could about the theatre, so I had studied the work that took place whenever I danced in a TV studio with Nigel Lythgoe. Even though being part of a 25-strong group of dancers wasn't really my thing, I'd used the hours between rehearsals, make-up and shooting to watch what went on: how the producers spoke to the cameramen, what dance moves had to be shot in a certain way, and so on. I never wasted a second, I always watched, listened and learned.

When I joined the *Not the Nine O'Clock News* team, that work paid off straightaway. I had an instinctive feel for what had to happen if 'The Nancy Boys' was to work and I felt comfortable behind a camera, issuing instructions, even though I'd never worked in a studio before as a choreographer.

'Flippin' hell,' I thought. 'I can do this!'

When it aired, 'The Nancy Boys' was a huge success – the critics loved it, the fans loved it. Directors and script writers saw my name on the credits and wanted to get in touch. Suddenly, a happy accident, twinned with my determination to learn, had created the perfect storm of creativity and demand. Through yet another lucky break I started to smoulder as a TV choreographer. The Equity strike was a dim and distant memory.

☆

My mind was in a whirlwind, I didn't know whether I was coming or going. Hurricane Bruno had struck force ten and I was careering around the place, what with all the craziness that was going on, both in my personal life and at work. To give you an idea of what it was like to be me back then, there are a couple little tales that I would like to tell you now because, well, they really sum up just how mental my life had become.

First of all Goldie Hawn called me up. Yes, you heard right, *the* Goldie Hawn, the bombshell American actress who was an Academy Award-winning global sensation because of her roles in films such as *Private Benjamin* and *Lovers And Liars*. Goldie was a Hollywood megastar – the equivalent of Scarlett Johansson now – and there she was, calling me in my Maida Vale flat from her glamorous mansion in Beverly Hills, or wherever it was she lived at the time.

My flatmate Ralph answered the phone first of all and I could see almost from the minute he cupped the receiver to his ear that something was amiss. He was turning a funny colour and staring at me with his jaw around his ankles.

'Goldie Hawn is on the phone for you Bruno,' he said, very slowly and quietly, like a man who had been hypnotised and told that he was a brain-guzzling zombie from *Shaun of the Dead*.

'What? Are you kidding me?' I whispered, barely daring to dream that the real Goldie Hawn could possibly want to talk to me. That's when Ralph seemed to snap back into the real world, probably because I seemed so reluctant to believe him.

'It's Goldie flippin' Hawn!' he screamed, now pacing frantically around the flat waving the phone in the air as if it were on fire. I took the call and made the first move.

'Er . . . hello?'

Well, I had the shock of my life, because blow me if it wasn't Private Benjamin. I had suspected that Alain or Pamela Stephenson might have been playing a prank call. Instead Goldie's deliciously silky voice was virtually kissing me on the ear and telling me she was due to be in London for a show. She wanted a one-on-one dance lesson and had called the Covent Garden centre because it was near to her hotel. The very nice girl on reception – who I really must reward with a fiver some time for her quick thinking – recommended me, so there she was, asking me if I could take her in for an appointment.

Was she crazy? Of course I would! But almost immediately I began to worry.

'Bruno, you can hold it together in front of famous people like Pamela and Rowan,' I thought in one of my many internal monologues that took place later on that night. 'But Goldie Hawn is Goldie Hawn, one of the most famous actresses in the world. How are you going to act?'

I'll tell you how, my darling: like a flippin' idiot. The thought of teaching her got me trembling like a leaf. I was a bag of nerves for days and as the meeting approached, I became increasingly fretful. By the time it came to our session, I was in such a state that I completely overdid my costume. When I left the house, I looked like such a pillock because I wore yellow towelling pants – the tightest you could imagine – red leg warmers, a bandana, a tight belt *and* bright red braces.

When I arrived at the studio, looking as if Timmy Mallett had dressed me in a power cut, there was Goldie, a picture of radiance and freshness, dressed stylishly in an expensive-looking tracksuit with a matching gym bag. She must have taken one look at me and thought, 'Who the hell is this clown?', but bless her, she was very polite. As I tried to cover up my nerves and the lesson got underway, she even seemed to be enjoying herself.

At the end of the session, she asked me how much I wanted for the workout.

'Oh, about twenty quid, Goldie,' I said, trying to act casual.

Goldie pulled out two twenties – this shows you the class of the woman – and she pushed them into my hand.

'Bruno,' she said, 'I think you should ask people like me to pay much more money for what you do.'

I thought that was very nice and an indication of what a lovely person she was, though she never came back, presumably because I looked like a prat. But at least she had paid me double.

☆

My flatmate Ralph hadn't exactly covered himself in glory during the whole Goldie Hawn phone call debacle, so it was some surprise when I got a message from my agent at Razzmatazz shortly afterwards, telling me that the Beeb wanted me for a talking part. Apparently, somebody called Ralph had recommended me.

'Ralph, of course!' I cried. 'He's come good. Flippin' heck, a part in a BBC show.'

I called my agent and told her that I'd love to do it – I liked being in character after all.

'What does the part involve?' I asked.

'Well, it says here you're the Boy With Lamp.'

Wow, I thought, the Boy With Lamp, that is fantastic.

'And what's the show called?' I asked.

'It's called *The Boy With Lamp*,' said my agent.

Well, that was it, I was ecstatic. Somehow Ralph had got me the lead role. That afternoon, I went to the BBC shaking with excitement. I walked straight to the production office and made myself known with a flamboyant and confident air.

'Hello, everyone,' I said. '*The Boy With Lamp*?'

They looked at me like I was mad.

'I'm looking for the show, *The Boy With Lamp* . . .'

The penny obviously dropped with some bright spark.

'Ah yes,' he said. 'Are you Bruno Tonioli?'

Well, I thought, *finally*, somebody has recognised the leading role in the show.

'Yes, yes I am,' I said, sighing like some prima donna actor with a strop on. 'Can I see my script?'

Now, this was where the biggest balls-up in TV history was about to be revealed to me, because my role as the Boy With Lamp wasn't the leading role at all. In fact it wasn't even a major role. The truth was, the show wasn't going to be called *The Boy With Lamp* at all. Rather it was an Oscar Wilde biopic, starring Michael Gambon, and I was playing a non-speaking, bit-part character who had been described in the cast list as 'Boy With Lamp'. The 'motivation' for my character was to walk around town, giving sexy looks towards a sexually confused Oscar Wilde, all the while holding a lamp like a wally. Talk about a kick in the teeth, but I took the part all the same.

It's funny because I recently sat on a flight from London to Los Angeles and who should park themselves in the seat next to me but Michael Gambon himself. This was too good an opportunity to miss, I thought, and having knocked back my complimentary champagne, I leaned across for a quick word.

'I don't know if you actually remember me, Michael,' I said. 'But I worked with you once when I was the Boy With Lamp in your Oscar Wilde biopic.'

A look of mild panic flickered across his face, before his Golden Globe-winning thespian abilities kicked in. Michael beamed broadly.

'Ah yes, that old thing,' he said. 'My word, the Boy With Lamp, eh? What a part that was!'

Shortly afterwards, he fell asleep, presumably to dream of Horcruxes and Hogwarts, and definitely not a boy with a lamp salaciously eyeing up a sexually disorientated Oscar Wilde. Either that or he was pretending to be semi-conscious so I couldn't bother him again.

CHAPTER 8

BOOM
TOWN

After that I was in demand. Big commercial contracts rolled in. There were choreography jobs for adverts, bands and pop promos. The music channel MTV had started up and everyone who was anyone in the pop world wanted to make videos to accompany their hit singles. Because people could see that I had an eye for choreography – that I had a modern and satirical outlook on dance – I was being called up nearly every day by somebody, somewhere, who wanted musical direction or a dance routine for their productions. The work was lucrative, too.

It all started when I was rehearsing in the Dance Centre with a pop band called Shock. The group had asked me to put together several dance routines for their live shows, and while they were never really going to crack the mainstream, they were very big in the New Romantic world. Robotics and body popping had just started to take off and it was something Shock liked to do in their

133

onstage show, particularly their brilliant dancers, Tik and Tok. They were very trendy, maybe a bit too trendy and a lot of people in London thought that Shock were too cool for school. Even so, Tik and Tok, Robert Pereno, LA Richards, Sean Crawford and the other robotic dancer in the band, Barbie Wilde, were asked to perform in a commercial for Wrangler Jeans. Naturally, when it came to putting the advert together, the group – which also featured Carole Caplin, who later went on to become lifestyle adviser to Tony and Cherie Blair (what a gig! Her work was cut out there) – wanted me to choreograph their performances.

The directors that day were a pop duo called Godley & Creme. They had previously been in the big rock band 10cc, and were very into their film-making. Godley & Creme had been producing their own videos and the work they were doing was considered very ground-breaking for the time. The Wrangler advert featuring Shock was going to be no different. It was called 'What's Going On', and during the commercial the production team would freeze the action – a clip of the actors walking down a street, for example – and with some technical wizardry, a dancer or another actor would burst out of that image, as if it were frozen, like a magazine page or large photograph. Computers and video editing would create the illusion and it was all very clever. Today, this idea probably sounds as backwards as the notion of an entire town gathering round the one black and white TV in the area to watch a man walking on the moon. But it was groundbreaking stuff back then and nobody had done anything like it anywhere else.

I'd never worked on anything that creative, it was on another level. I also think Godley & Creme were learning as they went along because very few people had used that style of film-making before, in adverts or in pop videos. It was the dawning of a new era and being around them as they created and devised a wild new form of visual expression was so inspiring. It also helped that they loved my choreography because once the advert was released, word soon got around – mainly due to their chitter chatter in meetings – that Bruno Tonioli was capable of handling big commercial productions with a large budget.

And that's when the ball started to roll down the hill. The next company to knock on my door were Lois Jeans. They wanted an advert that was choreographed and staged with beautiful models, including a young Nick Kamen who went on to record his own top ten single, 'Each Time You Break My Heart'. He was probably more famous for appearing in a very famous Levis ad where he stripped down to his boxer shorts and shoved his jeans into a launderette washing machine. If you're over the age of thirty-five, it's unlikely you'd ever forget it. Nick later ended up working with Madonna (she produced 'Each Time You Break My Heart'), when, presumably, he didn't have to use a launderette for quite a while. His smalls were probably hand washed in Evian and tiger's tears by an army of chamber maids.

Nick was beautiful, though. His co-star for that advert was a looker, too – a wonderful model called Caroline Cossey, or Tula, who despite being one of the leading female faces of the time, was actually a man. For years she had worked as a top model, despite the fact that she was a transsexual. Tula had even appeared as a Page 3 girl in the *Sun*.

I had known about her 'secret' when she was cast, but it never bothered me. As long as she was good at what she did, which she was, well, that was all I cared about. Later, when it all came out about her operation, there was an uproar. There was a big fight with somebody who took offence and she had to engage with the European Court of Human Rights to be recognised as a woman.

Anyway, enough of the political battles, darling. The Lois advert was a series of choreographed sexy vignettes. Every move carried a steamy undercurrent and was precisely designed to match the beat of the music. It was simple, but effective; the project was a huge success. It even won the Best Choreography Award at the Venice Film Festival, which was a very prestigious event and a real coup at the time because there were some very heavyweight directors making commercials in that era. In the 80s, adverts were considered a critically worthy sideline for a reputable film-maker and the quality was always very high. People didn't talk about commercials in the same way as they would discuss films or a TV show, but the technical skills, ability and imagination were often just as strong in an advert as they were in a movie blockbuster. The likes of Ridley Scott (who had made *Alien*, among other legendary films) and Freddie Young (a director of photography; he was godlike, he had worked on *Lawrence of Arabia* and *Doctor Zhivago*) often contributed to advertising projects. I worked on about twenty films later on in my career and they were hard work, but commercials were so much tougher because everything – every shot, every word, every dance move – had to be 100 per cent perfect.

Like the Persil advert I worked on in 1983, a musical in miniature called 'I Found My System'. Oh my flippin' goodness, it was as complicated as the whole production of La Grande Eugene! A director called Richard Loncraine rang me up out of the blue. I hadn't worked with him on anything before, so god knows how he

Bruno Tonioli

La Grande Eugene

Top left: Ripple & the Bodysnatchers. Surrounded by beauty, my favourite place to be.

Top right: Pole dancing in its infancy.

Above: Leaning lustfully on a Ferrari and wrapped in cellophane. Barmy, I know.

Left: *Le Petit*. My programme picture for La Grande Eugene.

Far left: Poster for La Grande Eugene.

Above: The look of 1976, when lounge lizards and stuffed tigers were all the rage.

Above right: Dancing in the 1980s. Ripped and toned for your viewing pleasure.

Bottom left: My gorgeous dancers from a Culture Club video shoot. I've always had an eye for beauty.

Bottom right: No words necessary – the package speaks for itself.

Top left and right: Cat people. With an impeccable pedigree...

... but who's the master? (It's Oliver.)

Left: Bruno 1977: the Brokeback Mountain years. And I'm still looking for my cowboy.

Below: Best mates. Paul with Keren and Sara of Bananarama. *Gorgeous.*

Above: Picture perfect: the happy couple in the early 80s. Paul was always going to be tough act to follow. As the famous song goes, 'He's a model and he's looking good.'

Below: A typical Bananarama warm up before yet another TV appearance.

Above: The Golden Girls and The Golden Boys.

Below: A picture of domestic bliss. Relaxing at home with Paul. Clothing was optional in the Tonioli household.

Above: Oliver, the king of all he surveys. 'Don't mess with me,' he seems to be saying.

Below: A night in Bangkok with Michael Summerton (left) and Paul. It was a long night, as you can tell by my face.

Above: Nature boy. Yet another promotional shot from the 1980s. I was a tart with a heart.

Above right: A dinner with Paul and Michael. They kept me sane during the hard times.

Right: Thunderballs. Daniel Craig stole my look but not my package.

Below: On the plane with Bananarama, hoping to conquer America. It took me 20 years longer than expected. I am *persistent*.

Above: In my beautiful garden with Mum and Oliver. Everything in bloom; my inner Titchmarsh unleashed.

Below: 'Moving On' – the last ever video with Keren and Sara. The girls never looked better.

Above: The four musketeers – Paul, Sara, Keren and myself – preparing to wreak havoc in London.

Below: Tony Ferrino and his dancing beauties backstage at The Royal Variety Performance in 1996; with my mother at the Tower of London. Some bitter people say they should have locked me in and thrown away the keys.

Above: My parents at home. You can see another one of my masterpieces hanging on the left hand wall. Mum made both the curtains and her blouse. Talk about versatility.

Above right: Trendy choreographer in silk and leather. The New Romantic era was in full swing.

Right: After I left home, my parents could afford to live a comfortable life. *I had been such a drain.*

Below: The *Ella Enchanted* cast. Now that's what I call a big movie. Where the hell am I? Did I actually do it? Or was it all a dream?

ELLA ENCHANTED 2002

had heard of me. He must have seen my work and liked it and decided to chance his arm. Oh, show business!

'Bruno,' he said. 'I'm doing a Persil advert and it's like a Broadway musical. There are going to be thirty dancers jumping around the place and it'll be like a massive 1940s Hollywood production. I know you've never done anything on this scale before, so it's a leap of faith for both of us, but I think you can do it . . .'

Well, I wasn't going to turn down such an opportunity (plus they paid well), so I agreed and quickly tried to get my head around the scale of the job. I knew it was going to be tough work. The ad was due to be filmed at the famous Shepperton Studios in Middlesex where the likes of *Ghandi*, *The Omen* and *A Passage to India* had been made. By the looks of things, the ambition of Persil's creation was just bloody huge. When I arrived, there was a massive set built to look like a giant laboratory. Cameras had been fixed to cranes and there was the biggest production team I had ever seen. Dozens and dozens of people were running around with clipboards. It was incredible.

'Oh my god, this is big,' I thought. 'I might be a bit out of my depth here.'

I threw myself into the process regardless, pretending to Richard and everyone else around me that it was nothing I couldn't handle. The idea for the commercial was that some washing powder boffin had discovered a new, super-strong formula that was guaranteed to bring a nuclear level of whiteness to the nation's washing lines. This news, of course, was a cue for him to scream, 'I've found a system!' at the top of his lungs before breaking into a West End musical-style dance routine with twenty-nine other 'doctors', all of whom were dressed in lab coats and unfashionable specs, just to

137

confirm to the audience that they definitely were detergent nerds.

Well, that was where my work started. According to Richard, I had to choreograph a minute-long dance routine for our assorted scientists to run through, complete with high jumps and excitable close-ups of delighted faces as pieces of paper (more top-secret formulas, I suppose) were thrown into the air. Now, sixty seconds of filming is actually a lot longer and a hell of a lot harder to fill than it sounds. The even trickier thing was that everything had to be done live, in a single take. We couldn't shoot five seconds here, ten seconds there. Oh no, everything had to be done in one go and if somebody made a mistake then we had to go back to the beginning and start again. Talk about pressure.

The funny thing was, once I'd worked out the dance routines with our cast, I knew I could do it. Everything was under control. The studio, despite its size, was no more complicated than the TV studio we'd used for *Not the Nine O'Clock News*. I was in my comfort zone. And once the cameras started to roll, everything fell into place perfectly. Scientists stared excitedly at bunsen burners and frothing test tubes! Dancers jumped down stairs and popped out of the floor! People climbed in and out of washing machines! It was a huge extravaganza and I pulled it through. Richard was pleased, I was pleased. I would later go on to work with him on a number of projects, including a movie called *The Gathering Storm* which starred Vanessa Redgrave. The advert was another huge hit and my star was rising even further. But if thought I had been busy before, my darling, I really had no idea.

☆

Spain, Paris, the Caribbean, Waterloo Station – the world became my canvas; my brushes were the advertising scripts and sound-tracks; my paint, the dancers. I was a choreographing Picasso – expressing myself and being paid to do so, which really was a wonderful bonus because I could stop making my own clothes. This was the freedom of creativity I had dreamt of as I spent my days in a frustrated strop, pretending to study in a German class at the *Ragioneria*. It was the fantasy life I'd discussed in Ferrara with Lia and Carla and Chinzia. It was heavenly. There were planes, champagne parties, fancy hotels, five-star treatment all the way . . . and I was bloody knackered.

Oh my goodness, it was exhausting. But before I go on, I don't want you to get me wrong here because I wasn't complaining, *amore mio*. I adored every single minute. I certainly didn't declare, 'Oh, my champagne's too cold!', or 'My bed's too comfy,' if ever I became uncomfortable in a luxury hotel (which I didn't because I was always too tired). No, I'd sip away and roll around to my heart's content, remembering the time when I was stuck in northern Italy faced with the prospect of a life in a dead-end insurance job. Had I followed my mother's wishes, that is. Thinking about it now, that job would have probably killed me through frustration and boredom. Now I was on the verge of being wiped out through sheer exhaustion.

My biggest problem was that I was terrified of turning anything down. Rejecting work gave me nightmares. I believed – and probably rightly – that if ever I knocked back a job, then I would live to regret it. My absence might open the door for somebody else. That meant I'd fall down the pecking order in next to no time. As a result I would struggle for work afterwards, my money would disappear, I would be homeless. Oh, the traumas in my mind! I wanted to be the best and I wanted to be busy, so I said yes to everything and worked myself to the bone like a flippin' cart horse.

Job after job, gig after gig. Yes, yes, yes. I was on a conveyor belt of commercials. British Airways, the Spanish Lottery, Braun, Chiclets Chewing Gum, Cadbury's, Air Canada, McCains Pizza, Scottish Power, BT, Tennants Special, Nutra Sweet, you name it, I thought of a dance routine for it. My list of clients was incredible. There were tonnes and tonnes and tonnes of businesses – big and super big – throwing ideas at me and I said, 'Of course!' to pretty much all of them.

At the time, a lot of the nationally owned companies in the country, like British Gas, were being privatised. I was often called up to concoct some advert or another for their new offshoot, and more often than not, the scale of their productions was incredible. The nationally owned companies who weren't yet privatised were just as ambitious. For example, British Rail once asked me to choreograph an advert entitled 'Gotta Go To Work' which involved 280 dancers twirling around Waterloo Station. Two hundred and eighty! There wasn't any computer-generated imagery or fancy video trickery on offer in those days, so when a director said that he wanted Waterloo Station to be packed with 280 dancing commuters, that's exactly what we had to get.

Well, can you imagine? What a pain in the backside. I remember we got permission to close off Waterloo during the dead of night and I called up just about every dancer in London, nearly all of whom readily agreed to running around a deserted mainline station in the early hours of the morning. And why wouldn't they want to do it? It was going to be a wonderful production, as I told them when they arrived at the Covent Garden Dance Centre for rehearsals.

'So, this is what we're doing,' I said as I relayed the plot of the commercial to all 280 of them. 'The doors fly open and a wave of commuters jump out, which will be you, followed by another wave, and another, all of you moving identically in a tap dance routine as you make the next step on your journey to work.

'Everyone will be dressed up. There will be umbrellas, bowler hats, stylish dresses, briefcases, high heels. Everyone looks fabulous. As this is going on, your voices will speak as one. "Gotta go to work, gotta go to work," you'll say, over and over in a rhythm identical to the sound of the train that brought you into London in the first place. Isn't it a brilliant idea?'

I genuinely thought it was, but putting the theory into practice was a whole other story. As you can imagine for a production that size, we had to rehearse and rehearse and rehearse. The planning was organised as if it were a military manoeuvre – Operation Trainspotter we'll call it. People had to learn the routines in blocks of 28. I would get the separate dancing teams into the studio and teach them the choreography as quickly as I could. Once one group had cracked it, I would bring in the next lot for rehearsals. Over and over. Again and again. Ten times I did it. It was like working with an army. In the end, as the cameras rolled, we had hundreds of people moving over the platforms and across the concourse in unison, and it looked brilliant. The only problem was, by the time filming had finished, I felt as knackered and world-weary as the fictional commuters in the British Rail advert.

☆

When thinking about that period, one of the most memorable commercials I put together was with the company Electricity Privatisation. It was a spoof entitled 'The Monster Mash' and it was a mickey take of both Frankenstein and the Munsters. It also got me working in Shepperton Studios once more, but this time I was a dab hand at operating in a big movie facility. Despite my growing experience, however, nothing was to prepare me for the chaos that later unfolded, and 'The Monster Mash' taught me a very valuable lesson: when it comes to making adverts, always expect the bloody unexpected.

On paper, the script looked pretty simple, but then they always do. The director wanted lots of people to dance around in monster outfits; there was nothing to really give me any sleepless nights (apart from the horrific make-up and costumes). But as filming got under-way, one of the leading actors, a poor boy who was playing the character of Igor, suddenly collapsed. He had been struck down with appendicitis and was in agony. It was obvious that he was too unwell to perform any more dance routines, no matter how many pain killers we forced down his neck, and he had to be operated on as quickly as possible. One of the production team rushed him to the nearest hospital before his appendix burst.

The problem for us was that the film shoot had been incredibly expensive to set up and suspending the recording to recast a new Igor would have been disastrous. It probably would have cost Electricity Privatisation hundreds of thousands of pounds, even then. So rather than cancelling the whole thing, we kept the cameras in place and as soon as our stricken actor was able to leave hospital a day or two later, we shoved him into a wheelchair and shot his scenes from the head up. He couldn't dance or throw himself about too much, because any excessive movements would have burst his stitches, but he did what he could and it was quite an impressive effort on his part. His lack of physical activity was offset by the really awful colour that had developed in his face — because of the operation Igor's skin had turned a funny shade of grey, which added to the realism of his character. It also saved us a few quid on make-up.

The biggest problem for the film crew was that he couldn't do any dance moves at all. There had been plenty of routines pencilled into the script for Igor, and all of them were incredibly technical and difficult to pull off. He even had to perform a series of moonwalks, the backwards, gliding shuffle step first used by Michael Jackson when he performed on MTV in 1983. It was a very popular move at the time.

It soon dawned on me that I would have to perform his routines myself. I would have to play Igor's feet. It didn't help that the director, the aforementioned Paul Weiland (from the introduction to this very book), was forever winding me up. Over the years our filming sessions would often descend into a tirade of filth; during the filming of a Walkers Crisps advert featuring Gary Lineker a decade later, we had to be separated because our messing around had become so disruptive. The producer could stand no more and we were forbidden from talking face to face with one another. Instead we had to communicate through an intermediary.

This time Paul was mocking me because I was about to degrade myself for a telly advert, and with a heavy heart I clambered into the Igor costume and boots, which were about ten sizes too big. Thankfully all my shots were filmed from the waist down. My face had to remain out of view to give the illusion that Igor was only half dead in fiction, rather than half dead in real life, which he was. The only way it could have been any less dignified was if I had been the back end of a pantomime cow. Still, we got the job done, which given the circumstances was a miracle in itself, but never again would I assume that a job was going to be easy based on the simplicity of a script.

What was my next ambition? Well, I wanted to buy my own place. I was tired of renting, and as much as I loved Ralph I simply had to buy Chez Bruno, which turned out to be a rather lovely flat in Maida Vale. It was the early 80s and it was summer, a glorious four months of rain and intermittent sunshine. Despite the grey clouds above, the apartment was beautiful, a one-bedroom place on a leafy street. It was everything a boy like me needed for his lifestyle, I was slap bang in the middle of the action. Only then did the bank tell me that I would need a £7,500 deposit for the flippin' place. At that time I was three grand short.

I'm very aware that £7,500 for an upfront sum would be a drop in the ocean for property these days. It probably wouldn't even buy a doorknob at Simon Cowell's summer house. But in those days, it was a lot of cash. It was even trickier for me back then because I was technically a freelancer and that meant I was forever waiting on money. During the week when I decided to buy the flat, I knew I had three grand coming in, it's just that I didn't know when exactly. The bank told me I would need the money immediately and so naturally I was beside myself. I could see my dream home slipping away, but fortunately Angela, a dancer friend of mine, had incredibly wealthy parents. She offered to get the money for me, which was wonderful. Within twenty-four hours the cash was in the bank, and the bank was buying the house.

The only problem was my parents, who hit the roof when they heard the news. The Toniolis were a proud family from northern Italy. We didn't *do* debt, especially not to the tune of three grand. Luckily, because I had been out of their hair for a few years, they had managed to save quite a lot of cash, so much so that my mother had even managed to buy herself a mink coat, which was considered quite a luxury. As it happened, they had enough money between them to advance me the cash.

'We'll pay off the debt to Angela's parents and you can repay us,' said my mother. 'Now how do we get the funds to them?'

Just by sheer coincidence, Angela's mother and father were holidaying in Italy at the time, around 300 miles from Ferrara. I made the flight home and the three of us – me, Mum and Dad – drove all the way to Sanremo where they were staying. We drove five hours there, paid the money, and then drove five hours back. But despite the stress of handing over all that money (in cash) it was lovely to see my parents so excited. They told me they were proud of me. Mum and Dad hadn't been able to buy their own place until much later in life, so it must have been incredibly reassuring for them to see me in a position where I could set up home. They also knew I had security and that I was safe, despite being so far away from their care.

As soon as I got to London, I sealed the deal. I was so thrilled that I worked non stop, moving things into the flat, arranging furniture, tidying away pots, pans and plates. I cleaned every single cupboard. In fact I was so thrilled at moving in that I didn't stop working for twenty-four hours, and at around five o'clock the following morning, I awoke on the kitchen floor surrounded by a lake of bleach, brushes and an overturned bucket, a rather large bump throbbing on the back of my head. In all my eagerness to move in, I had forgotten to eat, and as I stuck my head into yet another cupboard, rooting around for an untouched millimetre of dust, I fainted from exhaustion, falling backwards and cracking my head on the floor in the process. It was a miracle I didn't do more damage to myself.

My accident was a blip, though. I loved having my own lair, my place. It was great to be independent and I could do whatever I wanted, whenever I wanted. Sure, it wasn't a mansion in Hollywood or *Tre Ville*, Franco Zeffirelli's cliff-top mansion in Positano, but for me it was the equivalent. It was something I had worked hard for, and just like my parents had promised me when I was a boy, my hard work had been rewarded.

☆

Pop music was my calling. My inner Bryan Ferry had been re-awakened and I was asked to sing in a band. The year was 1980 and this time the group was called Duke & the Aces. I was an 'Ace', as was Nicola Martin, who would later help to create and manage the band, Bucks Fizz. I wasn't that enthused at the time. To my mind, being a backing singer was a waste of my talents. I was a star, and my role as an 'Ace' was a bit like Diana Ross when she was stuck in The Supremes – like her, I should have been out front, letting loose. Still, I said yes and screamed my head off in the studio during a desperate attempt to get noticed, but to no avail. I was very much a back-room player on that particular project; my dream of being Duke was cruelly shattered.

I had been chosen for the band by a very good TV choreographer called Geoff Richer who I'd previously worked with during my TV days. Geoff was hired to put together a group who could compete for Britain's Eurovision Song Contest place (or A Song For Europe, or whatever it's flippin' well called these days), and my name was put forward to him because I could sing. Geoff also knew that I looked damn good in a tight pair of pants, so I was placed in the front row of the Aces.

We recorded a track called 'Love Is Alive' – me bawling my head off with the other losers at the back – and of course, it was destined to be a flop. We came third in the qualifiers which I suppose was an achievement of sorts, but it wasn't enough for me. I have always been a first or nothing type of person as you may have guessed. Finishing third was a failure in my mind, and that's when the penny dropped

'Bruno, my darling,' I thought, having a little chat with myself. 'This is an avenue that you shouldn't go down anymore. When you bash your head on the wall a few times, you shouldn't keep on bashing your head on the same wall. Singing is something that might not be for you.'

The thing was, I loved pop music. I loved the idea of working with musicians. And that's when the lightbulb started to flash. A couple of years later when I choreographed the likes of Shock, I realised that pop videos were an avenue that I could pursue further. The fortunate thing for me was that MTV had really started to take off and we were entering the era of the pop promo. The Michael Jackson film for the song 'Thriller' in 1983 had really changed the game for everybody. It was a masterpiece, a mini movie where Jacko had turned into a werewolf and danced around with zombies, ghouls and other people who resembled the *Strictly Come Dancing* panel after a heavy night on the sauce. (But not me, darling, I barely drink.)

It was mind-blowing, a big-budget blockbuster; the most expensive video ever made at the time and at the centre of it all was this incredible singer and dancer who really was on top of his game. *Thriller* created a sensation, it inspired people, not just musically, but in dance and video, too.

I confess, I was inspired by it myself. I had never wanted to copy anyone, I always wanted to find my own way, but Michael Jackson was a game changer. He opened up dance, street dance, to the world; he brought in body popping and a raw vibe in a sleek and sophisticated style. I didn't rip off any of his ideas, but he inspired me to push my boundaries further, whether that was by being more ambitious as I choreographed monsters and commuters in a big-budget advert, or by working with musicians in a nightclub. I knew I could do the same thing with bands and pop videos, too. And that's when Paul Young came into my life.

For those of you too young to remember, Paul was an 80s pop star who had a number one hit with 'Wherever I Lay My Hat (That's My Home)'. He would later perform at Live Aid at Wembley in 1985. I'm not sure how Paul got to hear about me. Maybe, like Goldie Hawn, it was through the Dance Centre or maybe it was through a social connection, but when he rang Chez Bruno, it was clear he wanted my help.

'I need somebody to help me with my choreography,' he told me. 'I need a few moves for when I play live. And I could also do with some musical staging for when I perform on TV shows like *Saturday Superstore* or *Top of the Pops*.'

Paul was massive at the time. It was 1983, he was a teenage heart-throb, but musical staging was something he needed. Not all performers are comfortable when they're onstage. They often hold the mic awkwardly or wave their arms about in a silly fashion. The right choreography – just a move here, or a different stance at the microphone stand – could change all that. Paul readily agreed, it was something he needed, he said. We had a productive chat and he liked what I had been doing during my career, and what really struck me was how nice he was. In those days I didn't have a car, even though I was a huge car fan, and when we talked I explained that I wouldn't be able to get to his studio because of the location.

'Bruno, don't worry,' he said. 'I'll pick you up and drive you to the studio!'

The equivalent today would be for Robbie Williams to offer me a lift to the middle of nowhere for a dancing lesson (not that he needs it). It just wouldn't happen, would it? When Paul arrived, he was driving a bright red Mercedes SL. It was beautiful, a purring lioness of a car, sleek and speedy with an engine that sang like an opera star; when he revved the engine it sounded like a choir of angels in my mind. I made a decision there and then.

'One day,' I thought, 'I'm going to have a car like that.'

Anyway, we worked well together almost immediately, and as I tutored Paul, he became more and more comfortable with his musical staging. It was all very subtle stuff designed to make him feel more at ease, but it must have worked wonders because, before I knew it, I was being recommended to some of the biggest names in music. The singer Hazel O'Connor called and asked me to work with her on one of her videos. Hazel was friends with someone else who recommended me to another star, and so on and so on. It snowballed from there. Artists and their record labels were getting in touch because they had heard that I was able to get people to make the most of themselves whenever they sang live or moved around in a video. It was exciting stuff. What I didn't realise was that my newfound reputation was about to take me on a wild and incredible journey that would change my life forever.

CHAPTER 9

IT'S A
WONDERFUL
LIFE

I made hay during the music video explosion. It was boom time, the pop equivalent of Hollywood's Golden Age, the cinematic era which took place between the 1920s and the late 1950s and produced such movie masterpieces as *Casablanca* and *Citizen Kane*. Instead of propelling the likes of Lana Turner and Liz Taylor into superstardom, however, the 1980s became a period of intense creativity for Madonna, Peter Gabriel, Duran Duran and countless other bands. The music channel MTV had just opened for business and artists were determined to marry their latest music to a striking, visual masterpiece in order to attract the maximum attention. Meanwhile, every video director worth his salt wanted a choreographer to concoct a complicated dance routine for his latest muse.

Talk about performing a pirouette out of the frying pan and into the fire. I was working on pop videos nearly every week. Due to my previous work in the advertising industry, I was hot property among rock'n'roll's thrusting young creatives. Artists were getting in touch with me because they had heard that I possessed a natural feel for performance. Meanwhile my staging work with the likes of Paul Young and Hazel O'Connor caused the word to spread like wildfire.

Directors would chat and gossip at cocktail parties and fancy rock'n'roll soirées across the land. 'Bruno can get people to make the most out of themselves,' they would say (well, I liked to imagine). 'Darling, we must get him to produce our next video!'

And so I would receive phone call after phone call asking me to run along to some gigantic aircraft hangar of a studio in the middle of nowhere, often to work with the latest pop sensation of the moment.

Duran Duran were one of the first, and Duran Duran were big, just about as big as anyone could be. They had scored countless number one hits across the planet. They packed arenas with screaming fans whenever they played. If they weren't making hit albums or flying across the world for yet another sell-out tour, they could be found dating supermodels. Their music videos were just as ambitious, and Duran Duran promos were often made on 35mm film by renowned directors. The resulting mini-movies often included plenty of nudity, so naturally I thought they were fantastic even before I'd met them.

In 1985, Nick Rhodes and Simon Le Bon from the band reached out (as they say in *The Sopranos*) because they were working on another project, a spin-off group called Arcadia, which was an artier version of Duran Duran. They wanted someone to choreograph the videos for their latest single 'Election Day' and when they'd heard about some of the commercial projects I'd been working on, they were suitably impressed. In those days, the music industry was very different. It wasn't like it is now where a million people hang around a band and spend weeks arguing over what colour the lead singer should dye their hair. Back then, when somebody had to meet with the band, they actually met with the band. And because Duran Duran – or Arcadia – were apparently creating the whole video themselves, they were calling all the shots, which meant that they wanted to deal with me on a face-to-face basis. Naturally, I became very over-excited by this news, but having learned from my experience with Goldie Hawn I made sure to downplay my appearance for the first meeting. The bright red belt and matching braces stayed hidden away in the Tonioli closet where they belonged.

I can't remember where or when we met exactly, but once the band explained to me the concepts behind their new project (apparently it was based on the artist, poet and filmmaker, Jean Cocteau; their look was gothic, they wore vintage tuxedos and swept-back black hair dos. It was all very over the top) I became very excited about working with them. I thought it was flippin' fantastic and very removed from the more mainstream work that Duran Duran had been doing.

'Yes, boys,' I said. 'I'll do it!'

It was only when I saw the storyboards for the video that I started to get a feel for just how ambitious 'Election Day' promised to be. As I flicked through the pages, it felt as if somebody had spiked me with another acid trip, like the one I'd experienced in Munich. It was so surreal. In the sketches, hands were springing out of walls, men with horses were leaping up through the floor. There were gorgeous women everywhere. The video was going to be incredible, ground-breaking. At the very least it would be mind-bending.

The whole thing was shot in Paris and what with this being Duran Duran, filming was scheduled to take place on a huge studio set which featured some of the most beautiful models I had ever seen in my life. Even the casting process was glamorous, like something from a movie. A queue of fantastically good-looking girls snaked around the building as they waited to audition for the band. One of them was so beautiful my jaw dropped as she walked in to say hello. She looked amazing. Her hair was very long and her eyes were rippling pools of emerald green, like a pair of sparkling gems. Another supermodel, Yasmin Le Bon (who, as you may have guessed, was married to Duran Duran's lead singer Simon) was also there and looked striking as well, but this girl was something else.

I knew she would be perfect, almost from the second she sashayed across the room. The girl was treating our studio like it was her own personal catwalk! I turned to the band for a reaction but they were transfixed on this smouldering vision of hotness; their tongues lolled around their heads; a collective trance had taken hold.

'Er, boys . . .' I whispered, trying to jolt them.

They snapped out of whatever spell had been cast by our auditioning talent.

'Look, we have to have this girl in the video,' I said.

They all nodded silently, bewitched. Duran Duran being Duran Duran weren't about to disagree with my decision to employ a girl as sexy as that one.

'What's your name?' I asked.

She looked back coyly. 'It's Linda,' she said. 'Linda Evangelista.'

Well, back then Linda wasn't the world-famous supermodel she would later become, but I knew immediately that she was probably a phenomenon-in-waiting. I signed her up straightaway. In an instant she became the star of our shoot.

Once the casting was complete, my job was to get the various actors, models and dancers, as well as the band, to move around in a way that would work in front of the cameras. In the end we filmed Linda rising from a pit in the ground. She was perched on top of a column and was surrounded by muscular men wearing horse's heads. Her role was to look sexy in a grand studio that had been designed to resemble a post-apocalyptic nightclub. It was crazy. There was dry ice everywhere. The whole scene was made even weirder by the presence of dozens of very surreal actors: scary old men hung around in dark corners and played dice games, street artists sprayed Arcadia's album sleeve onto a crumbling wall. Linda's only job in all of this was to look at the camera and raise an eyebrow or two, but flippin' heck, she stole the whole show, which was some job on that set I can tell you.

The end result was incredibly over the top and wonderfully ambitious; it was also a fun experience. I loved working with Duran Duran because they were so friendly. I became one of the gang very quickly and I never felt as if there was an 'us and them' divide between the band and the crew. Everybody stayed in the same hotel, everybody mixed together. We all had a drink in the hotel bar when work was finished for the day and because the boys were sure about who they were and what they wanted, there was none of the rock star rubbish that tends to be associated with superstar bands nowadays. There were no insecurity issues or tantrums.

Duran Duran were one of the biggest acts in the world at that time and they were a pleasure to be around.

Despite the glamour and the temptations that were being afforded to me, however, I remained very professional. I didn't party heavily with the band; I didn't go clubbing with anyone in Paris when we finished work on 'Election Day', even though I knew the city quite well from my days with La Grande Eugene. My attitude was set: I was helping to put together an incredibly lavish production and I wanted to work hard, I wanted to be a success. Just as my father had taken pride in showing me the Ferrari Barchetta as he painted its bodywork in his garage, so I took pride in getting the choreography for Arcadia just right.

I also knew that I had to maintain a professional air if I wanted to succeed. During the shoot in Paris I had to organise hundreds of people. There was no way I could have functioned had I woken up with a banging hangover every morning. Word would have got around that I was unreliable and I didn't want that. I was a Tonioli, I wanted to be respected for my work. I'm still the same today. Even when I'm giving a 6 out of 10 rating to John Sergeant for a wooden tango performance on *Strictly Come Dancing*, I still have to give everything. It's all or nothing for me, darling.

Not everyone felt the same way, though. After Arcadia I began working with more and more pop acts. I began to see the bands and the artists that were falling prey to temptation: the booze, the drugs, the girls, the vices. Now, before we go any further, I've decided not to name names in this part of the book because a) I'm not in the business of dishing the dirt, and b) I don't want to get anyone into any trouble. I also wouldn't want to be accused of hypocrisy because I've previously buried my face in a bag of cocaine on a few occasions and I'd hate for people to accuse me of double standards.

Now, in case you're thinking of throwing this book away in disgust and reaching for a tamer literary work, I'd like to tell you that I'm not proud of my experiment, and I'm not going to make excuses for what I did back then. At the same time, I'm pleased to report that my brief, tempestuous Tangos with the white lady didn't consume me. In fact, I became aware that coke wasn't the vice for me. That would be fine wine, cigarettes and fantastic shoes, though not necessarily in that order.

Nevertheless, cocaine was a big thing in those days, especially in the music industry, Oh, my goodness, it was everywhere, like a snow storm in the North Pole. Lots of people were making plenty of money, and that's when the drug barons arrived at the party. Coke quickly became the fashionable thing, probably because it was so addictive, and it was scary. I knew people that were doing it daily and it became everything to them. One or two friends of mine even started taking cocaine for breakfast, which must have tasted awful when they sprinkled it over their Weetabix in the morning.

I still remember the night I fell into the drug's clutches for the first time. It was around 1984, and it was a disaster. I was invited to a dinner party by a group of very handsome gay men in the industry. I had a wonderful meal of fabulous food and then dessert arrived, and let me tell you, it was not the type of dessert I had been used to. It was a bowl of cocaine. When somebody asked me if I wanted to have some, I thought, 'Oh what the heck? When in Rome, I'll have a flippin' go on that.'

Well we did it and the transformation was instantaneous. My gums tingled and I was all buzzy; I had loads of energy. All of us felt like young lions and it was decided we should hit Heaven to dance the night away like the sexy, gay gladiators that we were. It was there that the trouble really began, however, because as I was dancing to Frankie Goes To Hollywood's hit single, 'Relax', I began to experience some rather unpleasant movements in my tummy. My lower intestine seemed to be doing some relaxing of its own.

'Hmm, that didn't feel good,' I thought, praying to god the bassline was causing my bowels to ripple and clench rather than something a lot more serious. Sadly it was the latter, and within seconds I was racing to the toilets like Lewis Hamilton burning his way to the pits during the Monaco Grand Prix in a desperate attempt to prevent myself from ruining my pristine white jeans in the most horrific of incidents. As I bolted the door shut. I did not feel like a sex god.

That didn't put me off cocaine, however, and there were one or two Waltzes during the next decade. The last time I did the drug was when I was at a party in 2002 and I could see that people were going flippin' mental on the stuff. There were stashes of it everywhere. People were snorting it off the tables, on the kitchen tops and in the toilets. It all seemed terribly unhygienic to me, but I bought a little bag and off I went into the loo with a rolled-up fiver to stick a line up my hooter.

'Sniffing drugs off the top of a toilet seat is hardly the height of glamour, darling,' I thought, but for the first five minutes it felt good. Everything changed when I staggered out of the loo – I was red-eyed and sniffly, like a hay fever sufferer at the Chelsea Flower Show. I wanted to talk to *everybody* even though I could see that a lot of the people around me had turned into raving idiots. They were banging on and on about how great they were and how *ah-maaaazing* their lives had become. It was fantastical nonsense and all of it had been brought on by the drugs. Everybody's ego was running wild. I was being blown away by the sheer noise of people shouting about how wonderful they had been at work that day, and as the talking crap got bigger and bigger, and louder and louder, I thought, 'Hold on one second, what the bloody hell is all of this about? This stuff is rubbish!' And that's when I ordered a taxi home.

That incident alone would have been enough to put me off the stuff for life, but the following morning I was struck down by the most incredible headache I had ever experienced. It felt as if Bruce Forsyth had been tap dancing on my bonce. I was in agony.

'Oh my god,' I wailed, hiding my head under a pillow. 'I've just paid for the world's biggest migraine.'

But that wasn't the half of it, darling. I was ill for days. Worse, I was unable to get out of bed. I couldn't function. In hindsight, I think that's what really scared me the most. I realised that if I ever got into drugs in a big way it would be the end of my career as a choreographer and TV judge. I'd be a slave to cocaine, and my work ethic, the one of which I was so proud, would have gone out of the window.

As the pop videos rolled in, I made another pact with myself. Whenever I mixed with the video crew or a band after work, I was happy to enjoy a glass of wine or two, but that would be it. No late night benders, and no drugs. I knew I would have to save my energy for the choreography. Of course, it would be boring, I understood that, but it also ensured that I remained disciplined and professional. Had I misbehaved every night, there's a very good chance that I might not have made it here to tell the tale.

☆

I didn't want to be a dancer anymore. In fact, I was done and dusted with it. I was so fulfilled with my choreography roles on exciting commercials and glamorous pop videos that the very thought of getting into the back of a van to drive into the deepest, darkest parts of London and beyond to dance in front of a club of sweaty drunks filled me with horror. I was also over being one in a dancing troupe of twenty-five other performers on a TV show. On the telly I was nothing more than moving wallpaper. Instead I wanted to be a success in my own right and working as a choreographer afforded me that chance.

But then 'I'm Still Standing' happened.

Out of the blue Russell Mulcahy, who had previously worked with Rod Stewart, Billy Joel and The Rolling Stones, got in touch. He was one of the biggest directors in the world at the time. He even made the promo film for a famous single by The Buggles called 'Video Killed the Radio Star'. He was quite a talent on the pop video scene.

Russell told me he was making a video with Elton John. It was for his latest single 'I'm Still Standing' and would I like to act in it? Well, talk about asking a silly question!

He later told me that he wanted me to play a character in his script who represented Elton's lyrics.

'Arlene is going to choreograph the video,' he said. 'I've seen some of your performances and I've decided that the role is ideal for you. Perfect in fact. It's going to be amazing, there will be cars crashing through windows. The video is going to be a mini movie. We'll be filming in Cannes.'

Oh, the glamour! Off we set to the south of France with Elton John, Cannes and a dancer on the cast who turned out to be Bonnie Langford's sister Cherida. Who could have asked for anything more? I was in heaven. The casting team had even picked up several dancers from a nearby ballet school as extras, though none of them spoke a word of English (which was fine for me because I spoke fluent French and they were all adorable). Everything seemed to be going swimmingly. But then . . . nothing. Zilch. Zero action. The production went dead.

However, Russell hadn't mentioned that he was working on another video during the run-up to 'I'm Still Standing'. That particular shoot had overrun, and that meant our entire cast and crew had to twiddle their thumbs until he finally arrived to save the day. God knows where Elton was in all of this. I didn't see him during the wasted days, not for a second. But let me tell you, it was not unpleasant. I was in Cannes, the weather was lovely and everyone was having a very nice time, strolling along the sea front and taking in the sights.

We didn't waste our days, either. Arlene decided that the dancers should rehearse various routines for the video, that way we could be prepared for shooting as soon as Russell and his team showed up. For a couple of days they danced and worked on their moves. I joined in, but nobody seemed to have any idea what was going on because most of the cast were French-speaking and didn't understand the basic plot of the video. In the end, Cherida and I took upon ourselves to explain the complicated dance moves to the startled children, who looked like rabbits caught in the headlights.

'Poor them,' I thought. 'And thank god I haven't got to do any dancing.'

At the back of my mind, I became convinced that 'I'm Still Standing' was shaping up to be a disaster and every day for three days I heard the same thing: 'Don't worry Bruno, we'll start work tomorrow.' But, of course, we never did.

When Russell eventually arrived, he hadn't finished the filming on his previous project. In his wisdom it was decided he should shoot the final scene on the Cannes pier. I could see his point, it did look lovely, but the large camera crew and our entourage of actors meant that he gathered a large audience wherever he worked. As he filmed the final scene – a tracking shot with Russell and his cameraman moving backwards along the pier as the action came towards them – a crowd of tourists gathered to watch the action taking place from a distance. Had they been any nearer, somebody, surely, would have shouted out a warning, because in his haste to finish the video, Russell had clearly forgotten the pier had no railing to separate the passers-by at Cannes from the crashing waves below.

Well, you can guess what happened next, can't you? The whole lot went tumbling into the sea – director, cameraman, camera, not to mention a lot of very expensive film. Because nothing was filmed digitally in those days, there was no back-up recording, and so the reels of videotape – which contained most of Russell's first video shoot – had to be stored in a bucket of salt water (don't ask me why, it was way above my head) and sent to Paris for repair work. What a disaster!

A very expensive camera had also been ruined, which meant that a massive spanner was in the works for 'I'm Still Standing'. Because we could only film for two more days without going over budget, Russell decided to scrap Plan A which seemed like a massive pain in the backside at the time, but with hindsight, his quick thinking actually resulted in one of the most iconic pop videos of the 1980s.

The new direction was clear: *we were to make everything up as we go along!* Anything that was rehearsed was put to one side. Elton was to drive around Cannes in his fancy sports car as loads of dancers paraded about the sea front dressed in brightly coloured suits and body paint. My role in all of this was to play a variety of dancing characters, including the campest hotel bell boy you could possibly imagine, complete with cap, black Y-fronts and a studded belt. The motivation for this role was to gyrate my crotch in just about every shot. With our script tossed to one side, Arlene had to make up several dance moves on the spot. Fortunately because I had known her for so long I was able to pick up what she wanted quite quickly, and our friends from the local ballet school followed my lead. Well, they had to, nobody else in the crew spoke a word of French.

It was a hoot. A nervous buzz took over the crew because all of us were up against it: me, Elton, Russell, the extras who couldn't speak a word of English, the entire cast chipped in to make sure that the filming got finished on schedule. I even stayed up all night to make sure the body painting was finished in time. Because there was no real wardrobe to speak of (the clothes that had been delivered were redundant due to the changed script), everybody had to make do with what they had in their suitcases. My bellboy costume was made from a pair of pants, a ripped vest and a cap I borrowed from one of the local hotels.

Elton seemed to really enjoy the anarchic vibe. The whole project carried a great spirit and looking back now, it reminds me of the first time I ever worked on *Strictly Come Dancing*. I knew something special was happening, I just wasn't sure what exactly, or where it would lead to. In this case, we pulled off the recording and the shoot looked fabulous. The manic energy that had driven us throughout the day poured from the screen. In fact, Elton was so pleased with the results that he took everyone out for dinner at the very expensive and incredibly exclusive Le Negresco Hotel in Nice. The food was fantastic, the wine was spectacular, but I was so famished after all my crotch thrusting and body painting that the only thing I wanted to eat was a flippin' burger and chips.

☆

I worked with some fantastic artists as a choreographer in the 80s and 90s, including Belinda Carlisle, Kool and the Gang, Donny Osmond, AC/DC, Culture Club (and Boy George) and Wham!. I even ended up on a shoot with Paul McCartney, but because Sir Beatle and his late wife Linda were vegetarians, the staff weren't cooked any meat products during meal times. You should have heard the grumbling! An English film crew marches on a diet of bacon and eggs. Tofu and aubergine didn't quite cut the mustard.

One of the greatest artists I ever had the pleasure of choreographing was Freddie Mercury, the Queen himself. Wow, what a performer he was. I loved Queen, I'd been a huge fan for years, so when I was asked to work on the video for Freddie's solo single, 'The Great Pretender', I jumped at the chance and the pair of us hit it off almost immediately, mainly because of our mutual love of opera. Oh my goodness, we would spend hours talking about the great tenors in his dressing room. He told me that Montserrat Caballe was his favourite singer; I told him that she was the only person I'd ever asked for an autograph when I once saw her on a flight from Barcelona to London. I thought he was brilliant company.

Anyway, when Freddie came to performing in front of the camera he became a force of nature. He was incredible, magnificent. It confirmed my belief that he was one of the greatest showmen the world had ever seen and it was a tragedy that AIDS eventually took him from us so early on in his life. As the cameras rolled that day, there wasn't a bad take. Bang! Everything was done perfectly; the shoot for 'The Great Pretender' caught Freddie at full power, stadium-sized and all-conquering. It was a treat to see up close.

The following day, when I got home after work, there was an envelope waiting for me on the doorstep. It was a gift from Freddie: two tickets for the Royal Opera House production of *Norma*. I couldn't believe it, it was an incredibly thoughtful gesture and one I wouldn't have expected from such a massive superstar. Whenever I think about Freddie today, I always remember that it wasn't just his personality that had blown me away. His generosity and kindness of spirit had knocked my socks off, too.

And then there were The Rolling Stones in 1986 – Mick, Keith, Bill, Ronnie, Charlie; the bad boys of music. I was so delighted to be working with them. I'd adored the band when I was a teenager growing up in Ferrara and when they arrived at Shepperton Studios to film the video for 'One Hit to the Body', they didn't let me down. They were rock'n'roll; each member of the group had his own tour bus and it was huge, like a skyscraper on wheels. I'm guessing it must have been pretty comfortable on those things because as long as there was sunlight in the sky, The Stones didn't step off the bus.

The first sign of any action taking place occurred when the models arrived for casting. (What is it with these groups? *Honestly.*) The idea for our production was that the band would perform on a massive ramp which was tilted at a 65-degree angle populated by fabulous creatures. On paper, it sounded like a great idea, but the girls the band had selected to perform were all beauty and no action. They had absolutely no training in dance whatsoever. As soon as they climbed the ramp they began dropping off the edge like flies. We knew there and then that it wasn't going to work.

That wasn't the only problem – we soon discovered that the track that had been delivered was the wrong mix. Despite all of this palaver, Mick thought it was hysterical. He was rolling around, giggling his head off like a naughty schoolboy. If he wasn't mucking about, he was gossiping and camping it up – I thought he was fantastic, a real laugh and I thoroughly enjoyed working with him. Despite the fun and games, though, I was starting to panic. I knew that if we didn't get the video finished, the filming could prove very costly. We worked for forty-eight hours non stop because I was trying to work out what we could do to salvage the project. Just by luck I had a shoot planned the following day which featured several dancers, so we ditched the models and my girls came in; the right music arrived and we were able to shoot for real.

Written in to the script was a scene involving some Geisha girls – kimonos, wigs and make-up included. In order to get a sense of symmetry during the dance routines, I needed an even number of girls. As I made a head count, my heart sank. We only had nine dancers. The shoot required ten. Then a light bulb went off in the director's head.

'Er, Bruno, why don't you dress up in a Geisha costume?' he said, chancing his arm.

Mick looked at me with a big grin on his face.

'Yeah, Bruno maaan, why not?'

Well, when I stepped out of the make-up department I couldn't believe it. I was standing there in a Geisha dress, my face was covered in white paint, complete with slashes of lipstick and eyeliner. It looked incredible. As I walked onset, I felt Mick's hands as he lifted my dress and lifted it up over my head. There was a flash of light, a photographer's bulb popped, and the following day my buttocks were splashed over the pages of the *Sun*. Fame at last.

When Mick got onstage, oh my goodness, he hit the cameras like a bolt of lightning. He was very similar to Freddie Mercury in a way: he had a kind of magic, something special, something that could not be replicated.

What a blast! I loved working with the likes of The Stones, Duran Duran and Freddie Mercury. I was motivated and inspired by them. Sure, I was behind the cameras for these projects and hardly the star of what were comparatively small-scale shows, but it was great fun. I felt fulfilled, happy and my life was thrilling and unpredictable.

I knew it was only rock'n'roll, darling, but I liked it.

CHAPTER 10

SOME LIKE IT HOT

The pop band Bananarama were hell cats, untameable vixens; a wild child to the power of three. As a band, they were absolutely fantastic. Their debut album *Deep Sea Skiving* was a top ten hit when it came out in 1983 and the trio – singers Keren Woodwood, Siobhan Fahey and Sara Dalin – had also recorded a few top ten singles at the same time, most notably 'Na Na Hey Hey Kiss Him Goodbye' and 'Ain't What You Do It's The Way That You Do It', which was recorded with another band called Fun Boy Three. Naturally, when I got a call from their manager Hillary Shaw asking me if I wanted to team up with the threesome for a video shoot in 1984, I was more than intrigued. (This was before Duran Duran: you'll have noticed that I've leapt backwards in time, but bear with me. The true order of things will right itself shortly.)

'Bruno, this is an emergency,' she said. 'You have a reputation for being able to choreograph *anyone*. Would you like to work with Bananarama?'

My experience had taught me that working with pop stars could be tricky, but 'What the heck?' I thought, 'what's the worst that could happen?'

'Hillary, I'd love to meet the band,' I said.

'Well they're on the set for their new single "Robert De Niro's Waiting",' she replied. 'I need someone who can make them do as they're told.'

I felt I could do the job. I wasn't stupid, though. I wasn't going to sign on the dotted line there and then.

'OK,' I said. 'But between you and me, I'll make up my mind about working with them when we've all spoken together.'

Well, when I arrived for filming, the girls weren't interested in talking to me one bit. Instead they faffed about and gave their very best impression of a 'Do Not Disturb' sign as they sat around their dressing room. Siobhan was reading a copy of *Smash Hits*; Sara was grumbling about being hungry. Meanwhile, Keren was chewing gum and twiddling her hair like a petulant schoolgirl. Every now and then she would blow a huge bubble which exploded over her face with a loud 'Pop!'. The dressing room was a bomb site. Magazines, bits of make-up and food cartons had been scattered everywhere. It looked like a teenage girl's bedroom. And not just any old teenage girl. Darling, I'm talking about the sort of hellion you might spot on *The Jeremy Kyle Show*, throwing a punch at one of her many acne-riddled boyfriends.

Call me stark, raving bonkers, but I fell in love with them straightaway. I couldn't help it because I sensed they were behaving naturally: Bananarama were being stroppy because that's what they *did*. At that time the music industry was full of fakes, liars, try-hards, show-offs and wannabes (I doubt it's changed much today), so it was refreshing to meet a bunch of people who were happy to be honest about what they were, just like I had been when I left home for the theatre all those years ago. Sensing that my window of opportunity was short, Hillary did the introductions and the girls all nodded in my general direction. Somewhat unsurprisingly, their interest in me was more fleeting than a Kim Kardashian marriage and it wasn't long before Bananarama had refocused their attentions on whatever it was they had been doing before my arrival, which, by the looks of things, was nothing more than a bit of sod all.

I had heard a recording of 'Robert De Niro's Waiting' earlier that day and my first thought was that this was a mid-paced pop tune – uptempo but not a floor filler for the clubs of Macclesfield or Romford. It certainly wasn't a track that would require anything too energetic in the dancing department. Still, to get things moving I suggested a few ideas on the spot.

'How about if we film you dancing in the back of a convertible car?' I said.

That was my first mistake. I was quickly shouted down.

'Nah, we're not doing that,' sighed Sara.

'We're not dancing to that song,' said Keren.

Then Siobhan piped up. 'We just want to eat pizza.'

I loved it. I wasn't put off, in fact I was strangely enthused. I loved a challenge; I was the sort of person who liked to speak my mind so I knew I could handle this bunch. I figured that if Bananarama couldn't care less about the video to 'Robert De Niro's Waiting', then I was happy to let them do whatever they wanted.

'That's all fine by me, girls,' I said. 'I really don't give a monkey's what you do because I'll still get paid. We can eat pizza all day long. I love the stuff anyway.'

And that was that, the ice was broken. I was on board. And when it came to making the video, I did exactly as they asked – very little. The basic plot of the film was based on a cinematic thriller: the girls were being stalked by a Mafioso type, a gangster in a long coat, wide-brimmed hat and a pair of Italian designer shoes. His hit man image was offset by a violin case, which he carried under his arm to dramatic effect – the audience were supposed to assume that a machine gun was stashed inside. All the girls had to do was walk down a darkened street in incredibly short skirts and stripy leggings. The choreography was a breeze – more effort was put into avoiding the dry ice that had been pumped into the studio than actually dancing – and when we finally increased the workload to something a bit more orchestrated, well, all Bananarama had to do was sit in an apartment and sing along to the lyrics.

'Robert De Niro's waiting,' they sang. 'Talking Italian (talking Italian). Robert De Niro's waiting. Talk-in'. It-a-lian. (*Italian!*).'

The band looked like street hookers in their clothes at times, but oh my goodness, what an easy gig! The closest that Keren, Sara and Siobhan got to any form of 'acting' was when they pretended to watch a movie, but even that was carried off with an intense air of disinterest. If you were to watch the video now – and it's still up there on the internet – you'll see what I mean. Keren looks so bored that she can hardly muster the energy to lip-sync her words; Sara can't see beyond a bleached fringe that has been hair-sprayed across her face.

While all of this was going on, the girls and I were having a laugh on set. I quickly realised that they carried the same naughty sense of humour as me; they wanted to play around all the time and I was all for it. That day I decided I wasn't going to present myself as a choreographer because the girls clearly weren't impressed by choreography. Instead, I decided to let them do whatever they wanted, which always got a much better result.

The girls even got their pizzas in the end. In the closing scenes of the video, when the cinematic gangster arrived at Bananarama's 'apartment', he was filmed standing with his violin case, while looming into the door frame ominously as if preparing for another mob hit. When Keren opened the door, the latch flipped and the case fell open to reveal three takeaway pizzas stuck to the inside.

The girls had great fun, and after our day in the studio they virtually welcomed me into the band. We became friends instantly, and wherever they went, I went with them and the next few years became a blur of parties, shows and video shoots. I think what I found so great about Bananarama was the fact that they were just three normal girls, the type you would find in any suburban nightclub up and down the country. They were attractive, but they weren't unattainable like Madonna. They were a real gang who preferred sitting in the pub to hanging out at a swanky, celeb-packed party; they would rather go bowling than film a TV commercial, and believe me they had plenty of offers. They did not care one bit about being cool and I admired them for it incredibly.

☆

Forgive me, if you can, because before I reveal the rest of my adventures with the 'Nanas I want to tell you about some important additions that arrived in my life around the same time: two new men and a fancy car. I'll tell you about the car first as it will probably be a lot easier.

I was earning a nice amount of money. Suddenly I could afford to go on wonderful holidays and every Christmas I travelled somewhere hot and tropical. I loved the Caribbean, the Maldives, Thailand and South Africa. I went everywhere, like an all-singing, all-dancing version of Judith Chalmers. To compliment my jet-set lifestyle, I also wanted an equally sexy car in which to parade around town, something that suited my passions and personality.

I knew exactly what I wanted, and as soon as I could afford it, I went down to the garage and picked up a Mercedes 350 SL convertible, just like the one Paul Young had driven when we started working together a few years earlier. It was sparkling white, the interior was a cool, blue leather; the silver trim on the bodywork gleamed. I was ecstatic. Whenever I drove around town with Bananarama, which was often, we would always have the soft top down. They would pretend to be my ladies of the night and I would act like a pimp, which always drew funny stares as we cruised around the west end of London, I can tell you.

The Mercedes was a dream and it made a change from my previous car. That was a Porsche 924, and what an animal it was. It looked great: the bodywork was black, sleek and very yuppie-ish; it was a sex symbol on a chassis. The only downside was that it happened to be the biggest pile of flippin' junk I'd ever had the misfortune to stick a key into. It was a VW in drag. I had bought it from a trusted director friend of mine, but I was shafted. The Porsche was a bitch to use, it was forever breaking down and every two weeks there was something wrong with the damn thing. I was furious.

Thankfully the Mercedes was able to satisfy my every demand, as was a new agent (the first new man in my life), the legendary showbiz figure Michael Summerton who I'd met around the same time. Michael worked with Iain Burton, the co-founder of a record label called Fanfare Records (which was also in partnership with Simon Cowell) and they had released Hot Gossip's single 'Don't Beat Around the Bush'; Iain and Michael were Arlene Phillips' managers. More thrillingly, Michael was also one of the original Dalek operators in an early series of *Dr Who*. Somehow I had come up in one convesation or another and out of the blue, Michael gave me a call.

'Bruno, darling,' he said – he would go on to refer to me as darling with every phone call, and every job he ever offered me was *major*. 'I hear you are doing good work, do you have someone to look after you? And by "look after you" darling, I mean do you have an *agent*?'

The truth was, I didn't have any representation. I had drifted away from Razzmatazz and now I was picking up plenty of work, I really needed somebody to manage my affairs, the things I was crap at in life – accounts, invoices, picking up the phone and hassling people. By all accounts, Michael was one of the great characters on the London showbiz scene. He told stories like Kenneth Williams, he could exaggerate gossip terribly (but in a nice way) and his tales would have people in stitches. I had heard from the likes of Arlene that he was at the top of his game, so I said, 'Yes, darling!'

We would become firm friends.

The other love in my life around that time was Paul, a very attractive and very funny Essex boy living in London. We were acquainted in Heaven in 1984. Elton John's 'I'm Still Standing' was being played constantly on the big TV screens that dangled above the bar. My crotch was on show every single night. What a treat! It gave me a licence to snog just about anybody I wanted. People saw the video, then they saw me dancing alongside them and before you knew it, Bob was my uncle. I had a great time.

Paul caught my eye straightaway. He was in London because he wanted to be a model and I spotted him one night as he lounged around in one of the club's ante rooms with a friend. Immediately I was struck by just how good looking he was and after a couple of drinks, I plucked up enough courage to introduce myself. Almost immediately we hit it off. It was another lightning bolt, like the one that had zapped me in the heart when I first met Scott in the very same club. At first I thought Paul might be a bit young for me because he was twenty-three, I was a few years older. But he seemed to be a lovely guy, so I thought, 'So what? Live a little, Bruno!' And I invited him out for a drink the following week.

I remember feeling very nervous before our first date. I hadn't really allowed anyone into my life after my relationship with Scott. Being so intimate and open with someone, anyone, even a person as nice as Paul, made me feel vulnerable and I really didn't want to get hurt again. I certainly didn't want to jump into anything big. But Paul wanted the same things as me and after our first date, we went on another night out and another, and then another. He fitted into my life quite well, everything was going so great, I was suddenly in love again.

As our relationship progressed, it was obvious that Paul was a happy fit for me. Even the 'Nanas loved him, and because of his hunky good looks and good sense of humour, they were forever asking the pair of us (along with another model called Bailey Walsh) to perform alongside them whenever they made personal appearances on the telly, though I soon realised the main reason for that was because they wanted an easy ride. We would always mess around with them as much as we could. Everything was going fantastically well. Within two years of our relationship, I had bought a new apartment in west London, and Paul and I decided to 'go steady'. He moved into my pad and for the first time ever I was living in domestic bliss.

☆

What I hadn't expected when I met the 'Nanas for the first time was just how flippin' huge they would become in America. Singles like 'Robert De Niro's Waiting' had done well in the charts at home, but by the time the band had released their third album, *True Confessions* in 1986, they were big stuff, especially over the pond where their single 'Venus' was a number one hit.

Working on that video was amazing, a blast. By that time, I had got to know the girls really well and I could understand their personalities and their moods. I had a skin thick enough to withstand their occasional strops. One time, for example, when we were working in Los Angeles, the band were filming a video. Sara was having terrible trouble with her hair and nothing seemed to be giving her the tangled, sun-kissed look she loved to wear at the time.

'I've got it,' she said. 'Sea water should do the trick, that'll tangle it up lovely.'

Well, that was fine in theory, but in practice it was much harder. We were in LA and the beach at Santa Monica was an hour's drive away, but poor Hillary, ever anxious to keep the girls happy, drove to the coast to bring back some fresh seawater, just so Sara could style her hair. Can you believe it?

It was for that reason that I rarely gave the 'Nanas any complicated dance steps or choreographed moves. They would kick up a fuss if they felt anything was beyond them. If ever I was planning a video or TV performance, I knew that if the dance steps seemed too elaborate or too demanding then they would give it short shrift. Instead I realised that any dance steps we prepared would have to suit their laid-back and accessible style. Simplicity seemed to go down very well.

I was happy too, because the message I wanted to get across in the 'Nanas' videos was that they were a bunch of girls who loved to dance rather than a bunch of dancing girls. There was a massive difference between the two and so I always devised moves that everybody would want to copy instantly. They had to be fun. More importantly they had to be *easily replicated* by the fans. Michael Jackson's moonwalk was a brilliant dance step, but let's not forget, very few people could pull it off. Especially after knocking back a can of Hofmeister or three.

With 'Venus', however, we struck gold. The basic concept for the video was of a series of vignettes which involved the girls dressing up as beautiful women from history such as Cleopatra, or fantastic fictional characters. At one point Siobhan even dressed up as the Devil, which seemed pretty apt given the girls' occasionally hellish temperaments. Throughout the video all three singers were surrounded by semi-naked men whose job was to writhe around on the floor among the fire and the dry ice. There wasn't really a story to the film as such, but who needed one when you had three girls as interesting as Keren, Sara and Siobhan running around, wriggling their tushes? After 'Venus', it was impossible to turn the radio on without hearing one of Bananarama's songs. They were everywhere.

One of the reasons for their increased success was a change of personnel behind the scenes. The band had handed song production duties over to Stock Aitken Waterman, the hit-making trio known to their mums as Mike Stock, Matt Aitken and Pete Waterman. SAW were the Three Musketeers of pop and had made records for the likes of Charlene from *Neighbours* (Kylie Minogue), Scott from *Neighbours* (Jason Donovan) and Rick Astley. 'Venus' was the first song from their partnership with the 'Nanas and after it went to number one in America, the two parties appeared to be a match made in heaven. They even recorded the band's fourth album, *Wow!* in 1987.

After that it was one smash hit after another. Their singles, 'Nathan Jones' and 'I Heard A Rumour' both went into the top 20; 'Love in the First Degree' and 'I Want You Back' were top 5 hits. And when it came to making the videos, we stuck to the same simple formula as 'Venus'. The dancing was uncomplicated, the girls were allowed to express themselves through their moves, and I invited as many boys in crop tops to dance around in the background as I could. I even stood in as a backing dancer when the band performed 'I Heard a Rumour' on *Top of the Pops*. Myself, Paul and Bailey could be seen quite clearly in cycling shorts, Aviator shades and leather cap (it was basically my uniform at the time); I even oiled up my chest for the special event, but nobody ever stopped me in the local Safeway for an autograph afterwards. They were probably afraid of what might happen if they approached me as I wandered down the frozen foods aisles.

We were all having such fun, even though we were in one another's pockets all the time at work. But then, work never felt like a chore, not for me anyway. I even gave the girls dance lessons in the Covent Garden studios, though I never dressed our sessions up as something they *had* to do. Oh no, that would have sounded a bit too much like hard labour and I wouldn't have been able to deal with all the moaning. Instead I told them we had to have some great moves for all the parties we were being invited to. They seemed to go along with my ruse.

And there were parties, plenty of them. *Oh, the parties!* One time when we went to see Madonna at Wembley and, my god, it was huge. The show was fantastic, the choreography was wild, and afterwards we were all invited to a backstage soirée to celebrate the incredibly glamorous affair. I used the term 'soirée' loosely because the gathering was actually an open invitation to anybody vaguely famous who might have been hanging around in the Wembley postcode at the time. Kylie Minogue was there with Michael Hutchence of INXS, and just about every band that had ever worked with Stock Aitken Waterman could be found gyrating around on the dance floor.

As I stood by the bar with the 'Nanas, all of whom were looking thoroughly bored with the whole palaver, I suddenly clapped eyes on Nick Kamen, the model I'd once employed for an advert promoting Lois Jeans (it was a few chapters back. Do keep up). At the time, Nick was getting a fair bit of attention from the tabloid press because he was working with Madonna and they were hanging around together. He was quite the star, and as I stood with Keren, Siobhan and Sara, Nick noticed my frantic attempts to catch his eye and came over to say hello, where, for few a minutes at least we had a very nice chat about life, the universe and launderettes. Well, talk about putting the cat among the pigeons. As we stood gossiping, I became very aware of a stirring in the crowd behind me. A major shift was taking place in the pop universe and my sixth sense was going wild with panic.

'Bruno, danger!' it screamed. 'Turn around! Turn around!'

Instinctively I looked behind me and that was when I came face to face with the queen of pop, the first lady herself: Madonna, arguably the angriest woman I had ever clapped eyes on in my life. She took one look at me and evaluated my importance like a dancing Terminator in a blonde wig and lacy top. The look on her face told me I wasn't important enough to warrant her acknowledgment; she grabbed Nick's hands and yanked him away from our conversation.

'Neeeeek!' she snapped, as he tried to explain that he'd been chatting with an old work colleague. 'I've been waaaaaai-tiiiiiiiiiiiiing!'

The poor boy didn't have a chance. He wasn't even able to bid us goodnight. The pair of them were off, Nick more by force than choice, and as they disappeared into the crowd I wondered how the working relationship would pan out for them both. My conclusion? Not bloody well, most likely.

☆

Bananarama were more like blokes than girls. When we weren't messing around at parties, we were playing cards. And when we weren't playing cards, we were getting drunk. With the 'Nanas, there was no saying 'no' to a party, despite the pact I had made with myself about mixing business with boozy pleasure. I was a terrible lightweight when it came to alcohol (a couple of glasses of wine is all it takes for me to be woozy and inappropriate), and I often found myself drinking the night away with Keren, Sara and Siobhan, usually after the gang had performed at one show or another.

The last time it happened was the worst time. We were in Newcastle having finished a recorded performance of 'I Heard A Rumour' on a music show called *The Tube*. Somebody had the bright idea of taking us to a local nightclub once the filming had finished (one of the posher ones in town, apparently), but when we got there, all the girls wanted to do was play cards along with Paul and Bailey. Honestly, it was like an addiction for all of us. Forget drugs, this was much more compulsive. Tour buses, trains, planes, airport lounges, backstage during the spare hours on a video shoot: all we ever did was play cards. This time, because the girls were near to a bar, it was decided that the loser of each hand, in whatever game we had involved ourselves in, should down a shot. And that's when the trouble started.

Neat vodka was the drink of choice and we all knocked back shot after shot after shot. I could barely stand, the girls could barely talk. We were so out of it. Suddenly the DJ put on a song the girls liked – god knows what it was, I could hardly see, let alone hear – and all of us ran onto the dance floor. Given that they were one of the biggest pop bands around at the time, it had been decided that we shouldn't draw too much attention to ourselves that evening, especially as the club was full of drunken, lecherous men looking for a snog, but that plan was suddenly well and truly out of the window. Matters got even more heated when the girls started ripping one another's clothes off. Sara ripped Paul's top, Siobhan ripped my shirt, I ripped Siobhan's dress. Oh my goodness, it was a disaster. There were bras on show everywhere.

Now, even though this was one of the posher nightclubs in Newcastle, it was still Newcastle and the year was 1987, hardly a vintage twelve months for metrosexuality. I don't even think the term 'New Man' had even been invented at that point. As the girls started to do their best impression of a cheap strip joint, the blokes in the club advanced upon them like a pack of cavemen. Our group were considered to be easy pickings and I knew I would be powerless to help if matters started getting a little rowdy.

I desperately looked for a way out. The girls' handbags were in a pile on the dance floor and having scooped them up, I shouted a warning at the top of my voice.

'Girls, run!' I screamed hysterically, at which point all six of us legged it for the exit as dozens of hairy, sweaty hands pawed at our clothes and naked flesh in an attempt to prevent us from escaping. It was like something from a zombie film. More horrific was the morning after, though. The next day we had to be awake at 6.30 a.m. for a flight back to London, and as I sat in an airplane toilet and vomited all the way home, I promised myself that I would never, *ever* try to keep up with the 'Nanas again.

☆

With hindsight, the 'Nanas didn't need a drink or ten to cause mischief. They were more than capable of causing trouble when they were stone cold sober. In fact, on one occasion they very nearly burned down the Sunset Marquis hotel in Hollywood, one of the most rock'n'roll hangouts in LA, when they hadn't even enjoyed a sniff of alcohol.

The girls were in the States to shoot a video and after a day of filming we all went back to the hotel to relax. We spent wonderful days in LA shopping, going to nightclubs and trying to avoid as much work as we could. Meanwhile, the record label, in their wisdom, had rented us a beautiful self-catering cabana and one night I offered to cook dinner, much to the delight of Keren and Sara – we were riding a 'Nana light because Siobhan was staying with her boyfriend, Dave Stewart of the Eurythmics, who lived in Encino. Anyway, drawing from my grandma's recipes I decided to rustle up a pasta dish, but there was very little in the way of ingredients. No meat, no stock, no herbs, no nothing. Well, there were some tomatoes and a little olive oil which I used to make a basic sauce, but I needed more oomph, more magic.

'Look, I'm going to have to get some bits and pieces from a grocery store,' I said as the girls began to play yet another hand of cards. 'Can you watch the tomato sauce cooking on the hob while I go out?'

Somebody mumbled something that sounded vaguely like a 'Yeah, whatever', and given that this was the closest anybody ever got to an acknowledgement when the girls were playing cards, I hopped in the hire car, safe in the knowledge that my gently simmering tomatoes were under control.

Except that they weren't. When I returned to the hotel, black smoke was belching out of the foyer; the fire alarms were going off. As I made my way to the cabana, I could only think one thing: 'What the bloody hell have they done now?'

I received my answer at the front door of our luxury pad. Hillary was gesticulating wildly and trying to calm an irate hotel manager. The girls were covered from head to foot in crap and soot. They were coughing, spluttering and wetting themselves laughing. Someone was dangling a large saucepan – the one I had been cooking with not half an hour earlier – in front of my face. It was charred, the handle had melted off. When I looked past the sorry scene I could see that the entire room was black and there was smoke everywhere. Apparently, the pillocks had completely forgotten about the pasta sauce until the flame from the hob had burned through the pan handle, setting the kitchen ablaze. My creation from the grandmother Tonioli recipe book was ruined. Not that the 'Nanas really cared. They just went off and ordered another takeaway pizza.

☆

In the midst of all this madness with the girls and Paul and the cars, I bought a cat. I'm not sure what made me do it, maybe I felt as if I needed an extra companion around Chez Bruno, and the chance purchase was completely unexpected and out of the blue, though not entirely out of character. I do like to shop. Anyway, the year was 1987, and I was still teaching and doing private classes at the Covent Garden Dance Centre. One of my clients, a pet shop owner, owed me quite a lot of money and when I went down to the store to collect my earnings, he had just received a litter of the most beautiful Himalayan Persian Blue Point cats.

My mouth dropped open. They were *stunning*. As I leaned down to look into the box, one of them, the oldest I think, jumped onto my shoulder and started purring loudly. He was incredible. Forget Linda Evangelista, this cat had eyes of turquoise, they were cool and piercing. I also noticed that he had a rough tongue and a playful spirit, because immediately he started licking my ear and rubbing his nose against my cheek.

How could I refuse him? This gorgeous kitten, this *temptress* had chosen me. I was besotted, but I could tell by the cut of his fur and his gorgeous eyes that the price tag would be huge, so I struck up a deal.

'I'll tell you what,' I said, trying to do my best impression of Del Boy from *Only Fools and Horses*. 'Forget the money, I'll take the cat.'

To my surprise, the owner readily agreed. I left the shop with the purring beast under my arm and dropped him onto the seat of my white Mercedes where he began to purr even more. I must have looked like Blofeld, the pussy-stroking villain from James Bond.

Once I got back to my flat, he made himself at home almost immediately. Some cats are jumpy and run away from everybody, but this one had a personality. I chose the name Oliver for him and immediately he became very assertive of his presence. If somebody came into the house, Oliver simply had to come in and check out who they were. And he didn't care for the occasion – dinner parties, social functions, afternoon meetings: he wanted to nose around and make friends whatever was going on. He was a real diva, and like most cats, at times, he thought he was a person. If I ever sat on the sofa, Oliver would jump up immediately and sit next to me. He was also barmy. Oliver didn't like to be held, but he liked to wrap himself around my neck like a shawl.

Then a weird thing happened. Not long after Oliver's arrival, I noticed that my telephone had stopped ringing. The work had dried up. I checked the line, it was definitely in order; I called Michael, he made noises about it being a 'quiet time, darling. *Nothing major.*' Then Paul, the twit, planted the seeds of doubt in my mind.

'Oh, you know what it is,' he said. 'It's the cat. Oliver's brought you bad luck.'

Well, this shows you what an idiot I was, because I genuinely thought he was being serious. I believed him, and in a fit of madness I took the cat back to the pet shop and asked for a refund. On my way home, as I picked the fur from my clothes and the Mercedes' cool blue, leather seats, I began sobbing uncontrollably. The tears continued until well into the evening, which was when Paul returned home from his work on a modelling shoot.

'Bruno, what's wrong?' he said, fearing the worst. 'Where's Oliver?'

I could barely speak through the waterworks.

'I . . . I . . . I . . . I took him back! You said he was bad luck.'

Paul looked at me like I was a pillock, which I was. He had clearly been joking, but I hadn't sensed it, and it suddenly dawned on me that I was suffering from Showbiz Dementia, a condition that can send a relatively normal person stark, raving mad because they have spent too much time with their heads in the clouds, surrounded by models in cycling shorts, champagne, free food and plastic glamour.

'Oh my god,' I said. 'What have I done? I need to get him back.'

It was late, so I called the pet shop owner at home. I was in hysterics. He understood my distress, but explained that, sadly, Oliver had already been sold to another buyer.

'To who?' I hissed. I sounded like an axe murderer. 'Where . . . is . . . he?'

I was told that the address was confidential.

'GIVE ME THE ADDRESS!' I screamed.

'Er . . . er, OK, Bruno . . .' he trembled, flicking through his contact book.

Even though it was the middle of the night, I got in the car and drove over to Oliver's new home. My eyes were bloodshot with tears and my face was puffy and flushed. I was unshaven, like a fury, obviously mental. When the owners opened the door, there were no introductions, there was no small talk. Instead they thrust Oliver's furry body into my arms, presumably because the pet shop owner had already warned them a maniac was on his way round to reclaim his kitten. But what choice did they have? Hell hath no fury like a pedigree cat owner scorned.

☆

And then the 'Nanas broke up . . .

. . . Well, kind of. I suppose given their anarchic way of living, it was inevitable that the relationship couldn't last between the three girls. Shortly after 'Love in the First Degree' in 1988, Siobhan started seeing more and more of Dave Stewart and that's when the cracks began to appear. She moved to Encino; Keren and Sara had always been closer because they had grown up together. While the girls got on fabulously for the most part, there was always a slight tension, but I always thought it was a great chemistry because that schism – however small – created an energy. It gave the band a vibrancy. I'm not sure if they would agree with me, but that's what I always felt.

When Siobhan left in 1988, that energy changed. A new girl came in called Jacquie O'Sullivan, who was lovely by the way, and while she understood all the dance moves and worked with Bananarama until 1991, it was never really the same, although the hits continued. Siobhan later went off and had her own solo career which was fantastic, and the two other 'Nanas, Sara and Keren, are still going today. I keep in touch with all of the girls because I loved them so much – Sara even went into labour at my barbecue a while back. But when it all changed, I knew it was time for me to move on. My brain needed a new adventure. My liver needed a rest.

CHAPTER 11

TO HAVE
AND TO
HAVE NOT

One photo I cherish dearly from my days with the 'Nanas was taken backstage at The London Palladium in 1988. It's a shot of me and Paul with the band – Keren, Sara, Siobhan – posing with another bunch of prima donnas from the time, the stars of America's favourite sitcom *The Golden Girls*. The picture was taken before the filming of the 1988 Royal Variety Performance, which was a big deal in those days, one of the telly highlights of the year, in fact. All the big names in showbiz at the time were invited to do a turn in front of the cameras (and the Queen Mum, of course) and I remember the line-up that year was a *Who's Who* of popular entertainment – Jackie Mason, Kylie Minogue and Russ Abbot all performed.

The greatest star on the bill in my eyes was Estelle Getty of *The Golden Girls*, or Sophia Petrillo (the Italian grandma), as her character was known. The main characters of the hit programme had been invited by the producers to do a live sketch and when we met them, oh, I was beside myself with excitement. It was like something out of a dream because I'd been a fan of the show for as long as I could remember; I had devoured every single episode. Even now, when I'm in the States and *The Golden Girls* comes on, I always make a point of watching it.

I'll never forget Estelle's grand entrance. We were sitting in the band's dressing room when it happened, playing cards, reading magazines, when suddenly the door burst open and her hurricane-like personality whooshed in.

'Oh, I can't stand those bitches next door!' she howled melodramatically and in character. It wasn't long before she was affectionately taking the mickey out of her co-stars, Bea Arthur, Rue McClanahan and Betty White.

'Oh they're such . . . They're such . . . *divas!*'

She eyed up the 'Nanas, then me. All of us were staring back at her, gobsmacked.

'So, what is it that you do then?' she said.

There was a brief moment of silence. We were dazed. One of the Golden Girls had burst into our dressing room for a chinwag and was now holding court. Everybody seemed to be taking in this surreal development. It was quite a moment.

'Oh, we're a band,' said Keren, nervously.

Estelle took a deep breath. Her nostrils flared as if the answer had offended her intelligence.

'Well, I didn't think you were *Christian Scientists* . . .'

Immediately the room fell about in stitches of laughter and it wasn't long before Estelle had settled into a chair for what she described as, 'some peace and quiet from those bitches'. She had picked the wrong place, however. For the next twenty minutes I bombarded her with question after question, I wanted to know everything about the show. It wasn't long before there was another knock on the door and this time it was the other girls – Bea, Betty and Rue – who then joined us for what turned into a fabulous gossiping session. Eventually, the two gangs and myself gathered together for a snapshot, the result of which is still hanging in my house today.

It was funny, despite meeting all those famous names during my time as a choreographer, I was rarely star struck. I had to stay composed. It would have been no good for my career had I sobbed uncontrollably, or collapsed into a puddle of my own sweat whenever I was introduced to somebody as famous as Estelle Getty, Freddie Mercury or Duran Duran. Word would have got around that I was completely off my rocker and I never would have been employed again. Of course, there was admiration for those people when I met them, but not hysteria. That was just as well really, because if I'd thought the job had introduced me to some seriously talented people during my work on all those pop videos, well, I was about to be blown away when Michael Summerton scored some work for me in the world of film-making. It was on a whole other level.

My first movie role, another big break – and I'm realising by writing this that I've had more of those than a flippin' snooker player – happened around 1989 when a director called Mike Ockrent rang up.

'I need a choreographer for a film I'm making called *Dancin' Thru the Dark*,' he said. 'It's written by Willy Russell. The plot is based on a girl who's having second thoughts about her wedding and during this crisis, she bumps into her ex-boyfriend in a club, played by Con O'Neill – who's the singer in a band . . .'

Mike wanted some musical staging for his rock star hunk, plus some choreography for the cast, who would be dancing in a nightclub scene. Because I'd worked with so many bands in the past, he felt I could bring some authenticity to the production.

Of course, I threw myself into the job. It was a challenge, it was something new, and I ran after it like Rin Tin Tin chasing a passing Ferrara postman. At that time, I was finding that the pop videos, while being fun, had become a bit of a travelator: a conveyor belt of shoots and bands, studios and hotels; the work had become repetitive at times, and as you know, my dears, I don't *do* repetition. Thankfully, *Dancin' Thru the Dark* was anything but. I was sent up to Liverpool for filming and straightaway I was dropped into a maelstrom of chaos. The hotel I was staying in, The Queen something or other, was a madhouse, an asylum. It was falling apart at the seams like a badly made dress. I would order tea and toast for breakfast at seven, and at 5 a.m. a bacon and egg roll would be delivered to my door by a troll-like man with a hunchback. The place made Fawlty Towers look like the Sunset Marquis in LA, before Bananarama nearly razed it to the ground.

In stark contrast to my humble and temporary abode, my role on *Dancin' Thru the Dark* ran like clockwork. The biggest job was to plan a scene that involved lots of extras in a club; a large number of dancers had to move around wildly as Con O'Neill's band ran through their gig, and while that might sound simple on paper, I can tell you it bloody well wasn't. For starters there had to be a certain number of good dancers to control the scene and move the speaking actors into the right place so they could deliver their lines on cue.

There also had to be a lot of not so good dancers to give the scenes some extra realism. Pulling all of that together was pretty tricky.

I learned almost straightaway – because I'm a quick learner, as you may have guessed – that choreography has many levels, and in film the trick is to manage and create a movement that feels right. The ambience on *Dancin' Thru the Dark* clearly had to seem natural. In some films, like the Anne Hathaway movie *Ella Enchanted*, which I will tell you about in more detail a bit later, I could use more elaborate, outlandish dance steps because it was a fantasy. If I'd really wanted to, I could have turned the scene into a West End musical because belief was supposed to be suspended among the audience. In a film based on realism, however, the acting and the choreography had to feel authentic, genuine. It wouldn't do if all the 'average' dancers in *Dancin' Thru the Dark* were able to jump around like Justin Timberlake or former *Strictly* contestant Dennis Taylor, would it? (That was a joke. Dennis Taylor was, of course, terrible. He danced like a lamppost lost in the Sahara.)

I felt as if I was exploring a whole new world. On set, I was helping to create another reality, but I was also building the illusion that the scenes and the dancing on show were real. Overall, though, I liked the way that I was working with 'characters' and not people. If that sounds crackers, let me part the curtains and reveal the wizardry working away behind the scenes: my darling, the truth was, when I worked with a group of dancers or a band like Bananarama, I was creating a routine with three, four, or however many people in the group. I always found myself working from the outside in, because a dancer is like a machine, trained to execute a plan given to them by somebody like me. The whole discipline was based on appearance.

However, when I talked with the actors from *Dancin' Thru the Dark*, I found that I was working with people pretending to be somebody else, which was another experience altogether. I had to work from the *inside out*, with the ideas and feelings of their character. So every time I spoke to one of the cast as filming was due to take place, I always asked them what they thought of their role; I asked them how their characters should behave in the situation they were in. After that, I found myself creating dance scenes through the eyes and personalities of fictional individuals, which was a fascinating experience.

When filming finished for the day, the scene had come together exactly as planned. I was delighted, ecstatic. I found the whole process so rewarding, so fulfilling, that I wanted to do it again and again and again because I knew that *Dancin' Thru the Dark*, or any movie I worked on in the future, would last forever. It would be there for people to watch for as long as there were video players and DVDs around, and to me, that was simply marvellous. Lights, camera, action! It felt as if I'd found a whole new calling.

☆

As David Bowie would say, ch-ch-ch-ch-ch-changes! They were taking place everywhere. With all the money I was making from the films, videos and adverts, I was able to buy a brand new garden flat down the road from my old place in 1991, but this time I could afford three bedrooms and three bathrooms – and I do love a bathroom en suite. The best thing about my latest fortress, though, was the garden. It was unkempt and a bit of a hole when I first arrived to be honest, but almost immediately I set about turning the place into a fantasy world of plants, flowers and foliage.

I think it must have been the peasant gene inside me, because I loved gardening from the minute I dropped to my knees with a trowel and a bucket. I instinctively knew what to do. I was a born again Alan Titchmarsh – I had it all down from the start. I could cut something, spit on a shoot and the flippin' thing would grow out of the soil before I knew it. It was clear to me that I had some pretty green fingers, plus plenty of memories of my grandparents' own gardening techniques. They had been farmers by origin and I must have stored lots of information in the back of my head from their conversations about sowing seeds. In my own garden, everything seemed to come to me naturally. I knew when to plant and when to cut, and I never used pesticides, apart from the odd slug pellet here and there.

Within a year it looked amazing, a riot of colours and fragrances. Some bolshy robins even moved in. I became obsessed with working away on my plants whenever I wasn't involved in a film or a video or advert because I found that gardening was a very calming experience. It cleared my mind of everything until I was as empty and as vacuous as Craig Revel Horwood on one of his many shopping trips. I even found myself painting with plants; I understood composition and colour. It was like choreographing or watercolour work, but this time I was creating with life.

I wasn't the only person who enjoyed the garden. Oliver quickly became a fan and when we moved in he changed from a preening, handsome show stopper into a trained killer, an unstoppable assassin. By then he was two years old and a big boy. Introducing him to a new world, a larger more colourful kingdom, seemed to unleash his inner tiger. No small mammal was safe, and if Oliver wasn't hunting and maiming and chewing, then he was parading along the walls and fences, showing off his glory to the world. His arrogance and beauty made him a celebrity among the neighbours. And he loved the attention, *the tart*.

Oliver also became the master of the house and if ever guests turned up he would always sniff at them like a dog; he would growl at people if he didn't like them, though that was rare. The biggest problem, however, was that nobody ever dared to leave their bags or coats lying around, because if they did, Oliver was sure to leave a grubby present on their property as a memento of the visit. I'm not sure what brought it on because he never did it to either myself or Paul, but some guests were clearly viewed with indifference and his unhappiness at their arrival was always displayed in the muckiest of ways.

I remember one night we had friends over for dinner. The pair of them were fashion designers, fabulously dressed and kitted out from head to foot in Prada. I knew instinctively that they would be bringing bags of clothes even though they were only staying for one evening, so I warned them before their arrival that they would have to shut the door on the spare room otherwise Oliver would unleash his funky fury upon them. Anyway, as our visitors put their coats away and I poured the first glasses of plonk that evening, I asked them whether they had remembered to shut the door on the way out. They looked at one another and shrugged. My heart sank.

'Oh no,' I hissed. 'Oliver . . .'

I dashed to the bedroom to find the door was wide open. There on the bed, staring at me defiantly, his crystal-like eyes brimming with attitude, was the cat. Straightaway I could see what was happening. He was piddling over thousands of quids worth of Prada coat like it was a luxury pet urinal. There was no shame in what he was doing either. He didn't even have the decency to move as I made a grab for his fur, lifting him from the scene of his crime, wee still pouring from him like a broken tap. Oh, it was rancid. Our friends from Italy were not impressed at all, especially as the coats had to be dry-cleaned. Looking back, I don't think they visited us again, not after Oliver had left his mark, the little anarchist.

My goodness I was working with some exciting and brilliant people. In 1991, shortly after my house move, I was asked to work on *The Ghosts of Oxford Street*, a made-for-TV film about Harry Gordon Selfridge, the shopping guru behind the store of the same name. The legendary punk impresario Malcolm McLaren – who infamously managed the Sex Pistols – was the director and I must admit I was a little nervous before I met with him because his reputation had travelled far and wide. I had heard all sorts of stories and I feared he would be an older version of the sneering, unpleasant band he had once managed. In actual fact, he was the complete opposite and Malcolm was brilliant to work with. He was professional, on the ball, very organised and very pleasant to be around.

He was also incredibly intelligent and well informed. Malcolm had a brilliant knowledge of all the art forms – not just fashion and music, but everything – and he was fascinating. I loved all of his stories about the Pistols and the punk era. I would often just sit there and listen to him talking because it was consistently mesmerising. To my mind, Malcolm was a cultural icon and he changed Britain when punk took over the world in the 1970s. Its influence can still be felt today and the movement has often been overlooked, but in my eyes his work was a catalyst for a huge cultural change.

My job on the show was to work with the great Sir Tom Jones, who played Mr Selfridge in the film. The movie was shot in a very surreal, pop promo style. It mixed the story and acting with some old, historical footage and several musical numbers which Sir Tom bellowed out in his unique way. He was the perfect professional, too. Whenever I told him what it was I needed him to do, he always got it immediately, then he would deliver on those instructions perfectly. Who would have thought it? Me working alongside Mr Thunderball and Mr Punk in a film about a department store? *Flippin' mental.*

I was having a great time working on those projects. I felt so free and excited, sitting behind the camera and organising the various dances and routines that were needed to bring some extra life to the acting. It paid well too, but (and this was important to me) I appreciated every part of it. My working class upbringing meant that I was never able to take anything for granted; I was always sensible with money because my overwhelming fear was that the good times might run out, or the work might dry up. I was forever making sure that I did everything I could to ensure that the jobs were coming in. As a result, I was in a good place financially and my mortgage repayments were sensible, but I still had the

Above: Putting Gary Lineker through his paces for a Walkers Crisps advert in 2010. I look like a serial killer. It seemed to have the desired effect: Gary did everything that was asked of him.

Above: With Robson and Jerome. As you can tell we had just enjoyed a lengthy lunch courtesy of Mr Simon Cowell.

Below: Backstage with Steve Coogan while filming *The Tony Ferrino Phenomenon*.

Above: Following Craig Revel Horwood into the toilet requires drastic measures.

Above: With Amanda Holden, Jackie St Clair and Carl Michaelson, preparing Simon Cowell's 50th birthday performance.

Above right: With Simon and Steve backstage at The Royal Variety. That's not Botox, he's just picked up the bill from dinner.

Right: With Len and Carrie Ann Inaba. Hollywood beauties, or so I would like to think.

Below: On *The Tonight Show* with Jay Leno with the delicious Carrie Ann. The girl is a *bombshell*.

Above: With Amanda Holden. Look at the stems on blondie!

Above right: The judges. *Strictly Come Dancing*'s original line up. Is Craig wearing lipstick?

Below: The judges in character for a photo shoot. Len as Del Boy... as for the others, who knows?

Above: Mirror, mirror on the wall, who's the most fabulous of them all? That will be me, then.

Right: The original Odd Couple. With my good mate, Len.

Below: A special moment with Sir Bruce. I love the man. We do have some giggles.

Above: Ascot-bound with the lovely Jackie St Clair.

Above right: The supergroup revving up.

Bottom left: Proving on *Jimmy Kimmel Live!* that I don't do fake tan.

Bottom right: Now that's what I call table dancing. Chris Hollins storms *Strictly*...

Above: Red and green should never be seen. We'll let that go because it's Christmas.

Right: Bewitched, bothered and bewildered.

Left: You're so vain. How to blow a record deal. Simon was *not* amused.

Below: Perfect 10s, apart from Craig. Typical.

Above: Darcey Bussell joins the party. But it does nothing to cheer Craig up.

Right: Backstage at *Dancing With The Stars*. Who says Hollywood changes a person?

Below: The gruesome foursome. Yet another spray tan for Craig.

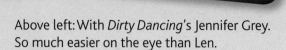

Above left: With *Dirty Dancing*'s Jennifer Grey. So much easier on the eye than Len.

Above right: The afterglow. Miranda Hart joined me on the dance floor before the recording of *Strictly*. Our impromptu duet turned into a picture-perfect impression of chapter one of the *Kama Sutra*. The girl's a pussycat doll.

Left and below: The perfect score. It happens so rarely, but when it does, it's *special*.

worries and insecurities that dog every working person. I certainly didn't want to go back to my grotty Stockwell flat with the cling-film windows.

I was so comfortable in my new house that I invited my parents over for another holiday in 1993. We had a great time, we ate out every night and cooked some glorious barbecues; I took them to see wonderful shows in the west end of town. It was weird though: I was living with Paul and we were quite clearly a couple, but nothing was ever said by my mum and dad about my lifestyle choice. It was as if my sexuality, my relationship with Paul, had been assimilated in their minds. I could see that the fear and the doubt had gone out of them and there was a sense of acceptance of who I was and who I was with. It made me so happy. I felt that they were proud of me, that the arguments and the hard years had been long forgotten. They were also pleased that I had security, which is something every parent wants for their children.

And then, a year after their visit, my world caved in.

I remember the day well. It was the 19th July 1994. I was sitting outside in the garden with some friends who had come over for lunch when the phone started ringing. I could hear Paul shouting from the house.

'Bruno, it's for you,' he said. 'It's a call from Italy.'

'Italy?' I thought. 'Who would be calling me from Italy today?'

I spoke to my mother on the phone every week, but we would always chat on a Sunday. It was all very confusing. I went inside and took the call and that's when everything blew apart because as I held the receiver, the news from the other end was so shocking and so devastating that it changed my life forever.

'Bruno,' said the voice. (It was the husband of my mother's

sister. I hadn't spoken to him for twenty years.) 'I just wanted to tell you that your mother's dead.'

Silence.

That was it, there was no softening the blow. The information was blunt, definite, final. There was to be no negotiation or explanation of what had happened. No more was to be said. It was a statement of fact and I knew that nothing could be done to change it. My mum had gone.

As I stood there, the ground seemed to fall away from underneath me. My senses were overloaded, I felt as if I had been struck by an electric shock of huge proportions, but not in a physically painful way. Instead it was as if all of my being was being shaken violently by an invisible pair of hands. I can't imagine what it must be like for a parent when they discover their son has been killed in Afghanistan or somewhere equally horrible.

The news was so unexpected that I instantly collapsed onto the floor in hysterics. I knew that my mother had been suffering some problems with her blood pressure, but I was under the impression that everything had been been sorted out. Though I also knew that if there had been a problem with her health, she never would have told me. Some families are like that, they like to keep the bad news from their nearest and dearest to stop them from worrying. And that was my mother's way. Contrary to the common perception of all Italians as being over-emotional and wildly passionate in times of crisis, Mum and Dad were people who dealt with problems quietly and privately. As I've said before, if there was something wrong, they just got on with it.

I wasn't as strong. Paul and my friends rushed to see what was wrong, but I could barely get the words out to explain. I didn't want to hear myself say them because I didn't want them to become a reality. I knew one thing for certain: time was standing still and I wasn't in control of my body. I was a wreck.

'I have to book a flight to Italy,' I said, tears streaming down my face. 'My mother has gone. I have to get on a plane to Ferrara.'

I booked the earliest ticket I could, for a flight which was leaving the next day, and for twenty-four hours I didn't know what the hell was going on. One minute I was in shock, unable to talk or do anything. At other times I would be crying and wailing into my pillow. The incredible lows were mixed up with flashes of clarity where all my emotions seemed to come into focus. I would feel a hit of adrenalin and suddenly I could function perfectly again. It was in those brief moments that I would do something rational. I packed my bags for the trip and made phone calls to Ferrara even though I could instinctively tell that my senses were being fried by grief. At one point it really felt as if I was looking down at myself from the outside and from there I could see that I was going through a storm of emotions – anger, guilt, depression and helplessness. There was nothing I could do to stop them. My feelings changed every five minutes and it was like being stuck on a tiny boat that was lost in the middle of a huge, scary ocean.

When I arrived in Ferrara, everybody was in a state. My father was catatonic. He was absolutely devastated, the man was a zombie; my grandmother was also in shock. As soon as I arrived home that day there were tears as she explained what had happened to my wonderful mother.

'It was a very, very hot day,' she said. 'A heatwave. And at eleven in the morning your mother cycled into town to get some groceries for lunch. It must have been 35 degrees. She came back and cooked the meal, but she said to everyone, "I'm going to bed because I think I have indigestion". Bruno, she never woke up. She passed away in her sleep from a heart attack. Your father went to the bedroom to wake her, but she was gone. He called an ambulance but there was nothing they could do.'

That night I went to bed wracked with guilt. Being raised as a Roman Catholic meant that I was burdened with a lot of unnecessary moral pressure throughout my life (even though I was not religious at all myself). Naturally, that night I battered myself about the head with a series of self-harming questions.

Did I do enough?

Was I a good son?

Should I have seen them more?

Should I have noticed the signs that she was ill?

Was there anything that I could have done to help?

The following morning I knew I would have to help to arrange the funeral with the rest of the family. I also had to deal with all my mother's belongings, her clothes and the other things that were lying around the house. I knew it would be shattering because my father didn't know what to do with himself. To help out, I promised to stay there for a couple of weeks, just so everything could be dealt with, but because I had been away from Ferrara for so long what I hadn't realised was that my dad had never made himself a meal in his entire life. He didn't even know how to cook a potato. As I've said before, such was the division of labour in our traditional Italian household that my father did nothing in the way of domestic work, his job was to earn the money. Meanwhile, my mother had controlled everything. She did the washing, the cooking, the cleaning, the banking, the lot. Now she was gone, Dad was stranded.

'Oh my god,' I thought. 'What is going to happen here?'

I was terrified that my father would be helpless. I cried every five minutes through the heartbreak and the stress. In the end, the family organised for somebody to visit his house once I had returned home to London so they could cook and clean for him every week. My grandmother was also around to help him. It wasn't the same as having my mother there, but at least it helped.

☆

It wasn't until I got back to London a couple of weeks later, once the funeral had taken place, that the enormity of my mother's death hit me like a ten-tonne truck. The house was quiet. Paul was out at work. I got into the house and lost my mind. I cried non stop all day because there was the shattering realisation that the bond between my mother and me really had been the purest form of unconditional love. From the minute I was born, I had never really been separated from my mother, even though she was in Italy and I was in London. It's the same with fathers and their children I know, but there's something a little bit different with the mother – I knew my mum would always be there for me, whatever happened. Now that she had gone, I felt desperately alone, even though I still had my father, Paul and my friends.

It was a month before I could get back to work. I spent my days wandering around the flowerbeds and staring at the ceiling in the house. As I got stronger, I threw myself into my gardening obsession more than ever. Creating and planting flowers and bringing new life into the garden became very therapeutic to me. It was meditative and a healthy way of keeping me sane. It allowed me to empty my mind and accept the pain and the loss that was threatening to consume me. Then one day, as I was losing myself in the flower beds, Michael called.

'Darling, there's a job for you,' he said. 'It's a Sting video, it's going to be *major* and it's being shot in Almeria in Spain. Bruno, I really think that you have to do this. It will be good for you. It will take your mind off things.'

I knew he was right; I knew I had to start living my life again because it's what my mother would have wanted me to do. I also knew that I couldn't wallow in my misery anymore, so I accepted the job, but when I got to the location I felt totally bewildered. And when I walked up to Sting to introduce myself, well, that's when I really lost it. I was all over the place in the head.

'Hello Bruno, I'm Sting,' I said, offering a handshake.

I think he must have assumed that I was completely demented, because he didn't speak to me for the rest of the day, but I wasn't too bothered. I was out of my mind with grief.

The single I was working on was called 'This Cowboy Song', and to be honest, I hadn't bothered to listen to it before I'd arrived on set. When I heard it for the first time, I didn't think it was that good. I still don't. Sorry, Sting. Thankfully, I didn't have much to do on the day. My job was to get some silly girls to jump up and down for a bit, which wasn't very challenging at all, but blow me, I was relieved when it was all over.

The good news, if I could call it that, was that I could operate again, albeit not quiet at 100 per cent. It was a start, but I soon found that my grief was bewildering. Some days I could go for an hour without thinking about it, there were other times when it didn't leave my head for a second; it was always the first thing I thought about when I woke up in the morning and the last thing I thought about at night. To be honest, I was like that for years, but as time went by, I started to get over it, although whenever I made some kind of recovery, it would hit me again, like a blow to the stomach and usually when I least expected it. The smallest incident could trigger it off – a song on the radio, a line from a film, anything that reminded me of her voice, her face, her soul. I would always lose it to the tears shortly afterwards. I'd like to say that I'm over it now, but I don't think anyone gets over the loss of a parent. That day in July when my mother died, a big part of me died, too.

CHAPTER 12

LITTLE
CAESAR

I would love to say that my mother's death was a one-off shot of misery, but it flippin' well wasn't. In fact it was only the beginning, and my relationship with bereavement began to resemble an old famous saying about London buses. I had been free of pain and loss for nearly all of my life, but not long after mother's passing, two more hammer blows came along at once when my grandparents died shortly afterwards.

Like my mother's death, I can clearly remember the date that my grandmother left me. It was 31 January 1996, and the day is etched into my brain because I loved her as much as I had loved my mother – I really felt her death just as keenly. She had raised me as a child while my parents had gone to work like the classic, warm, loving Italian grandma that she was. Her heart was as big as a country and she hadn't a bad bone in her body, even though she suffered a fair amount of stress and tension during her life, what with the feud that had torn her two sons apart. Decades had passed since my father and uncle Silvano had first fallen out over their house and my grandmother had been caught in the crossfire for over thirty-five years.

Typically, nobody had told me that there was even a chance that another tragedy might be coming. As with my mother's blood pressure, I hadn't been informed of any illness or health problems. My grandma had apparently gone into hospital for an operation (god knows what for, they didn't tell me that, either) and she never woke up. She was eighty-six years old and the news hit me hard.

'Oh my god,' I thought. 'When is this ever going to end?'

Despite the passing years, I was still rocked by the loss of my mother, and my grandmother's death reopened all those old wounds. It was destabilising for my father, too. He had been relying upon his own mother's good soul for companionship and support ever since Mum's heart attack, and now he was all alone in the world. Thinking about it today, the news was probably a turning point for him. Everything he had managed to hold together for his entire life was gone and he started to break down without it.

Not that he showed it at first. My father had never been an outwardly expressive man; he was very internalised and rarely displayed any sign of emotion if things were going wrong in his life. Because of his reluctance to be open, all the hurt and the feelings of heartbreak were bottled up inside where they were able to fester and become poisonous. I was very different. I could cry and wail and sob, and I found that expressing my pain helped to release all the negative emotions that came attached to the death of a loved one, like guilt and anger. My dad couldn't do that. Despite his calm exterior, I knew he was devastated, but I also knew that by internalising his emotions, he was making himself very ill.

From a distance – to a passing acquaintance, say – he probably seemed fine, but when I met with him for the funeral I could feel him unravelling before my eyes. But then, I felt like I was unravelling as well. Going to Italy was becoming a soul-destroying journey. The last time I had been to Ferrara was in 1994 when I'd buried my mother. Now I was going back to say farewell to another family member. I felt as if the place was cursed, I was bewildered, but the sensation was to increase further because when I got back to London to piece my life together once more, it wasn't long before I was making yet another miserable journey back to northern Italy, this time to attend the funeral of my grandfather, who died two months later. It was all too much.

Mercifully, after the heartbreak came some much needed comic relief, and I mean that almost literally. In 1996, I was called by the BBC because the comedian Steve Coogan had created a new character called Tony Ferrino and he needed some choreography for a one-off TV programme entitled *The Tony Ferrino Phenomenon*. For those of you who don't remember the show, Tony Ferrino was the parody of a Portuguese crooner, a Lothario who infamously won the Eurovision Song Contest with a fictional song called 'Papa Bendi'. The character was sleazy. He had shoulder-length hair and a droopy moustache and he wore sparkly suits; he had an eye for the ladies like you wouldn't believe.

Steve was great to work with, but like most comedians I remember being struck by just how serious he was when it came to perfecting his craft. He was very clear about what he wanted to do. There was no messing about, or laughing and faffing; there was no joking. It was all very professional. Before filming started, Steve

211

told me that the show was a spoof – part of it would be filmed as if it were a documentary, the other part as if it were a live show, which nobody else had really done before. Remember, this was an era before Ricky Gervais's award-winning show *The Office*, which was done in a similar style.

Given that this was such a high-profile project, I was determined to make my mark on both the production team and the cast when all of us hooked up for a meeting before the filming started. Everybody had gathered in the BBC canteen (very glamorous, darling) for coffees and pastries, and all the important heads were there: the producer Geoff Posner, Steve, the cast – which included Julia Davis of *Nighty Night* – and all the dancers I'd be working with. I had spent ages planning my choreography and all the moves were worked out. I was so incredibly well prepared that I'd even brought my notes and papers to the meeting, just to look extra professional.

Well, of course it all went horribly wrong. As I grabbed myself a coffee, a nice big steaming mug of frothy, decadently chocolatey cappuccino, I steeled myself. I was determined to make my mark on the meeting. Steve was somebody I had admired from his early shows, such as *Knowing Me, Knowing You With Alan Partridge*, which I still love today. I really wanted to impress him with my work on his latest project. Geoff Posner was also a comedy genius. As you may remember from a few chapters back, he had previously worked on *Not The Nine O'Clock News*, as well as *The Young Ones* and *Victoria Wood*.

Anyway, it wasn't long before I'd made a big impression, because as I turned to face the gathered crowd, my notes in one hand, a cappuccino in the other, I put so much impetus into what was supposed to be a dramatic twirl that everything went flying. My papers seemed to shoot up in the air as if gathered together by a mini tornado. The froth from my coffee flew off, landing with expert accuracy into the lap of Julia Davis, who looked at me as if I was the biggest pillock to walk the earth. Thankfully, this being BBC coffee, its temperature wasn't remotely hot and so I only faced the indignity of a dry-cleaning bill rather than an apologetic visit to the nearest burns unit. It was embarrassing all the same.

Thankfully, it didn't put Steve off my inclusion on the show and we had a ball as filming got underway. Working with him was a real eye opener because everything was planned meticulously. The dancing, the clothes, the wigs he wore, his outfits and the comic glances and nuances were all choreographed in advance. When I saw him in action, I realised that *Alan Partridge* had been planned in perfect detail and that there was a great method to the madness, and it was all done with incredible skill and care. In the planning stages everything was rigorously rehearsed and analysed, but when Tony Ferrino's wig and outfit came together, that was when the character sprang to life. After that, I didn't see the technique anymore. I saw the character, living and breathing, and pinching girls' bottoms.

Once we'd completed *The Tony Ferrino Phenomenon*, Steve asked me to help him out with a very grand live tour he was planning called *The Man Who Thinks He's It*. The show was incredibly ambitious because it was due to feature all of his characters, Tony Ferrino, Alan Partridge, the chav siblings Paul and Pauline Calf (both played by Steve), and a stupid but hilarious individual called Duncan Thicket. Most of the characters had been perfected on telly over the years, but the one role that seemed to be giving Steve a lot of difficulty for the live show was Pauline Calf.

If you don't know her, Pauline was the woman from hell. A chain-smoking, man-eating, binge-drinking fishwife scrubber. Steve always played her in drag and I remember when I first saw the character it took me back to my days in Ferrara when Lucy the town trannie used to parade around the Piazza Trento Trieste. Steve had always managed to get his routines with Pauline 100 per cent right when they had filmed her for TV, but in a live environment, he was having trouble perfecting her walk as she prowled the stage like a street hooker drunk on cheap gin. I could see that Steve didn't look like a randy woman in rehearsals. He was walking like a trucker. As I watched him, I thought, 'Oh dear, I've got to tell him.'

'Steve, darling,' I said. 'You look amazing, but you walk like a builder. The joke only works if you walk like a woman and at the moment you're strutting around the stage as if you have a big willy swinging between your legs.'

I steeled myself for what I was about to say next because it was going to be *filthy*.

'Steve, you have to walk as if you have a foof. You have to imagine that down there is a foof that wants to have fun. It wants to have fun all the time. All day and every day, and definitely all night long.'

I had gone all the way, and after my gynaecological explanation, Steve walked across the stage like a cheap tart that wanted to roll in the hay. And he looked simply fabulous.

☆

Typically, there was another night to be had at The Royal Variety Performance, this time with Tony Ferrino in 1996. As I sat backstage with Steve I bumped into Simon Cowell, the pop impresario who went on to have huge successes with a number of acts such as Il Divo and Leona Lewis. He later became a judge on *Pop Idol*, before creating *The X Factor* and *Britain's Got Talent*. Simon even founded the television company Syco TV which actually made *The X Factor* – talk about savvy. He was a boy with some serious talents.

At the time, though, Simon was very much a work in progress. He had been working with the record label BMG as an A&R guy, but I had become friends with him some years earlier when he was in partnership with the record label, Fanfare, which was owned by Iain Burton who, along with my agent Michael, also looked after Arlene Phillips. Our paths had crossed many times. I had even choreographed a video for one of his acts, Sinitta, and he soon fell into our circle of friends where I would see him socially.

What were my first impressions of him, I hear you cry? Well, my darling, I didn't fancy him, if that's what you're thinking. I was with Paul and I never had a wandering eye (I most definitely was not like Tony Ferrino), but I liked Simon as a person. He was very quiet and polite and back then he was still finding his way in the world.

I remember the moment he hit the jackpot very clearly. I was at Mike Stock's studio (he of Stock Aitken Waterman) and Simon was there for a meeting or some other business. He began telling me about a new act he had signed for BMG.

'Oh, I'm doing a single with Robson and Jerome,' he said.

I thought he'd gone mad in the brain. Robson and Jerome were the two actors, Robson Green and Jerome Flynn. They had appeared on the TV show *Soldier, Soldier* which was all the rage with the nations' housewives. Well, the ones who had a bit of a thing for men in uniforms anyway.

'Robson and Jerome?' I said. 'What the flippin' heck is that all about?'

Simon clearly had more business acumen in the music market than me, because despite my withering assessment of his finely tuned ears, the duo released a cover of The Righteous Brothers' 'Unchained Melody' which then stayed in the charts for seven weeks in 1995. It sold nearly two million copies and was the best-selling single of the year. Shows you how much I know.

But then, Simon was unique. He had become brilliant at spotting things that the public wanted, things that other record labels wouldn't have signed up ordinarily, and he made a lot of money, very quickly. Sure, there were some flops, but when he cleaned up – as he did with those two army boys – he cleaned up big time. Which was one of the reasons why Simon signed Tony Ferrino for a one-off album. He could see it as a potential success.

That day at the Variety Performance, as everyone rehearsed, Simon was there with Robson and Jerome; I was there with Steve. And seeing as he was the record label guy, we demanded that he take us all for late lunch, before the show started. When Simon agreed, we went to a Chinese restaurant around the corner and ordered everything on the menu. Thinking about it, I don't think we ate very much, but myself, Steve, Robson and Jerome got such a kick from being complete bitches to him that it was worth it. Not that he minded, he was a generous host. Back then Simon wasn't the character he is on the telly today because that ruthless side of him is only a small part of the person he is. He's someone altogether different.

I'll explain in more detail. When I first saw *Pop Idol*, I realised Simon had made a very clever move. He'd changed his character. I thought, 'Well, that's flippin' brilliant!' because what he had done was actually an example of drama at its very best. Like an actor, when he builds a role for himself in rehearsals, Simon had taken a part of his personality – in this case the business, marketing side – exaggerated it by a million and then created an alter ego. He had turned up the ruthlessness (a facet required in his job) and made it his TV persona. The thing was, he did it so well that everybody believed it was his real character. Well, everybody apart from the people who knew him personally, like myself and Michael.

It was for that reason that I understood his success when it happened. The power of his *Pop Idol* persona came from sheer determination and self-belief; Simon had created something out of nothing. He had a knack of giving the people what they wanted and that persona – the man the public loved to hate – came out of the blue, fully formed. Sure, a lot of people might have slagged him off for it, but the fact remained that he'd made a good business decision. *Pop Idol* was a success.

Despite Simon's triumphs, he was always the same person to me. Whenever I see him today we always go back to how we were when we worked together in the 80s and 90s. His public and private persona have never crossed over when we've been together and when he lets his hair down in private, he's very funny, he's always honest. He's really quite generous. Despite my behaviour that afternoon before the Royal Variety Performance, Simon has since taken me out for a Chinese meal. So on top of everything else, one could consider him rather brave, too. Well, how else could he have signed Robson and Jerome?

☆

By 1997 I could tell that my dad was really falling to pieces, so I did what any good son would do: I made sure that he was comfortable; I ensured that somebody was able to look after him when I went home. But shortly after my return to London, I received a phone call from a family friend telling me that a number of people in the town had become increasingly concerned about his behaviour. He wasn't acting right. Apparently he had been found wandering through the streets in the middle of the night. It wasn't long before he was diagnosed with Alzheimer's and, oh my god, I didn't know what the flip to do. I couldn't move to Ferrara because my life was in London; Dad definitely couldn't move in with me because he wouldn't have stood for the drama and the hectic way of life, and there was no way that he was going to move into a care home. That was a no-no. What tends to happen when people develop Alzheimer's is that they can become very stubborn, probably because they're fighting to keep hold of their identity and independence. They want to retain their lives. It's understandable, especially as most of the time they can't see that something bad is happening to them, but it was tragic to watch as my dad battled and argued to stay in his house when it was clearly the worst place for him.

It was then, as I went to visit him once more, that something miraculous happened. My father suggested that he should move in with Uncle Silvano, probably because he was so muddled. Through his confusion and illness, he seemed to have forgotten the dispute that had divided them for thirty-five years. What was even stranger was that Uncle Silvano seemed happy to live as if nothing had happened, too. He probably needed all the family contact he could get because he had lost his parents like my father. The tragedies that had befallen the family meant that all those years of resentment and bitterness had been erased.

It was the perfect set-up. Uncle Silvano now had a house just outside Ferrara in the countryside. It was beautiful and peaceful and my dad could wander around in the fields as much as he liked. With my help he sold up the home I'd been raised in and we gave the money from the sale to Silvano, so he could care for my dad properly. Packing up his things and rediscovering so many bits and pieces that my mother had once used – pots, pans, towels, note-books, old schoolbooks of mine – was heartbreaking. But the silver lining to the cloud was that through the tragedy of death, the Tonioli brothers were friends again.

☆

Michael called me not long after with news of another job.

'Bruno, darling,' he said. 'It's a film this time, called *Bring Me the Head of Mavis Davis*. I hear it's a black comedy and it stars Rik Mayall and the wonderful Jane Horrocks. It's going to be *major*.'

The script arrived in the post and when I read it I was spellbound. In the movie, Jane played a pop star called Mavis Davis and by all accounts everybody wanted to kill her. Talk about doing exactly what it said on the tin. Typically for a film of that nature, there were one or two musical numbers to prepare for. Ordinarily there wouldn't have been a problem, but I soon learned that Jane was struggling to come to terms with her footwork.

'Broo-ner,' she said, speaking in her delicious Lancashire burr when I first met her for rehearsals. 'I just kerrrn't do it derrrrling. I just kerrrn't dance.'

I used the skills I had picked up from *Dancin' Thru the Dark* to help her make those first, important steps.

'I'm sure you can, Jane,' I said in my most soothing voice. 'You have to remember it's not you that's dancing here, it's Mavis. And you certainly don't have to dance like a performer from *Swan Lake*, my dear. I'm not going to give you a barrage of instructions and expect you to leap around in time to the music. Just get into the mind of Mavis first . . .'

Well, it worked. In the studio we clicked instantly and she soon found her feet. Jane was totally unassuming and 100 per cent approachable. There were no airs and graces and ours was an intangible connection that sometimes happens between a dancer and their choreographer. Once we'd operated from Mavis's point of view rather than Jane's she was brilliant. I realised that she could be anything I wanted her to be, provided the intentions behind the role were in her head, and the results looked heavenly on screen.

Our work on Mavis Davis was so good that when Jane scored a lead role in the 1998 movie *Little Voice*, she specifically asked me to do her choreography. Well, you would, wouldn't you, darling? And what an experience that was. The cast was star-studded and featured the likes of Ewan McGregor, Michael Caine, Jim Broadbent and Brenda Blethyn. The plot, meanwhile, revolved around the life of Laura Hoff – or Little Voice – a young woman who suffered from anxiety attacks and agoraphobia. Without giving the game away for those of you who haven't seen it, in the script she spent all her time listening to her late dad's old records in the family home; she lived through his music to escape from her horrific mother. She was later forced by her mum's boyfriend to perform in a local club, where she wowed her audience with a dramatic and emotional performance.

As you can imagine for a script of that intensity, the film was full on, powerful, moving. All the things that *Hollyoaks* is not, and we started work on the production in 1997. As she had been in *Bring Me the Head of Mavis Davis*, Jane was amazing and mind-blowing. Her singing performances had to mimic some of the great performers, such as Dame Shirley Bassey and Judy Garland, but we managed to work her scenes so it looked as if her mannerisms and character changes were happening naturally. She really did manage to pull it off spectacularly well.

While I was on set, I had the amazing opportunity to watch Jim Broadbent (one of the best British actors ever in my mind), Brenda Blethyn (who was in full battle-axe mode) and Michael Caine, who performed one of the most powerful scenes I have ever witnessed on a film set. At one point in the movie, his character had to break down and sing a howling, emotional song, completely out of tune. When the cameras trained in on his face, what I saw as I watched him was a man emotionally cracking. It was so believable that it was actually frightening. But what really amazed me was his star quality. He was able to turn it on like a hair dryer.

I used to see him in the pub in Scarborough where the cast and crew would gather after filming, drinking and having fun. He was very quiet and very reserved, but at the same time ever so friendly and charming. But when the cameras went on, a light seemed to flash in his brain and that's when he flicked on the thespian magic. Suddenly he became a dynamo of the stage, an acting explosion, and watching him was like watching something hypnotic. That's when I appreciated the power of the huge movie star for the first time. It wasn't something I had ever seen up until then.

Watching those people – Michael, Jane, Brenda and Jim – even Ewan McGregor who had a small role in the film as Little Voice's boyfriend – was a gift. They were on the top of their game. And like Franco Zeffirelli, Steve Coogan, Freddie Mercury and the dancers I had seen in Paris, New York and London, they inspired me yet again. I wanted to be as good as them. And that, in a nutshell, was the wonder of film.

CHAPTER 13

LIFE WITH FATHER

Darling, I can't kiss bottom. Whenever I've tried, I've failed. Nearly all my jobs have come from a recommendation or the word of a mouth. If I have to turn up out of the blue and charm a director or producer I've never met before, it usually ends in tears. Like in 2003: there was one film I was keen to work on. It was called *Finding Neverland*, a story about J.M. Barrie, the playwright who wrote the children's tale, *Peter Pan*. It starred Johnny Depp and Kate Winslet and it was certain to be a smash. Well, when I went to see the director, Marc Foster, he told me that there were several scenes that required expert choreographing. After that he called me in for another meeting, and then another, and then another. Flippin' heck, I was in more meetings than Gordon Brown and David Cameron put together.

Anyway, not long afterwards, I got a call asking me to meet with some producer or another, but when I went along I must have said something wrong (I think I may have asked for something that was way too expensive for his tastes) because I never heard from Marc again. I was furious at the time, but I suppose I should have been more careful. The thing is, *amore mio*, as you may have guessed from my appearances on *Strictly Come Dancing* – when I jump over desks and shout and faint and fall over myself with excitement – I don't have a self-censorship button. Oh my goodness, that filter got broken for good a long time ago, probably when I first heard my Uncle Silvano swearing and bitching like a docker in the Tonioli home. Privately I've always been the same. I am grotesque, I really am. My language is terrible; I swear, I rant and I rave, not that I would ever do it around you, because I like to keep my filth away from the public eye, but I am not embarrassed about who I am. I never have been and I never will be.

But at least I'm painting an honest picture of myself here, which is more than can be said of some people. Not long after I was shunned by the production team of *Finding Neverland*, I received a call from Michael.

'The *Finding Neverland* job went somewhere else,' he said.

Well, I was furious and after a couple of minutes of ranting and raving, I said, 'Fine, I'm going to do a spot of gardening to clear my head.'

Now, what I'm going to tell you next will give you a clear indication of what Michael was like, because out of that one simple line, he constructed a whole story about me, an absolute fantasy, which he proceeded to tell at dinner parties. It went something like this . . .

'Darling, after the phone call, Bruno went into a rage, screaming and shouting and spitting poison. Then he went into the garden and with his bare hands he ripped off all the ivy from his wall which was fifteen feet high and fifty feet across. He was covered in blood and filth.

'When he heard Paul walk through the front door he yelled, "Paul, bring me the axe!" At which point he chopped down an apple tree in the corner of the garden. To top it off, still bleeding, covered in filth and axe-wielding, he then went for poor Oliver, giving him a scalding hot bath and grooming him to within an inch of his life.'

The cheek! It was a complete lie, but it was passed around at dinner parties and cocktail events for years. Forget *Finding Neverland*, Michael had created a fantasy masterpiece all of his own.

☆

My father just wasn't the same after moving in with my Uncle Silvano. I went to visit him on several occasions, but with every visit a little piece of him seemed to have died. He was fading away, like an old photograph, and his memories and personality were retreating into his body. It was awful, he was a shell of the man I had once seen gliding across the kitchen floor with my mother as they danced the Waltz to his favourite records. It tore me apart every time I met with him.

The worst time took place during my last visit to Ferrara during 2001. He didn't recognise me. He looked at me as if I were a stranger, or somebody he vaguely remembered, like a passing acquaintance or an old work friend from years gone by. It was as if

I wasn't his son anymore, and he couldn't place my face or my voice. Oh god, when it happened it felt as if somebody had stabbed me in the heart. I hated the fact that my father had been wiped out: his mind, his passions, his pride had all been erased, all his history and his thoughts had been taken from him. You cannot imagine.

I started to feel guilty again.

'Oh Bruno,' I cried during several terrible, long, dark nights of the soul. 'Maybe you should have done this, maybe you should have done that?'

It's a natural thing, I suppose. I think a lot of people who suffer this same experience often bring doubt and stress upon themselves. They beat themselves about the head for not being there for somebody they loved. It was an incredibly stressful time for me and when my father eventually died in 2001, I have to confess that it was almost a relief. The man was free again. His spirit wasn't shackled to a brain that couldn't bring back the beautiful memories of his childhood, or his friends and family.

By a strange coincidence, he died almost to the date of my mother's passing. Seven years had gone by, but in my head, it was a loss as horrific and traumatic as all the others and I went to some gruesome places in my soul. As I said earlier, I began to doubt my worthiness as a son and whether I had been there enough for him. But with hindsight, I realised that I had to live my life and make decisions and the choices for myself – it's what my parents would have wanted after all. The experiences in those depressing years also taught me that life wasn't always gloss and perfection, glamour and beauty. It was a lesson for sure, but it didn't help me at the time. I would often have crying fits as I thought about what

I should have said and done, or not said and not done to him during my life. It was even harder given the fact that everything seemed to have happened during such a short period of time. My mother, my father, my grandmother, my grandfather: they had all disappeared in an instant.

I think the sense of loss was made even more acute by the realisation that I was alone, an orphan almost. There were no siblings to lean on, all my remaining family members were uncles, aunts, cousins and they all lived in Italy. I was lucky in a way, because I'd always been a loner in life, I've always liked my own space. I certainly wan't somebody who craved constant attention or companionship. That didn't make my grief any easier to absorb, however. What I quickly realised was that by losing my parents and my grandparents, I'd lost a link to another life, one that had been going on without me in Ferrara, but one that was happening nevertheless – a life where people I loved were existing in happiness. With the tie now severed, I found that I was losing myself to grief. I was drifting in that huge, scary ocean again.

I stopped going out, I tried to digest everything that was happening to me. I knew that I had to work and, weirdly, I never thought of my job and my passions as being trivial in the light of my loss. It was quite the opposite, in fact. I loved what I did and I learned that work was very important to me because it stopped me from wallowing. It gave me a sense of purpose. I knew that if I ever lost that drive then I would really fall into a downward spiral and that would have been dangerous.

To keep myself vaguely sane, I decided that I had to work and work hard. That part of my life I had sorted. In a TV studio or on set somewhere, I was fine. I was in my element. My problems began when I went home at night and closed myself away, just like I had done as a child when I entered the fantasy land of the toads and the butterflies. This time, my mental retreat was into the kingdoms of yoga and gardening, and I loved nothing more than to lose myself completely.

I threw myself into yoga like a man possessed. It gave me peace of mind; it centred me. There was an institute of meditation down the road from my house and I would go there whenever I could. Sitting there gave me peace and solitude. It stopped the chatter in my head. As I had with dance lessons in Paris and New York, I soon became possessed by yoga because I loved it. The discipline seemed to tap into my spiritual side and for a few brief moments a day, I was free from pain.

'Spiritual side?' you're probably saying as you pour another glass of crisp, chilled white wine. 'What the flippin' heck is he on about? He jumps about on the telly like a lunatic. As if he's got a spiritual side.'

Well, let me tell you, I bloody well have, and I think it's probably the right time to reveal to the world that I'm actually a little bit like Simon Cowell in a funny way. Now before you get any strange ideas, that doesn't mean I wear my trousers above my belly button in a ghastly manner whenever I wander around Chez Bruno. Dear god, no. But rather, like Simon, I have two personalities, a public image and a private persona – one for the TV and another for me. Well, I have to; if I was as excitable at home as I am in front of the cameras I'd have driven myself mental by now. The truth is, I'm almost the opposite of the person that people see on the telly and I'm proud to say that one part of my private personality carries a certain sense of spirituality.

I don't really follow any single faith. If I had to choose one though, I'd say that Buddhism is the closest religion to my own individual style. I like its simplicity and purity; I find I can apply its ideas and values to modern-day living quite easily. It is non-judgemental and it makes me feel as if there is something very natural at its roots. I also find it very refreshing. (Don't worry: I'm hardly wandering around the house in my ballet shoes and tuxedo tapping little cymbals and chanting like the Dalai Lama.)

Looking back, I guess I've always wanted to be in tune with life. By doing yoga and taking in everything around me – living in the moment – I've managed to find a nice mental balance, but I am far from enlightened, and I'm definitely nowhere near a guru. I'm hardly a saint, either. Screw me, I'm the opposite! Still, there have been moments in life when I've felt totally aligned to something higher, *something else*, and when it's happened, it's happened in the craziest places, like when I've been alone in the garden and planting a flower or cutting back a bush. The overwhelming sensation during those rare minutes is that I've been existing in a moment of perfection.

The very first time I experienced it was when I went to Africa. I saw the fog lifting over Mount Kilimanjaro, a huge herd of zebras ran past, and it reduced me to tears. It happened when I saw a blood red sunset over the Indian Ocean. Sometimes it's even happened to me when I've been working. I've witnessed a dance move so perfect, so graceful, that I've felt as if I've connected with something bigger and more powerful than anything I've ever encountered before in my life. And yes, that includes Sir Bruce Forsyth.

After the death of my father though, I found my biggest problem was that I was shutting myself off from the outside world.

I was seeking solace alone, all the while reserving my energy for work – the films and the adverts and the pop promos. Thankfully I had a group of very good people around me, like Michael and Paul, who cared for me dearly. Michael was always much more than an agent. He was a friend and was forever calling me up in an attempt to make me laugh. He would constantly ring me with funny stories and bits of idle gossip because he knew that if he allowed me to wallow in my misery, it would only damage my fragile state of mind further. We went to the cinema together; he was always inviting me and Paul to parties.

Paul, meanwhile, was the most honest person I knew; he was really instrumental in helping me to come to terms with everything – he gave me another life outside of the world of show business and I trusted him above everybody else. He was a rock. He gave me safety. He was family.

With time, the grief and the pain began to subside. With the help of Michael and Paul I soon began entering the real world where I could rebuild a life that had been completely shattered by heartbreak and loss.

☆

Amid all the tragedy of my father's death, I managed to get myself another film. Well, one has to keep going, and the production in question was *Enigma*, which starred Dougray Scott and Kate Winslet (again – bloody hell, she must have taken up half the shelf space in Blockbuster Video during the early noughties). The script was based upon the very clever man who had cracked the Enigma code – a type of communication used by the Germans in World War II – but what was great about the movie was its dance scenes. It featured a couple of filming sessions in a 1940s style dance hall, where American GIs were supposed to move around with a number of swooning British girls as their hubbies fought abroad. *The harlots!*

Well, I loved it because it meant I could work with the Jive, a dance I had adored for as long as I could remember. It also meant that I could research the history of that particular dance thoroughly. Working on a period drama or a film that was based on historical fact always required a lot of homework. I knew that if I ever got a detail wrong, or used a step from another era, then I would soon be bombarded with complaints from various eagle-eyed so and sos with nothing better to do. Anyway, during one scene, the gorgeous actress Saffron Burrows had to dance with an extra. It was his job to 'Jive' her into the right position so she could deliver her lines in front of the cameras, which had been expertly positioned to capture the shot. A word to the wise: film is lit very precisely. A cameraman has to find the perfect angle on which to train his lens. The actors have to get to an exact spot to deliver their lines, but this poor extra just could not get his positioning right.

Anyway, after much toing and froing and faffing, the director broke the pair of them up.

'Bruno, this is no good!' he shouted. 'Get into uniform. You'll have to do it.'

Well, I was thrilled. I went into make-up and had my hair slicked back like an American GI; I fitted into the costume perfectly. And when I got in front of the director once more, I discovered yet more joy. I had to deliver a line in a Brooklyn drawl! Oh my goodness, that was fantastic news because it meant I could banish the disappointment of the Boy With Lamp forever, even if my American accent was a bit suspect.

'Never mind about that, Bruno,' I thought. 'You have to go for it!'

And so I put my heart and soles into it, whisking Saffron around like a dervish before saying my one and only line into her ear.

'Hi Claire,' I slurred like Kojak after a few too many bourbons.

That was it. Oh dear! In my head I sounded awful, though it must have been fine because 'Hi, Claire' made it into the movie's final cut, though it's only just dawned on me that I was never paid for my speaking debut. *The cheek.*

☆

They say that when one door closes another opens. That was certainly the case with *Finding Neverland*. Shortly after being ignored for the choreographer's role – one in which I would have been a triumphant success, for sure – I got a call asking me to work on the fantasy film *Ella Enchanted* which starred Anne Hathaway, Steve Coogan, Vivica A. Fox, Minnie Driver and Eric Idle. The cast was fantastic. It was like another *Who's Who* of British and Hollywood talent.

What I loved about *Ella Enchanted* was that it had a lot of musical numbers throughout the film; the movie was a bit of a retelling of the Cinderella story. It was filmed in Ireland, in a studio just outside Dublin, and as soon as we started working I began enjoying myself. Dublin was fantastic. The people there used to drink the city dry every weekend and they always had a story to tell you. The only problem was, the more they drank, the faster they talked and I didn't have a clue what they were going on about half the time.

Anyway, the star of the show was undoubtedly Anne Hathaway. She was only a young girl at the time, not even nineteen, but she was beautiful. Imagine a cross between Judy Garland and Julia Roberts. Annie had huge eyes and gorgeous lips; star quality seemed to radiate from her whenever she walked into a room. What was more impressive, given her tender years, was the fact that she could do everything: Annie could sing, she could dance, she could act. The director placed her in rehearsals with several acting veterans like Joanna Lumley and she never looked out of place. Not for a second.

When the cameras started rolling for real, Annie's star seemed to burn even brighter. She was word perfect, character perfect, and mark perfect; the girl wasn't even out of her teens, it was unbelievable. Clearly the director, Tommy O'Haver, knew what he was doing when he cast her for the role because Annie was the ultimate pro. She had a large number of choreographed scenes which caused a minor panic as far as I was concerned because our time together was so limited during the filming schedule. There were countless moves for her to learn and I was genuinely worried that we might struggle to complete her scenes in time, though it soon became apparent that I needn't have fretted. I would only have to show Annie a dance move once and she would learn it immediately. I almost hated her.

'This is insane,' I thought. 'This *girl* is insane. How can she be that good?'

As we worked together more and more, I noticed that whenever Annie asked a question it was always a pertinent one. *Oh, so she's clever too! Typical.* Her inquisitive mind always wanted to know what we had to do to perfect a certain move, or what she should practise in order to improve a step. Once I'd told her, the answer was immediately absorbed, computed, executed and . . . Next! We were on to another thing. I often wondered if her performance was down to my ability as an incredibly brilliant choreographer or whether Annie was the best thing since a pair of Bologna shoes (I'd like to think the former, though I suspect it was the latter). I even suffered a heavy, panicked nightmare where I imagined that she was, in actual fact, a mechanised dancing robot, like one of the replicants from Ridley Scott's brilliant sci-fi movie *Blade Runner*. In my dream, Annie began spinning and pirouetting perfectly in front of an audience of dazzled production staff. Suddenly her head twisted off to reveal a jumble of sparking wires and computer circuits. What a horrific vision! At breakfast the next morning, I was sure to put that surreal thought out of my mind before another day's work began. The truth was, though, I loved working with her. It was a pleasure to be in the same studio because she was so flippin' brilliant.

If there was one major headache, it was the final scene of the movie. An executive from Miramax films (the company responsible for funding the production of *Ella Enchanted*) decided that the show should have a huge number at the end. He wanted the entire cast, all 180 of them, to dance around to Elton John's brilliant single, 'Don't Go Breaking My Heart'. It certainly was an exciting idea, but if the thought of Anne Hathaway being a robotic creation from the future wasn't enough to freak me out, then choreographing a routine featuring 180 people soon reduced me to sleepless nights. Of course, I had worked with a bigger number of performers when I planned the British Rail advert, 'Gotta Go To Work' (that number had been 280), but back then, all of the people involved had been trained dancers. The vast majority of people I'd be working with this time were actors.

What a puzzle! Suddenly I had to plan my rehearsals with all 180 cast members in-between filming sessions. Organising the schedule was harder than any Sudoku challenge you could possibly imagine and the questions rained down on me every day.

'So Joanna Lumley is in tomorrow, we can rehearse with her from eleven 'til one o'clock.'

'But Annie is only in tomorrow from twelve 'til two and we need to work with her for at least two hours.'

'What happens if I have a nervous breakdown?"

In the end I put it together as simply as I could and although there were nearly 200 people involved, the majority of the filming actually focused on Annie and the other lead actor, Hugh Dancy who played the character of Char. Hugh, bless his heart, was a good actor, but he could not dance. Well, he thought he couldn't dance, which I'd realised was the common complaint among all actors. Thankfully, I had RoboAnnie by my side and she was able to lead him through the entire scene. At one point, she even picked him up, that's how confident she was.

After filming that day, Tommy, the director, decided to have a party in his hotel room to celebrate the successful completion of a very tricky scene. It was a Saturday night, and as is the way in Ireland, the drinks were quickly produced. Everybody was having a great time when all of a sudden we couldn't find Annie. She had disappeared. The star of the movie had gone! Everyone started to panic, we checked the bathroom; she wasn't answering her phone. Nobody knew when she had left the party. She wasn't in her hotel room. It was as if she had vanished into thin air.

When we eventually found her, Annie was passed out under a pile of coats in a spare room, snoozing peacefully like a Sleeping Beauty. I breathed a sigh of relief. My nightmare wasn't going to come true: Annie, bless her, was cream crackered and had passed out with exhaustion which, according to *Blade Runner*, made her 100 per cent humanoid. Thank the stars.

☆

One of the other leading lights of *Ella Enchanted* was the actress Joanna Lumley. Oh my goodness, what a star she was. I loved her during our brief moments on the set because she was so genuine. But then, I had always adored her from afar. In the 60s she had summed up just about everything that was sexy about England, especially when she appeared in the hit TV show *The New Avengers*. I thought Joanna was incredibly cool – she had been an actress and a model during the time when British style had been transformed into a world sensation, like a sticky larvae into a resplendent, globe-conquering, colourful butterfly; she was acting in the 1970s and 80s when Britain changed from punk to new romantic. The woman had seen it all.

It's easy to imagine someone with that much experience and style as being a little awkward; someone as worldly as her could have easily disappeared up her own buttocks, but that's the last accusation one would throw at Joanna Lumley. Honestly, I don't think there's one person in the TV industry who would say anything bad about her. She was so wonderful. I would love nothing more than to sit and chat to her about the time she was a model in the 1960s as we smoked countless fags together. She had enjoyed such a rich life that I just wanted to hear her talk. My mouth would drop open at some of the stories she used to tell me.

And her manners! Oh, even a saint would have learned a thing or two from Joanna Lumley. I remember a few years later in 2004 we worked together in the ITV Miss Marple drama *The Body in the Library* and there was a terrible kerfuffle involving Joanna. We had given her an allotted time schedule so she could learn some dance steps and she'd driven into the studio on her day off to perform them with me. Anyway, just as we were about to get underway, another actor (who will remain nameless, because I don't air kiss and tell) *simply had to be seen immediately*. Something had happened to his schedule and he had to be seen there and then and blah, blah, blah. Well, I fired a nervous glance over to Joanna who simply shrugged her shoulders as if it were no problem at all. She was all class.

'Bruno, I will go away with my newspaper,' she said. 'I will smoke my cigarette and when (actor who will still remain nameless) has finished, we can go to work.'

As an actress, she was fantastic, too. I remember Jane Horrocks asked me to work with her again when she was due to appear in the comedy show *Absolutely Fabulous*. Joanna played one of the main characters Patsy, a vile chain-smoking, booze-guzzling hell raiser of a woman who made the 'Nanas look like a bunch of nuns.

She was about as far removed from Joanna's real personality as you could possibly imagine but – oh my god – when she stood there on set, lippy smeared all over her trap, a cigarette dangling from her lower lip, well, the transformation was incredible.

It's funny how one thing leads to another, though. *The Body in the Library* carried a massive cast. Among the actors involved was the brilliant and very funny David Walliams. At the time, David was just about to make a name for himself with *Little Britain*. And while he wasn't a major role in the show, he was always hanging around. During fag breaks we hit it off like a house on fire, but flippin' heck, if I thought I had a cheeky sense of humour, then I wasn't prepared for David. He was *naughty*. So naughty that I couldn't possibly repeat any of his jokes on these pages.

I've always loved that type of personality though, and David and I became good friends. During the recording of *The Body in the Library*, I didn't really work with him in a one-on-one capacity, but afterwards I soon started bumping into him at all manner of social occasions – parties, premieres and the suchlike. Whenever we got together, it was rarely long before we were trading cheeky retorts and wading around in a torrent of innuendo. He was incorrigible! I am very difficult to shock, as I've already mentioned, but David used to make my hair stand on end with his gags. I even traded muck with him at Simon Cowell's fiftieth birthday celebrations in 2009, when, somewhat typically, there were two parties to celebrate his living through a half century – one for his close friends and family and one . . . *for all the world!* I was invited to both and the two couldn't have been further removed from one another. The smaller, more personal party was a nice meal with friends – myself, the actress Amanda Holden, Pete Waterman (previously of Stock

Aitken Waterman), and former newspaper editor turned TV journalist Piers Morgan (there will be more about how I met him later). The dinner had been organised by one of Simon's close friends, Jackie St Clair – it was a wonderful barbecue in the garden on a lovely summer afternoon. And when I say 'personal party', the gathering took place in a magnificent garden in Jackie's Holland Park mansion. It was a vision. The garden was decorated with white tents and shimmering muslins. The tables were covered in just about every delicacy known to man; the 100 guests were an example of sophistication.

The highlight of the occasion arrived when a supergroup organised by Jackie and her husband Carl Michaelson and composed of myself, Pete, Amanda and Piers serenaded Simon with our version of 'You're So Vain' by Carly Simon. We wore cut-out masks of his face (though mine was positioned over my crotch, just to be different and much to the thinly-disguised discomfort of the guest of honour). Even to this day I'm bitterly disappointed I wasn't offered a Leona Lewis-sized contract on the spot.

The Party For All The World! was an altogether different affair, a glamorous, decadent, extravagant event that, in my mind, echoed Las Vegas at the height of The Rat Pack's excesses mixed with the wildest excesses of ancient Rome. People were flying in and out by helicopter; there were ice sculptures, Glamazonian cocktail waitresses, reservoirs of champagne – France was dry. There were acts from New York and Sin City. Top entertainers from pop stars to strippers wowed the crowd. The pop band Westlife even did a personal performance. Everyone was there, and I mean *everyone*. Kate Moss, Sharon Osbourne, just about every band Simon had ever managed, the Lloyd Webbers, Leona Lewis, and all the stars of telly (but only the ITV ones). If a bomb had gone off, every TV in Britain would have gone dark and it's unlikely any albums would have been released by Simon for a long time, although some people might have been thankful for that.

In the midst of all the chaos and the fire breathing and the canapes, David Walliams sidled up to me. In front of everybody, he drooled salaciously, 'Oh Bruno, I just want to feel your big willy.'

That wasn't going to unsettle me, however

'Oh, but David, are you sure you can handle it?' I said, which kickstarted a typically filthy gossip. The man was unstoppable. And I loved him for it.

CHAPTER 14

IT HAPPENED
ONE NIGHT

In May 2004, my life suddenly changed forever . . .

Ring, ring!

. . . I was given a role on one of the biggest variety shows the country had ever known!

Ring, ring!

. . . My face and raging enthusiasm was projected into the world of Saturday evening entertainment where it would be celebrated forever alongside other telly greats such as Forsyth, Daniels, Grayson . . .

Ring, ring!

. . . Will somebody answer the flippin' phone?!

Ring, ring!

Oh . . .

'Hello, darling?'

'Bruno, my dear, it's Michael.'

'Oh hello, darling. How are you?'

'Bruno, I have the most fabulous news. The BBC have called because they're making a new version of *Come Dancing*. All the top choreographers in the country are up for it. Arlene is going, they're all going for it, they're all doing it And they want you Bruno! They want you to be a judge!'

'I'm not sure, Michael. *Come Dancing*? That's ancient! I used to watch it when it was on before. It was so camp and a bit stiff for my tastes.'

'It's going to be *major*, Bruno. A big hit. I really think you should go . . .'

'Well, if you say so.'

And that was that. I was on the list, trying out for what was about to become the biggest show on Saturday night telly. Isn't it funny how life can change with a lightning bolt out of the blue?

☆

I really didn't know how *Strictly Come Dancing* was going to work out. Nobody did. Before my first ever live performance on BBC One that fateful Saturday night in May 2004, none of the judging panel – myself, Len Goodman, Arlene Phillips and Craig Revel Horwood – really understood what kind of show it was going to be. Back then there was no '*Strictly*'; the word hadn't been added to the title, and as soon as I'd hung up the phone, I rummaged around in my videos (yes, my dear, I still had a

VHS player) for an old tape of *Come Dancing*. I wanted to know exactly what I was letting myself in for.

I'd bought the old episode for research purposes from eBay when I was studying a number of ballroom dances for a period drama I'd been working on at the time. I was always drawing on different styles whenever I planned those programmes and as I sat there, watching the Waltz and the Jive, I was struck by just how old-fashioned it all was back then. The show was basically a ballroom dancing competition. It was hysterical, as camp as Christmas. It seemed to be from another era, well, probably because it was.

'How the flippin' heck are they going to bring this back to life?' I thought. 'And how the hell am I going to fit in to the judging panel?'

What I noticed immediately was the way in which the show was judged. I quickly realised that ballroom, when organised into a competition format like *Come Dancing*, was turned into a sport. It was an event every bit as competitive and as disciplined as figure skating or gymnastics. It was very specific and very stylised. The moves were so technical that the judges were often marking the contestants in the same way they would mark a team of synchronised swimmers. I really wasn't sure what good I was going to bring to the format. After all, I was a choreographer with no real experience of ballroom dancing competitions and this was all new to me. But in the end I thought, 'What the heck?' And I went along to the BBC auditions anyway.

Michael was right, everybody who had done anything relevant on the choreography scene in the UK had been interviewed for the show. A pilot – a practice programme, for those of you not in the know – had already been filmed and it featured Arlene Phillips (who would later join me on the panel for real) and a few others, but apparently the recording had been really, really bad. Nothing seemed to fit.

Anyway, when I arrived, a producer sat me in a room and asked me to 'judge' a number of ballroom dancers who were prancing about on a TV screen. Alongside me were a couple of other hopeful panellists, all of whom were going for the same job. I was my usual excitable self and I didn't pull any punches, but I was nowhere near the Tasmanian Devil-type I would later become. Still, I must have done something right because the BBC called me back again. My biggest problem was that I didn't know why, exactly, or what they actually wanted from their judges.

I went for my second audition. To my shock, I was asked back for another, then another, and another. I was placed alongside all sorts of people on the panel. I worked next to Arlene for one sitting. Another time I did a casting session alongside one-time professional dancer Len Goodman: tall, chipper, articulate, Cockney Len with his smart suits and elderly gravitas. There was something I liked about him. He had an easy charm and authority. He was every bit the ballroom judge. Len's demeanour and manner exuded confidence; he was The Godfather of Ballroom, and that's when the penny finally dropped.

'Ah, so that's what they're after here,' I thought. 'Len is perfect for *Come Dancing*, not me.'

He fitted the role like an elegant, manicured hand into a silk glove, and I could tell that the panel was being formed into several distinct characters. In those days, judges were either luvvie duvvies, Simon Cowell wannabes, or the considered, but easy going type. The *Come Dancing* team presumably was going to contain elements of all three, and given that the wildcat character hadn't existed back then (because I'd yet to invent it) I was set to be an also-ran, or so I thought. Out of the blue I was called back for about the 10,000th time, and that's when I decided to do something drastic.

'I need to alter my personality for the panel,' I thought on the eve of the next screen test. 'I know I can't be like Simon Cowell, I'm not the ruthless kind, and anyway, Simon is Simon – I don't want it to appear as if I'm copying anyone. Hmm, maybe I should use a side of my personality and multiply it a million times like Simon did with his *Pop Idol* image? But how exactly?'

I pondered for a while, smoked some fags, drank a glass of wine and then . . . Eureka!

'Bruno, you must explode your fiery Italian side onto the screen. You must take the passion, and the excitement and the sexiness and blow it up, up, up! It might not work, but it's worth a go . . .'

So that's what I tried to do. I knew it was a risk because there wasn't another anarchic or funny judge doing the rounds in those days; those panellists weren't in demand yet. My character was hardly well formed, either – it really was only a hastily put together idea in the mind, so I knew that the next audition would be a shot in the dark, a gamble. Whatever it was, it seemed to work because for another week or two, I went backwards and forwards, backwards and forwards, attending more and more auditions, all the while expanding my natural flamboyance to the point where I felt like a mad man.

I was enjoying it, though, the filming was fun, but with every test I became more convinced that the producers didn't want somebody like me. I didn't fit. But then the funniest thing happened. A week before the show was due to go out on air live, I received another call from Michael.

'Bruno, my darling, we've got the gig,' he said. 'You start on the show next week.'

And that, as they say in show business (and just about everywhere else for that matter), was that.

☆

The first live recording of *Strictly Come Dancing* was chaos, complete and utter anarchy in the UK. Nobody knew what they were doing, people were running around, spinning about and it was absolute bedlam. I sat next to Arlene on the end of the panel alongside Len and Craig Revel Horwood and none of us had a clue what to do. Well, how could we? I hadn't even met Craig before opening night, and you can't exactly prepare or practise for a show that you haven't seen before, can you? We hadn't the time to experience *Strictly Come Dancing* (as it was now being called) in its new live format, and I certainly hadn't been given the time to perfect my TV character.

How that character was going to fit into the show was a whole other story, though. *Strictly Come Dancing* was based on its stuffy, strait-laced predecessor, but this time the contestants (of which there were eight) were celebrities and they had been paired up with professional dancers. For each show, the couples had to perform a certain style of dance. The performer with the worst score every week was bumped off by a voting process that included the judges and the viewers at home.

It was exciting stuff, and my imagination ran wild because it seemed so rock'n'roll to me. The different Latin dance styles featured the Jive, Cha Cha Cha, Rumba, Samba, Paso Doble; the ballroom dances were the Viennese Waltz, Quickstep, Foxtrot, Waltz and the Tango. I knew all of those off by heart because my father had performed a lot of them in the Tonioli kitchen when I was a child. I'd also researched several of the dances when I was working on period dramas and movies, so I knew about the moves and the steps. I had danced the Jive myself as a performer on Nigel Lythgoe's TV shows; the Cha Cha Cha was my favourite style when I used to dance in Ferrara. So in that respect, I knew that marking the performers would be easy.

My main problem, however, involved the cast of 'celebrities' involved with the competition. I didn't have a clue who any of them were! The first season included the late Jason Wood (comedian), David Dickinson (TV presenter), Verona Joseph (actress), Claire Sweeney (actress), Martin Offiah (rugby player), Lesley Garrett (opera singer), Christopher Parker (*EastEnders* actor) and Natasha Kaplinsky (newsreader). I didn't recognise any of them, apart from Natasha and Lesley. I always watched Natasha on the news and obviously being an opera lover I knew who Lesley was. I wasn't the only one, however. As performer after performer ran out to shake their stuff for the first show, Len was forever nudging me in the ribs.

'Who the hell is that?' he would hiss under his breath.

I would shrug my shoulders every time. We still do it now.

Straightaway I knew that I liked Len. His directness was funny and I could tell that, despite our different approaches to life, we were actually very similar. We both came from no nonsense backgrounds, we were both working class; there were no airs and graces to either of us. We also shared an ability to spot the bull**** from a mile off, and very quickly, Len and I got on. Almost from the minute we sat at the panel for the first time in fact.

But oh my god, the opening show was a blur. I don't remember a thing about it. The last time I'd experienced that kind of amnesia was during my debut performance for La Grande Eugene, when I had been thrown into the lions' den while wearing painfully tight boots and a dress made from broken mirrors. And as with that first performance in Milan, I had to make everything up as I went along during my *Strictly Come Dancing* debut. I'd been thrown into the deep end and it was sink or swim with the crazy sharks time.

As the show got underway, I decided to approach the experience as if it were a live theatre performance. Well, I really had no alternative because there was going to be no take two if ever I fluffed a line. What a departure! If I worked on a film and something went wrong, I could always reset the actors and the dancers in their original positions and start again. With *Strictly Come Dancing* I was screwed. There would be no rewinds and definitely no second chances. And once I was on the ride, I was stuck on it for two hours, but flippin' heck it was a thrill because millions of people were watching at home as they scoffed their dinners.

'Well, Bruno,' I thought looking across at the 'On Air' light in the studio. 'If you're going to make a fool out of yourself, make sure you do it in style.'

I allowed myself to get carried away. I also made sure that I focused only on what was in front of me. I forgot about the people staring at their tellies all over the country. Instead, I concentrated on the job in hand, which was to react to the dancers and their steps. Then I knew I had to let my character run wild. Of course, that meant there would be an element of sticking one's neck out, but at the same time I knew I couldn't worry about that too much. If I did I would have become stifled, constricted with nerves, so I went for it, deciding to show the courage of my convictions as I judged the dancers. I was excitable and enthusiastic. My new persona gave me an adrenalin buzz and I experienced the rush of excitement I'd once felt as I waited in the theatre wings of Milan, Paris, Hamburg, London and Berlin.

When the 'On Air' signs were switched off, I honestly thought the show had been a disaster. Everything flashed by so quickly that my brain hadn't the time to assess my own performance. I didn't have time to gather my thoughts. I knew that when it came to reviewing the dancers, I'd blurted out whatever had entered my head at the time. God knows what that was. My judging technique was also a little off. I'd had to tune into the performance and the dancers, distilling my points and comments upstairs, in the head. Then I had tried to talk to the cameras, all the while making my quips very funny. It's easy for me to do that now, but back then it was a nightmare.

As I sat backstage afterwards, I understood the show for what it really was: theatre. *Strictly* certainly wasn't like some of the ballroom championships I had seen in places such as Blackpool, because the celebrity contestants weren't professionals. The marking process had to be much more relaxed, while maintaining an air of authority and insightfulness among the panel. If we were to have judged the likes of Natasha or Martin Offiah by the standards set by the Ballroom World Championships in Blackpool, for example, I wouldn't have given a mark of 10 *ever*. Not in the history of the entire show, probably. Nobody would have got close. In fact, I doubt if any of the show's professional dancers would have scored 10s on a regular basis.

So, my first show was really done on basic instinct. But I am a quick learner. I knew that the more I performed, the faster I would perfect the role. And once I'd done that, I would be a real success on the show, so over the next few weeks I worked at refining my telly persona, but it was so hard. There were no rehearsals. We would turn up before the filming of each show, catch the running order of dances for the evening, and then . . . showtime! That was it. I would come out after filming had finished, blinking and startled.

Every night I went home adrenalised and excited. My mind was racing. If I had thought my days of dance classes in New York and Paris had been tough, I was in for a shock. Live telly was in a completely different league, though this time the efforts were mental rather than physical. I always sipped on a glass of wine when I came home to keep the adrenalin at bay because the rush of excitement that had carried me through the live recording often continued for hours. The thrill ride had taken on a life of its own and I found that it was almost impossible to sleep. And as I tossed and turned in bed every Saturday night I had only one overwhelming thought.

'If only my mother and father could be around to see me now. They would be so proud . . .'

☆

A day or two after that first show, I received a call from Michael. The TV ratings had come in for *Strictly* and they were off the scale. Millions had tuned in. I would love to be able to tell you that I'd known instinctively that the programme would become a hit, that I had seen it coming, but the truth was, I didn't have a clue. It was as big a shock to me as it was to everyone else, but I've learned in my life never to expect anything. I could never tell whether a show or an advert or a pop video was going to be popular until the fat lady opened her mouth and started singing like Montserrat Caballe.

A lot of people seemed to like *Strictly*, though. It was crazy, and it wasn't long before I started appearing in the tabloid papers. Not a week after the show started, I received a phone call from a friend saying they had seen some quotes about me in the paper and I was headline news. It was quite flattering. Suddenly I was the one being written about and it felt *lovely*. Up until that point I'd always read *The Times*, because it was a nice way to teach myself English. Overnight, I was having to read every daily under the sun.

The recording process was all very thrilling for me at the time, because I had taken on a new challenge and it was shaping up to be a success. As you know, *amore mio*, I've always loved something new and exciting. Even as a child, I liked a fresh adventure, I think it must be the gypsy in me (if there is one). The film choreography, like the adverts and the pop videos, and the dance classes before that, had become a bit repetitive. It had been getting a bit boring. *Strictly Come Dancing* gave me a shot in the arm, a new challenge and I could tell straight away that the buzz would be long-lasting because the format of the show was ever-changing: the cast were chopped every season, the dances changed every show; every scene was different.

Why was the programme becoming a success? I used to ask that question of myself every day. I think the answer to that was because *Strictly* was a variety show first and foremost. It had the glamour, the quality and the entertainment factor, a bit like a lot of the big shows of the 1970s. It had the feel good factor. It was glossy, uplifting and funny. It provided an escapism from the reality of life. The celebrity element was important as well, especially as it was presented by Sir Bruce Forsyth, the king of light entertainment, and Tess Daly as his sidekick. There was also an element of pantomime to the whole affair. British audiences have always loved watching famous people falling on their backsides, sometimes literally. They were to get plenty of that on *Strictly*.

The other key element was that people could be inspired by the show. It didn't look elitist, in fact it involved everyone who watched. One of the greatest side effects of *Strictly*'s success was that it opened up a whole new audience to dancing. Suddenly people wanted to go to classes at every level. Viewers wanted to go to shows. We really changed the whole ballroom scene in that way and I'd like to think that the Cha Cha Cha, the Tango, the Waltz, all of them, are more popular than ever before, thanks to the programme.

☆

As the season progressed, I managed to develop my TV persona more and more. I became wilder, more enthusiastic. I leapt around the desk like a hyperactive child on Red Bull at Christmas. Though the first show had felt like a bit of a shambles, by the second performance, I was really on it. The main reason for that, my darling, was the producers and their chopping and changing. In the first show I was at the far end of the panel, furthest away from Bruce and next to Arlene. But for the next show they moved me along the desk and I was placed on the other end, next to Bruce and in direct view of the TV cameras. As soon as that happened, everything fell into place because I could react. Like an actor I could see exactly where I was supposed to be looking whenever it was my turn to deliver a verdict. I was able to stare into the contestant's eyes. I could look at Bruce and Tess while I was talking, whereas before, I had been a little out of the way.

I sprang into action. I began to view my delivery in a different manner. Like some of the actors I had worked with previously, such as Jane Horrocks for example, I found that once I'd approached the judging process from the point of view of my TV persona rather than the persona of Bruno Tonioli, I was able to bring my lines to life. (Please excuse my talking about myself in the third person: I know it's the first sign of showbiz dementia.) I then realised that everything I'd done in my career had always come back to help me at some point later down the line. In this case, my years of working in film had paid off, big time. Having studied the likes of Michael Caine, Ewan McGregor, Jim Broadbent and Steve Coogan I had learned that once an actor finds the character, then the character carries him or her throughout their scenes. My character was dragging me along by the scruff of the neck every Saturday night, like a teacher scolding a particularly naughty child, and it seemed to be helping. If I were to distill exactly who my alter ego was based on, I would say it was one part Uncle Silvano, another Michael (my agent) and a whole electric blast of me. The shouting, the moving around, the excitability, the asides were all things I'd absorbed from people as I'd grown older. I found that when combined, they created a nice balance. Once I'd got my first laugh and a response from the audience, well, I knew it was a flier.

It was quite far-removed from my real personality, though. If you were to see me backstage before a show you would notice that I'm definitely the quietest. Before recording, I hardly speak. I swear a lot, that's true, but I'm also very matter of fact in my preparation for the programme. There's no messing around with me. I like to be alone; I have to be on my own to get my energy together. Then I have to digest everything – the show ahead, the contestants, the dances – hopefully with my head clear of distractions.

The others are a whole other story: Len's much more jovial than me, he's always bloody whistling. Craig likes to faff about and dress up in different outfits, stuff he's usually bought from the nearest shop with a sale (but I'll tell you about that shortly). We're all different, but once we get to our seats at the panel, the transformation is instantaneous, like a group of suave, urbane, tuxedo-clad chameleon-like creatures from an episode of *Dr Who*.

Len can turn on a sixpence. His moods are more unpredictable then the British weather. Craig turns into a bitch, and I go stark, raving mental. But something in the chemistry obviously worked back then, because after season one, the BBC quickly commissioned another run of shows. It was official: *Strictly Come Dancing* was fast becoming a phenomenon! Or, as Michael would say, 'It was *major*, darling.'

CHAPTER 15

THERE'S NO BUSINESS LIKE SHOW BUSINESS

Shortly after it was announced that the BBC were commissioning another series of *Strictly Come Dancing*, I received a phone call from Michael.

'Bruno, darling,' he said. 'America have been on the phone.'

Now, before I go on, I'd like to give you some background to this little story, because Michael loved to tease me about America. He knew about my fascination with Hollywood and the silver screen, and there was nothing he enjoyed more than to call me under the pretence that my stellar talent had been noticed by one of the big movie directors in Tinsel Town.

'Bruno, darling, the States are calling,' he would say. (Not just a movie theatre in LA, *the whole flippin' country* was calling.)

'Really, Michael?' I'd say. 'Can it be true?'

'Yes, darling . . . *Spielberg*. He's on line two . . .'

The pillock. I'd fall for it every time and he would laugh his bloody head off.

This time he wasn't kidding.

'Bruno, it's for real,' he said. 'They love the show, bloody love it. They're crazy for it, darling. And they want you to be one of the panellists over there. ABC want it. They can see it as being a hit. It's going to be *major*.'

I was beside myself with excitement. America. Hollywood. It had meant everything to me from the minute I had seen La Liz and L'atomica at the pictures with my parents. I had bought the books, watched the movies. I had been so eager to see Stanley Kubrick's *2001: A Space Odyssey* when it first came out in 1968 that I had cycled into town like a lunatic to catch the first screening I could. As I was racing down a hill, a car came out of nowhere and struck me hard on the side. Oh my goodness, the noise of the screeching tyres and the crunch of my bike hitting the bonnet! Miraculously I was fine, unhurt. And when the poor driver, shaken and shocked, asked me my name, I told her that I was in a rush to see a movie and cycled off as fast as I could. So, as you can imagine, making it to the land of the silver screen, the movie Mecca of Hollywood, was a challenge I could not resist.

When the news came through about the ABC contract I was so excited, but I couldn't say anything to anyone, because at the time they only wanted me for the show. Arlene, Craig and Len would be staying in London. The American version – which was entitled *Dancing With the Stars* – only featured two other panellists, and they were going to be American. The idea was that we were going to do the recording for six weeks, starting at the end of May, and the format would be identical to *Strictly Come Dancing*. As the paperwork was sorted and the fantasy started to become a reality, all I could think was, 'Are you kidding me?'

Hollywood, to me, was the ultimate dream factory. If they call you, believe me, you jump. There were tonnes of actors from the UK who were working in LA, constantly moving backwards and forwards from California to home. I knew it was the ultimate place to work because everyone who did go there was at the pinnacle of their profession. You couldn't top the place, but I was also very aware that not everybody who had been there had made a success of themselves; it was not a given thing that I, or Dancing With the Stars, would be a hit. A performer can be a big name at home, but when they head to America, they might fall down like a sack of coal. It's like wine – some wines travel well, others are only meant to be drunk in their own country.

When I landed and got to work I was overwhelmed by the place. Everybody was so enthusiastic and they worked to the belief that anything was possible, a bit like I had when I was growing up in Ferrara and travelling around Europe with La Grande Eugene. I found that positivity very refreshing. I was also warmed by the fact that they understood my temperament. They could connect with me and my spicy TV alter ego, probably because there were a lot of Italians and Hispanics in the country. They enjoyed my fire-like energy because they had seen it all before.

But, flippin' heck, the work ethic! If you read another showbiz memoir after this one (and I do hope I've turned you on to the genre) and Mr or Mrs X tells you that a Hollywood existence is easy living, well I can guarantee you that they're telling porky pies. The real LA life is a hard-working one. People are up at five or six in the morning, usually to go straight into the gym. They're in the office or studio at eight, working until nine, ten, eleven at night and beyond. Then they do it all over again, Monday to Friday, weekends, too.

I think a lot of people have a vision of LA in which TV executives and movie directors plan their latest productions by the swimming pool as they chomp on expensive cigars; glamorous tarts walk sexily by in bikinis, there are cocktails *everywhere*. Not a chance! Actors or directors who head for the City of Angels expecting that type of existence are very quickly disappointed. The people who try to follow that type of lifestyle often disappear very fast. Nobody gets successful in America by being lazy.

When planning work got underway on *Dancing With the Stars*, I was put in a room with two other judges (who didn't make it to the final show) to explain what it was that we did in the UK. We also ran through a screen test and recorded a pilot. This was midweek, the show was due to go live the following Wednesday. I did my thing, they did theirs, but we could tell that it wasn't going to work, mainly because they were trying to be something that didn't come naturally to them – they couldn't capture the magic and easy-going charm of Len Goodman. I knew they had to find their own personae, like I had, and inevitably, when we watched the recordings after-wards, it made for grim viewing. The chemistry simply wasn't there.

I knew we were in trouble because time was running out. The producers could see the issues too. They asked me what I thought.

'You can't have somebody imitate Len because, it won't work,' I said. 'You have to get the real deal. Either you have someone that's totally different but just as powerful, or you get Len. You can't force this thing. What we do is a very specific style of perform-ance and it needs a specific personality to do it.'

The call was made and Operation Goodman sprang into action. Len was in LA the following day, moaning and grumbling about the jet lag, the airline food, the hotel, and the heat — I knew he was happy to be there really, and I was happy to have him there. I knew we had another great show on our hands. A third presenter, the former dancer and choreographer Carrie Ann Inaba was also brought in. What a vision of beauty! She was funny, sexy, sassy. Len and I fell in love with her straightaway, and a new, exciting panel was up and running.

Our first show was real seat of the pants stuff, as it had been in the UK, but by the time we settled into our chairs for the second live airing, everything ran like clockwork. The experience of Len and myself carried Carrie Ann through for the first week or two and the chemistry bubbled and fizzed like a bottle of champagne. Ballroom dancing was a hit once more.

☆

What with the Hollywood lifestyle and the travelling backwards and forwards between the two shows for a couple of years, my life became even more of a cyclone of emotions. Everything had taken off at a crazy speed and I ran with it, as I always did in those situations. I was jumping from one adventure to the next: there were calls to do *Strictly Come Dancing* in Australia; I was spending three months on the show at home and three months in America, which was particularly tough when the two contracts overlapped, which they did for a couple of months every year. By May 2006, it had all become a little overwhelming, even for a creature of chaos like myself.

One week, as I got home after yet another commute from LA, Oliver was waiting for me at the door as he always did. Every time I got back, I would only have to put my key in the door and he would be there, the master of the house, waiting for his human pet to return. This time, though, I could tell something was wrong. Oliver wasn't grumbling or complaining, but he was definitely off colour. He was moving slowly, he couldn't jump onto the sofa to sit with me. He wasn't as bolshy as usual.

One of the concerns of having a pedigree cat is that they need special care and attention. And because Oliver had long, beautiful fur, I would often bathe him like a baby. He didn't like it. His face was always a picture as I dropped him in the water and scrubbed him with shampoo, but he never scratched me. He was aware that it was a job that had to be done. When I washed and lavished attention upon him that night, the fur clung to his body and I noticed how thin he had become. He also had a pot belly.

'Oh no,' I thought. 'This is not good.'

I called the vet immediately. Oliver was nineteen years old – around 133 in cat years – and I knew he was on his last legs.

'The cat has a tumour by the sounds of it,' said the vet. 'We can perform an operation, but at his age he's going to suffer and nothing is really going to change.'

I was heartbroken. I kept an eye on him for a few weeks, and not long afterwards it got to the stage where he couldn't walk. He looked permanently startled at his inability to do things that had been so easy to him before, like running and jumping across the kitchen tops. It was then that I knew what had to be done. I held him in the vet's as they put him to sleep. I didn't stop sobbing for days afterwards.

When tragedy strikes – and losing a pet is sad, like losing a close friend – it can force a person to reassess their life. Mine had been moving at warp speed, and Oliver's passing suddenly forced me to stop, albeit for a few brief moments in time, and consider where I was and what I had been doing. I was all over the shop: on planes, in different time zones; Paul was working well in London, he was running his own model agency at the time. What I realised – and only then did it come into sharp focus – was that the pair of us were leading separate lives. He had his own circle of friends, I had mine. We were living in different places most of the time. The pair of us had changed and I realised that our relationship had turned into a habit.

We had been together for twenty years, but there was no point pretending. We were friends, nothing more. That can sometimes happen in a long-term relationship and although we were the same people, we had changed over time, we had grown apart. There wasn't one particular incident that highlighted the fact that a distance had grown between us, but after the moment of calm that took place once I'd returned home from America and Oliver had died we realised that the pair of us had been pretending to be something that we weren't anymore – a unified couple. We made the difficult decision that it would be better if we lived apart because we didn't want to move along the way we had been. I also knew that attempting to paper over the cracks and stay together would lead to resentment and bitterness. The last thing I wanted was for Paul and I to hate one another.

It was a painful and life-changing decision. I am a sensitive soul, so I took it badly; because of my Catholic upbringing, I blamed myself. I thought it was my fault. I was convinced that I had done something wrong. It took me a while to realise that it wasn't anything to do with either of us, nobody was at fault. It was just two people growing and developing in healthy ways, but those changes had created a vacuum in the relationship. Fortunately we were able to accept those changes for what they were and we decided to accept that our union was now at another level. We were friends, and both of us were happy with that, although it took some time before the sense of loss disappeared.

I was lucky in a way, I've always liked being alone. I don't need another person in my life to make me feel complete. I can easily go on holiday on my own for a couple of weeks, where the only time I ever talk to another person is when I go to the restaurant to order food and a bottle of wine. I can spend days without talking to another soul. I'm so busy with my work and the social life I do have that I feel full. I don't need to be in a relationship just for the sake of it, or to fulfill any craving for companionship. I'm happy to fly solo, which is probably the reason why there hasn't been another special person in my life since Paul and I broke up.

I've decided I'm not going to settle for second best. It's not worth it, and it's not me. Unless it's 100 per cent right, I'm not interested.

☆

By the time series two of *Strictly Come Dancing* had begun, the show had taken on a life of its own. It was a monster, a King

Kong-sized variety show striding across the landscape. Everybody seemed to love it, and the scale of its success really struck me as I carried on my normal, day to day routine. People would stop for a chat whenever I went to the supermarket. I would sign an autograph if ever I went to the garden centre to pick up some seeds or a new watering can. But everybody was being so lovely that I enjoyed every second, though I did learn not to look at the internet. When I put my name into Google once, I got the shock of my life.

'Flippin' heck!' I thought. 'There's 88,000 pictures up here of me apparently! When did I ever pose for 88,000 photographs?'

As the second series got underway, however, that's when I began to really appreciate the spirit of *Strictly Come Dancing*. The show had been well cast again, though like the first series, Len and I had no idea who was who, or who did what. As each celebrity dancer was announced, we looked at each other and scratched our heads once more.

TV presenter, Quentin Wilson!

'Who?'

Singer, Aled Jones!

'Oh, is that the choirboy who sang 'The Snowman'? Bless him. Hasn't he grown up!'

TV gardener, Diarmuid Gavin!

'Oh, well, that's wonderful! Maybe I can get some tips . . .'

And so on and so forth. But it really didn't matter what Len and I thought of the people on show because the BBC had drawn together a fascinating gang of characters, a trick they had learned in the first series. It didn't matter if none of them could really dance. What I'd learned was that a person's personality could shine through in his or her routines, and that was the most important thing. The winner of series one, Natasha Kaplinsky, for example, had been a closeted rocket, an unexploded bomb waiting to go off. Who'd have thought it? The girl sitting behind the BBC's news desk gravely wittering on about Mad Cow's Disease was a rhythmic typhoon! Meanwhile the runner up that first year, *EastEnders* actor Chris Parker, was an actor, a man of expression, but he had been terrible. Bless the little thing, he ran around with a cape during his rendition of the Paso Doble. I didn't know what the heck was going on. 'What is he doing?' I thought as he puffed and panted and threw himself around. 'The poor child is demented.' But the audiences loved him and wonderful Chris got to the final on charm alone.

He wasn't the only awful dancer to win over the crowds. Astrologer Russell Grant – who appeared in series nine – was another example. Oh my god, he wasn't a dancer, he had about as much style and grace as a Tellytubby on LSD, but what he lacked in technique he more than made up for in effort. He put everything he had into his performances and by the end of a session under the BBC glitter balls, he was a sweating, panting, heaving, *behemoth* of ballroom. Of course, nobody gave Russell a score of 10 for his efforts, and I remember Craig was particularly bitchy about one performance, claiming that, 'Dumbo springs to mind,' but the entertainment value and the joy he gave to the audience made him as good as anyone else. He later landed himself a role in the West End version of *The Wizard of Oz* at the London Palladium.

I suppose the most memorable example of personality over performance was TV journalist John Sergeant in the sixth series. Oh my lord, John Sergeant: his dancing stank like rotten vegetables and out-of-date fish. He was wooden and awkward, like Pinocchio after a night on Geppetto's whisky. Every week, the judges voted him as the worst dancer on display, but every week the viewers voted him back into contention. Not that I would ever grumble about that – it was all part of the fun of the show and if the public wanted somebody to stay on for another week then that was their prerogative. I never had any problems with it, though I can't speak for the others of course. When John eventually withdrew, I was quite surprised. I thought he should have stayed on and tried to win the whole series. (When John pulled out he said, 'The trouble is there is now a real danger that I might win the competition. Even for me that would be a joke too far.')

The funny thing was, I could never tell how a person was going to do just by looking at them, that was impossible. People would always ask me whether I had a hunch about this dancer or that dancer, but the truth was, I didn't. Then there was the debate about pop stars and their experience of choreography: did it give them an advantage? That question was raised more than once by *Strictly Come Dancing* fans and I could understand why. After all, pop stars who eventually appeared on the show included Rachel Stevens and Jason Donovan. They would have experienced a lot of choreography during their singing careers. Jason had even performed in *Joseph and the Amazing Technicolor Dreamcoat*.

The thing was, I didn't agree with that argument at all. Maybe a musically talented person might have had an advantage when it came to the music – they might have had more of a *feel* for the rhythms of a certain song – but the ballroom and Latin dances featured on the show were so specific, that it wasn't like doing a dance routine on *Joseph*, or the moves required to make a fantastic S Club 7 video. A new technique had to be learned, and one that

267

was often bloody difficult to master. It was incredibly hard to deliver a performance that married timing and technique with personality and power. A background in pop wouldn't have given anyone a headstart over contestants such as Russell Grant or John Sergeant.

There was plenty of learning for everyone to experience, which was why the rehearsals could take quite a toll on the contestants. The training, I soon noticed, was full on. At times it was almost like the dancers were going into an army boot camp because they had to work for several hours a day, every day of the week. Mentally it was draining too. They often put an incredible amount of pressure on themselves because they were all desperate to win. That desire, plus the adrenalin and nerves that came with doing a live performance on a Saturday and Sunday night, could be a real strain. My old friend Pamela Stephenson danced on the show in 2010/11 and came out of *Strictly Come Dancing* a completely different person. (She even scored four 10s for her Viennese Waltz and made it to the final.) Nobody expected her to do so well, but the way in which she applied herself was incredible – she was over sixty years old, her stint on the show required some serious levels of commitment. But the work had an incredible impact on her and the weight fell off her body. She shrunk, and I could see her changing over the course of the series. Pamela looked like a bombshell by the end of it.

What some people didn't realise about the show was that physically, ballroom was almost like a sport. The dancing was continuous and vigorous and that could take its toll on the body. And as in any sport or physical activity, people had to be careful because injuries could happen. Whenever somebody spends a lot of time working with their bodies, they can hurt themselves, people can fall, but it was all part of the discipline. It's all part of the game.

Some people took to it and others didn't; some people surprised me incredibly, and some people struggled, but that was interesting to watch, too. What was more impressive was that a lot of our contestants were taking up the challenge while maintaining their day jobs. I was always amazed at how the morning TV presenters would get up at dawn's crack to work on a show like *Daybreak* and then manage to go through a whole day of intense training in the Cha Cha Cha. It boggled the mind.

What I was beginning to love most about *Strictly Come Dancing*, though, was its unpredictability. That was one of the biggest draws. It was part panto, part soap opera, part Broadway musical. All those elements came into play as soon as the show started, and once the judges had their say, that's when the spanners started getting thrown into the works. I also loved the fact that the individual personalities of each contestant on the show became important, as did the relationship with their professional partners. At that time, partnering in dance had gone out fashion – there was no interplay between people whenever they stepped out on the dance floor in nightclubs. That style had disappeared because of the individualistic moves used by pop stars in their videos and live shows.

Suddenly the concept of having a dance partner had been reignited by *Strictly Come Dancing*, and I for one, was delighted. Dance, particularly ballroom and Latin, has always been about the relationship between two people. It's about storytelling, and during those one and half minutes where I was judging a performance, I looked for the mood that each dancer was creating within themselves. Was it a love story or a hate story? Was it the tale of a jilted lover or a swooning heart? The mystery was what excited me. It took two to Tango after all, and that's what kept the viewers hooked every week.

CHAPTER 16

FROM HERE
TO ETERNITY

The good, the bad and the ugly – I saw it all on *Strictly Come Dancing*. Some of our contestants were fantastic, some of them were terrible, hopeless even. But nobody was quite as bad as the politician Ann Widdecombe who appeared on the show in 2010. Oh dear, Starship Ann: watching her dance the Tango was like watching the Millennium Falcon as it came in to land. She turned like a ferry in a storm and nothing could be done to improve her style, no matter what her dance partner, Anton du Beke, did to help. She was a natural disaster and most of Ann's dance routines involved her either being hurled gracelessly through the air or dragged around like a mop. It was great fun.

Ann wasn't the only one, though. There have been plenty of other horror stories to write home about, most notably the gruesome twosome from *GMTV*, Kate Garraway and Fiona Phillips.

I don't know what their catering crew were giving them for breakfast in the mornings, but they should have considered introducing plenty of iron into their diets because physically they were all over the place. They seemed limbless, filleted, as if every bone in their body had been removed by an expert surgeon. When the pair of them danced they looked limp and listless especially as they were pushed and pulled around by their professional partners like a pair of damp dishcloths. They brought tears to my eyes.

Throughout the disasters, I noticed that sometimes contestants could start on the show without a prayer, but after five or six performances they improved beyond recognition. And then there was Nancy Dell'Olio in 2011.

When Nancy showed up I was surprised that she had wanted to take on such a challenge. I had met her socially at a dinner the year previously and my first thoughts were, 'High gloss, high maintenance.' She was bathed in glamour and when it came to her performances, she was hardly anonymous. The girl twirled like a pair of brightly coloured knickers on a washing machine spin cycle. It wasn't pretty, and after a wooden Rumba with Anton du Beke (poor Anton, he does get the rough end of the stick sometimes) on Halloween night, where she dared to emerge from a coffin, I had no choice but to let loose with both barrels.

'Oh Nancy, emerging from the coffin looking like the Queen of the Night,' I said. 'But you danced like the walking dead. It was like the Zombie of Bond Street!'

I later told the world that Nancy danced like she had 'inhaled two gallons of Veuve Clicquot', which caused some offence, I can tell you. Suddenly there were rumours that she was going to sue me over the critique, but it was a storm in a teacup. We later took

Strictly Come Dancing on tour, a roving circus called *Strictly Come Dancing Live!* where we moved the show around the country to places as remote and fantastic as Birmingham, Nottingham, Glasgow and Belfast. We packed out cavernous venues like the O2 in London. We felt like rock stars. It was great fun. But if Nancy's decision to join *Strictly Come Dancing* in the first place had been surprising, then her arrival on the touring show was even more unexpected. Talk about a revelation! Nancy was fantastic. She was always the first one on the set and the first one to rehearse. She embraced her comedic side and as a result she became the star of the show. She almost became a good dancer, too.

If I'd learned one thing from my experience of working with Nancy, then it was that my tongue could sometimes get me into trouble. 'Clicquogate' clearly caused a stir but throughout my near decade on the show, I have always hammered the contestants with weird and wacky references, in both *Strictly Come Dancing* and *Dancing With the Stars*. During that time I have never held back, but I'd like to think that I've always been honest rather than wilfully bitchy. And I've never failed to shoot from the hip.

'It was like Godzilla and the praying mantis,' was how I once described Bill Turnbull, the *BBC Breakfast* presenter.

'It was the boy from Brazil let loose and bootylicious,' I told athlete Colin Jackson.

Jill Halfpenny, actress, was summarised even more wildly: 'I can't judge that! I was transported by an explosion of talent.'

Jill got off lightly compared to the bombshell actress, Pamela Anderson.

'I can only think of sex, sex, sex, and more sex. Stripperella is back home. Do it to me girl!' I yelled.

The comments left an indelible mark. *Strictly Come Dancing* fans started quoting lines back to me in the street; people wrote headlines in the papers about the catty comments I had made. The scary thing was, I couldn't remember saying any of them. Because I'd put so much energy and mental concentration into my performances, I quickly forgot anything I'd said during recordings, often from the minute I'd first said it. The moment it had passed my lips I was thinking about the next thing and once I'd exited the studio I was often unable to recall any of my critical comments. They had been left behind, hanging in the ether. It was crazy.

☆

There have been occasions when good dancers have blown the chance of winning *Strictly Come Dancing* with a misguided choice of routine, particularly in the freestyle section of the show which always takes place in the grand final. That's the moment in the series where the remaining contestants can do any dance of their choosing. It's their chance to shine! But sadly for Colin Jackson in 2005, it was the moment when he imploded spectacularly, which was a shame because to my mind he had a real chance of winning the whole event.

Colin, along with the cricketer Darren Gough, had been fantastic that year and both of them made it to the final. I discovered that a lot of the sportsmen on the show often did quite well because they could apply themselves to the practice sessions and rehearsals. Their pain thresholds were high and they often had a good level of base fitness. Learning the Waltz or the Foxtrot was like training to them. Mark Ramprakash, another cricketer, was the same.

Anyway, in the 2005 final, Colin attempted one of the most misguided freestyles I had ever seen. He strode onto the dance floor with a life-sized, blow up doll attached to his feet and proceeded to dance wildly, like a man possessed. (Or in dire need of some medication.) I mean, *really*, what was he thinking? It was one of the most insane and ridiculous things I had watched on *Strictly Come Dancing* and during his painfully brief stint on the dance floor, the judges were left nudging one another and pointing.

'Is this for real?' I thought.

Of course, Colin was hammered repeatedly by all of us, and deservedly so because we were frustrated. Everybody knew that he had been in with a chance. The freestyle section is crucial in the final because usually it's the part of the show that can give a contestant an advantage; the person who nails the freestyle often wins the competition. In this case, Colin had stuck a pin into his hopes of success and the showing was as lifeless and floppy as the grotesque inflatable stuck to his shoes.

☆

I was having so much fun with the recording of *Strictly Come Dancing* that I didn't expect another hammer blow of tragedy. But of course, it would have been foolish for me to imagine that my woes had finished forever and in 2009, my agent Michael was taken by cancer. The last time I saw him, he was in hospital, ravaged, a shell of the man he once was. Michael just wasn't Michael anymore and when I spoke to him he couldn't open his eyes, but he squeezed my hand and I just broke apart inside. I hated having to say my goodbyes to a friend I loved so dearly.

I was in pieces afterwards. As I sat in my flat the day after he passed, the phone rang. It was Simon Cowell. He knew I would be in a terrible state and wanted to bring me out of myself.

'Darling, we're all going to Ascot for the day,' he said. 'You have to come, it'll take your mind off it. I know what you will do otherwise: you'll stay at home and sit in your garden and wallow.'

I couldn't do it. I told him that I was in a bad way and I didn't want to face anyone.

'Now darling, that's not going to happen,' he said. 'You have to come, it's the best thing for you. I'm going to send a car because I'm not going to have you there, alone and hysterical. My mum will be with me, and some close friends.'

I knew Simon's mum Julie very well from his days at Fanfare Records; she was also good friends with Michael and was there when he died. But I wasn't sure who the rest of the crowd would be.

'It's just going to be some old friends of ours . . . and Piers Morgan.'

I wasn't happy about that. Piers was the former editor of the *Daily Mirror*, a judge on *Britain's Got Talent* and a successful TV presenter in his own right. I wasn't sure I could face a conversation with somebody who had so many show business ties, especially as I hadn't met him before.

'Oh bloody hell, Simon,' I said. 'I don't know . . .'

'No excuses now, darling,' he said. 'Trust me, you being here with us will be the best thing for you. You can stay here all day and take your mind off it.'

In the end I relented and when I eventually arrived at Ascot, I was bewildered, stunned, desolate in the head. Straightaway Simon threw me into the action and I was immediately introduced to Piers. Understandably, I was a bit apprehensive about him at first, but we soon hit it off and I ended up spending all day with him and his then girlfriend (now wife), Celia Walden. What a character! I found him funny, intelligent and charming company, though I was even more struck by Celia. She was beautiful.

As I've told you before, I don't have a self-censorship button, especially with a glass of fizz inside me, so when she was introduced as his other half I blurted out something typically inappropriate.

'Oh my god,' I said. 'But you're so beautiful, what are you doing with him?'

And that's when she delivered the best line ever: 'Bruno, some people do charity. I do Piers.'

It killed me, but Piers took it on the chin with a laugh and it wasn't long before we had become good friends. Over the coming years he would often invite me to events and charity functions. One of those shindigs was a charity dinner in 2009 at the Harbour Club in south London, the very fancy leisure establishment that Princess Diana used to visit. Piers was very interested in cricket and as the function got underway, I was introduced to the sport's greats, not that I had a bloody clue who any of them were.

It wasn't long before I had struck up a conversation with the very funny Freddie Flintoff and it was then that I discovered I really had the best locker room sense of humour ever. I could outgross all of them with my Uncle Silvano-style language; my innuendos were beyond anything they could comprehend. I got on with Freddie like a house on fire and when he introduced me to the former Australian international, Shane Warne, I just couldn't help myself.

'So Shane,' I said. 'Have you ever thought about batting for my team?'

Well, I had enjoyed a glass or two of fine champagne, darling. Shane should have seen it coming. He didn't know what to say. I later heard it was one of only a few times that he'd ever been lost for words.

☆

In the midst of Michael's death, a controversy began to brew which affected *Strictly Come Dancing* and my fellow judge Arlene Phillips. I had been bouncing around the walls with grief, as had Arlene — she had also been affected by the news. Michael had been her agent too. It was then that I received a call from a girl at the BBC. She needed to know whether I wanted to do another series of the show.

That wasn't anything unusual. As judges, we're not employed by the Beeb, we're actually invited to turn up on the panel every season, but because of my bereavement, I didn't know what I was doing for the next five minutes, let alone the next five months.

'My dear, I can't talk about it right now,' I said. I was tired and emotional. 'Michael used to handle all that stuff. Give me a day or two to get my head around it. I can't do it today.'

I was mentally whacked out, exhausted. I didn't know whether I was coming or going, and my natural instinct was to turn the offer down because I couldn't face the thought of doing another intense show in the middle of all my grief and pain. I called Paul for some advice. He was always a good barometer on these things and he quickly brought me back into the real world.

'Of course you want to do it,' he said. 'Don't be so stupid.'

Anyway, that's when the messy stuff hit the fan, because that same day, maybe the day after, I can't remember exactly, Arlene called. She told me that there was an article in the papers claiming she was going to be replaced. Apparently she was off the show. I had no idea what she was going on about because I was in such a state. The last thing I'd been thinking about was my next stint on Strictly Come Dancing. I hadn't picked up the newspapers for days, so I shrugged it off and thought nothing more about it. The following day I saw the story. It claimed Arlene wasn't going to feature on the panel for the next series.

'Well that's weird,' I thought. 'Maybe Arlene was right . . .'

The BBC called not long afterwards about my appearance, and once I'd asked the usual formalities – when does it start? How long will it go on for? – I mentioned the judging panel.

'What's this about Arlene?' I said.

'We can't tell you anything about it,' came the reply.

'What do you mean?'

'Nothing is official,' I was told.

Now, I know what I'm about to tell you will sound like a cop out, but I honestly can't recall the order of events in all of this. It was one of the most traumatic and emotional periods of my life. Once Michael had died, all the memories of my parents' deaths and the passing of my grandparents weighed down on me again. The events were so overwhelming that I didn't really pay much attention to what was going on with Arlene, apart from the fact that I knew she was also hurting from Michael's death. The news of her role on the show was another shock for her though, and nobody saw it coming. A big fuss kicked up because some people started claiming that the decision had been based on her age (Arlene was sixty-six), but I had no idea what was going on. And the first I knew about Alesha Dixon becoming a judge was when everybody else was informed.

Alesha had been a singer with the pop band Mystique and a contestant on the show in 2007 where she won the final with professional dancer Matthew Cutler. She was good, fantastic in fact. She picked up record scores (her average was the highest so far: 36.5 out of 40) and wowed the judges with her performances. Naturally, that wasn't going to stop the critics from having a go at her when she first started on the show because of the Arlene situation. She was hammered initially. She had replaced someone who had done a very good job and everyone wanted to knock her. Still, Alesha stuck it out, she survived, and after that first wave of negativity, she found her place in an established panel of personalities.

I couldn't make any judgements about her. It wasn't for me to form a critique of Alesha at the time, or her performances. As a friend to Arlene I was upset that she wasn't on the show anymore, but at the same time I wasn't resentful towards Alesha for coming in because the girl had been offered the job and that's the way show business works. Things like that happen all the time. Movie stars are dropped, record labels finish with bands. I've even sacked people as a choreographer. It's the nature of the business, and it wasn't as if Arlene was going to be out on the street. She was an industry in her own right and an incredibly successful one at that, though I know she was wounded by the situation.

Once I found my energy with Alesha though, we hit it off. We ended up being the naughty school kids at the end of the table and we were forever messing around. She reminded me of one of my gorgeous, best friends from Ferrara, Lia, and we spent our whole time laughing and sniggering. There was a health and safety risk with Alesha sitting next to me because I very nearly bruised her boobs a few times as I gesticulated wildly. One time I virtually stripped her naked with my crazy arm-waving. But despite the injuries I very almost subjected her to, I loved working with Alesha and our final season together in 2011 was my favourite on the show.

When she eventually left, it was because she had been tapped up by a source close to home. Simon Cowell had admired her talents from afar and enticed her away for his latest show *Britain's Got Talent*. Well, he would, wouldn't he? She was on top of her game, a fantastic personality and drop dead gorgeous to boot. When the news filtered through, I dropped him a scolding text.

'Cheeky move, you sneak.'

I didn't get a reply.

☆

For nearly ten years I've sat on that panel. It's flashed by in a blur and every minute of it has been a wild, crazy ride, mainly because of the people I work with. Len, for example, is a godsend, a curmudgeonly angel. He's the person I spend the most time with. We commute to America and back for three months out of the year and without him, I'd have probably gone insane by now. To look at we're the original Odd Couple, but we both have a get-on-with-it attitude that works well: we do the job, we finish the job, and whatever happens onstage stays onstage.

Thanks to Len I have become a master grump. The one thing I picked up during my early spell in Britain was the wonderful art of moaning, which I took to like a duck taking to water. I later perfected the art under Len's tutelage because he is so bloody good at it. We're both permanently jet-lagged during the eight weeks when both *Strictly Come Dancing* and *Dancing With the Stars* are running concurrently. All we do is gripe and moan, gripe and moan. I come out with things that I would never repeat to you as we drag our bags through departure lounges and into taxis, but we always say the same thing to one another as the misery turns into demented laughter: 'Well, we can always say no.'

The one thing I have learned about Len during our travels is that he's a very good ironer. He always looks dapper in his crisp suits and sharp shirts. Everything is perfectly pressed and there's rarely a crease on him. Not that he's immune to looking occasionally ruffled. During one stint in LA, we shared apartments that were next door to each other, and one morning he popped round to borrow some sugar, as you do. Given that this visit took place at a relatively early time in the morning, Len must have been in a rush to get out (to the golf course, most probably) because in his haste, he neglected to get dressed. Instead, fresh out of the shower, he padded across the landing that separated our two flats with nothing more than a towel wrapped around his waist and when I opened the door, it dropped to the floor with a sense of comic timing, revealing 'Big Len' in all its glory.

'Len,' I said, as he desperately attempted to cover his manhood. 'I think we should live in separate apartment blocks. I don't think I can have this every morning.'

The septuagenarian stripper is not alone in his eccentricity though. Craig is just as bad, albeit in entirely different ways. For starters, he's nothing like the spiky, barbwire assassin that people see on the screen. In fact, he's actually a very funny and warm character. But, oh god, the booze. Give him a drink and he's happy. Sometimes I cannot comprehend his ability to knock them back, and whenever we go to lunch Craig will always head straight for the wine list.

'Well, we can stay for a couple,' he'll say, scanning for a particularly fruity number.

The first time that happened, I was under the impression that Craig was referring to 'a couple' of glasses. I learned very quickly that he only deals in bottles.

If he's not knocking back the plonk, then Craig can usually be found battling his way through the crowds at the latest shopping sales. He can't resist them. He's like an addict, our very own *Queen of Shops*, and whenever we share a car together as we travel towards the next step on the *Strictly Come Dancing Live!* tour, Craig will always fill the boot with twenty-seven bags of half-price crap.

'Listen Craig,' I've said to him on more than one occasion. 'If it's in the sales, it's because nobody wants it.'

But Craig has never listened to me. If there's a '50% off' label stuck to a newly-purchased pair of fluorescent lime leggings then he's happier than a pig in muck, though there have been one or two occasions when his shopping sprees have been wildly miscalculated. On one trip he bought a pair of shoes that looked like oil rigs in miniature. They were so awkward and ill-fitting that he could barely squeeze his feet into them. I thought they were something out of a science-fiction novel and he couldn't take a step without grimacing like a constipated chimpanzee. It was to get worse, because when Craig stepped out of the car for the first time, he nearly fell flat on his face. He could hardly balance on the silly boots. Every time he took a step his body weight was propelled forward with an uncomfortable jolt.

Luckily, I have managed to pass on a few fashion tips to him in recent years, but really, these have been nothing more than a gentle reminder to wear more black (it tends to be slimming). Most of the time, he pays heed, but Craig does have a tendency to go off message, and one afternoon he turned up to a meeting in a brand new pair of shiny, slim cut, black jeans. He looked as pleased as punch.

'Darling, see what I've just bought in the sales,' he said proudly as Len and I eyed him grumpily.

I admit it, from the front, his new purchase looked really rather nice. When he did a quick twirl, however, the full horror of his latest shopping spree slapped us across the face like a wet fish because stitched across his backside was an embroidery that resembled a garish version of the Bayeaux Tapestry. Far worse was the colour scheme. The designer had used the most lurid and vivid shades you could possibly imagine. Len turned away in disgust, Craig's arse looked so big in the shiny fabric that he resembled a walking IMAX cinema. *Avatar* could have been played across his buttocks.

'What do you think?' he said, full of joy.

'Yes, Craig,' I said. 'It's fabulous for you, but an eyesore for us. Your backside looks like a walking art installation. And not a good one.'

I also had some great times with Arlene when she was on the show. I'd known her for years and years, we went a long way back, and we were often screaming with laughter at some of the antics that went on during the making of *Strictly Come Dancing*. I remember an occasion, during the live tour, when Arlene was being particularly scathing to one of the contestants. I can't remember which one it was, but she absolutely demolished her victim. It was shocking, Arlene at her most brutal. She didn't pull any punches.

The thing with Arlene was that she was always scribbling something down on her notepad when she worked on the panel. This time, she was so absorbed in her notes that she didn't notice the other panellists had started giving their final scores. Craig gave his verdict.

'Ugh. Two.'

Arlene was next, but she was in her own world, writing some list or another, blissfully unaware. Craig nudged her hard in the ribs and as she came to her senses, she dropped her pen, her paper and all the paddles, the handheld placards that score the dancers with a number from 1 to 10, to the floor. As she scrabbled around to pick one up, she held up the first paddle that came to hand.

'Er . . . a ten!' she cried, looking flustered.

I glanced across at Craig, who stared back at me, his jaw touching the floor. Remember Arlene, not five minutes earlier, had absolutely ruined this contestant.

'WHAT?!' he shrieked.

We all laughed like madness.

One of the greatest joys of *Strictly Come Dancing* is working with the presenters, because in the midst of all the furore and high drama is the lovely, glamorous and delightful Tess Daly, and Sir Bruce Forsyth – the doyen of light entertainment, the top dog of British telly. Bruce is the last of a dying breed: an all-round entertainer who can do everything. He can sing, he can dance, he can act. He could probably juggle on a bloody unicycle, if somebody asked him. He's got everything because he perfected his act on the working men's club circuit years and years ago during a generation in which entertainers had to be versatile. He's also energetic. Every night, before the show, he warms up the crowd with a comedy routine that has everyone in stitches. He's a national institution, like toad in the hole and spotted dick. But this treasure is unique. They don't make them like Bruce anymore.

He's fun to work with too. Sometimes, when I'm sitting at the end of the panel, it's like being alongside an uncle. He tells me off whenever I'm being naughty (which makes me even naughtier), he tries to calm me down whenever I get over excited (which seems to be all the time).

'You should be strapped into that chair,' he'll say.

Or, 'You are being very, *very* naughty today Bruno!'

But I love it and whenever Bruce talks me down if ever I've been a bit over the top on the telly, it gives me an energy I can feed from. After all, being bad is so much more fun than being good, which is something I've realised throughout my entire life.

☆

What a departure! When I think about what I could have been, it scares me sometimes. What would have happened to me had I stayed in Ferrara with Lucy the town trannie? Where would I have got to had I fulfilled my parents' hopes and worked towards becoming an accountant? I would have been bloody miserable for starters. Chances are I would have died inside and lost all my enthusiasm for life. Thank god I had a rebellious streak that helped to turn my ambitions into a reality.

I know that if it wasn't for my desperate attempts to escape Ferrara as a teenager, chances are I'd never have made it into choreography, or pop music, or television. Nobody would have spotted my talents from afar. I never would have given dance lessons to Goldie Hawn, or dressed up as a Geisha girl for The Rolling Stones. Instead I would have remained in a world where the Kessler Twins were nothing more than a fantasy creation and Hollywood was but a distant dream. Now all of those dreams have become my reality.

Who knows what's next? I haven't got a flippin' clue. As a stroppy, combustible, intense teenager, I made a pact with myself to follow the path that fate had made for me, dealing with what-ever was thrown in my way. And like a dog chasing a bone, I've followed it faithfully because as long as life continues to be exciting and new, then I'm interested. Exploration and adventure is what feeds me. It keeps me alive, it keeps me eager. It gives me a *life force*.

That path has led me through some crazy times, as strange and as disorientating as the acid trip that spun me out in Munich, and there have been plenty of highs and a fair few lows, but now I'm here I can see that all of the hard work and enthusiasm was worth it. So my aim is to stick to that path. And why wouldn't I? My darling, I'm happy, fulfilled, experienced, as well as being the member of a very special, but very exclusive club: I'm one of the lucky few to have seen Len Goodman starkers.

PICTURE CREDITS

The author and publishers are grateful to the following for the use of their pictures:

(numbers refer to plates; t = top; c = centre; b = bottom; l = left; r = right).

Plate Section 1

© Fiona Macpherson – 3tr & br, 4tl, bl & br, 6b, 7bl
© Lila Mann – 4tl
© F. Sanjar – 5tl
© Johnny Rosza – 5bl
© Michelangelo Giuliani – 8br

Plate Section 2

© Fiona Macpherson – 1tl & c, 2tr & bl
© Daniel Boudinet – 1bl
© Theatreprint – 1bfl
© David Appleby – 8b

Plate Section 3

© PepsiCo UK & Ireland – 1tl
© BBC Photo Library/Guy Levy – 20b, 21t & br, 22 (all), 23t & b, 24 (all)
© Paul Drinkwater/NBCU Photobank via Getty Images – 2b
© Disney ABC Television Group – 5b
© Rick Baptist – 4c

'White Party' photographs courtesy of Carl Michaelson and Jackie St Clair.

All other photographs courtesy of the author.